ARMED CITIZENS

ARMED CITIZENS

THE ROAD FROM ANCIENT ROME TO THE SECOND AMENDMENT

Noah Shusterman

University of Virginia Press
Charlottesville and London

University of Virginia Press

Printed in the United States of America on acid-free paper

First published 2020

ISBN 978-0-8139-4461-6 (hardcover)
ISBN 978-0-8139-4462-3 (ebook)
1 3 5 7 9 8 6 4 2

Library of Congress Cataloging-in-Publication Data
is available for this title.

Cover art: "The true portrait of his Excellancy George Washington Esqr. in the Roman Dress," John Norman, hand-colored etching and engraving, ca. 1783. (Mabel Brady Garvan Collection, Yale University Art Gallery)

CONTENTS

ACKNOWLEDGMENTS

DECIDING MIDCAREER TO WRITE A BOOK on a subject outside of my training required seeking help from many people—more, even, than would your typical history book. I can thank only a small fraction of those who were kind enough to set aside their time so that they could share their knowledge with me. I have benefited from feedback from my colleagues, first at Temple University and then at the Chinese University of Hong Kong; the scholars at the McNeil Center for Early American Studies; and all of those who attended the talks I have given in Hong Kong and Philadelphia. I also want to thank the scores of students who have sat through my courses during this time, especially those who have taken my classes on the history of militias and had to follow me down more than a few rabbit holes.

To list just a few people specifically, I'd like to mention Philadelphians Daniel Richter and Audra Wolfe, who gave me advice from their own areas of expertise in which I was sorely lacking; and fellow Hong Kongers Jeremy Yellen, Elizabeth Ho Pui-yin, and Bryan Mercurio. I'd also like to thank my fellow historians of the French Revolution, including Malcolm Crook and Micah Alpaugh, along with John Abromeit, all of whom gave me feedback on the parallel projects I've been working on yet whose insights worked their way into this one as well. Stuart Semmel, James Morton, and Stuart McManus all read chapters of this book and provided invaluable feedback. I also want to thank everyone I've worked with at the University of Virginia Press, especially Angie Hogan, Ellen Satrom, and George Roupe.

While writing this book, I took full advantage of the new digital world. Without the scores of podcasts and e-courses I listened to and the insights and feedback I received from the friends I have made among twitterstorians and other gun scholarship tweeters, it would have taken me far longer to learn everything that went into writing this book.

I do want to give special thanks to two friends in Philadelphia. First, David Waldstreicher, who encouraged me to pursue this project back when we were both at Temple and has helped me with it ever since. Second, Bill Hangley, who read over the first draft of the book and helped me bring an unwieldy collection of stories into a coherent whole.

Moving to Hong Kong turned out to be one of the great experiences of my life. Seeing the changes there during the production phase of this book was both inspiring and heartbreaking. The people of Hong Kong have taken on a far greater burden than the world should ever have asked of them. Add oil, heung gong yan. Add oil.

No one has helped me more than my wife, Helen, and our son, Zachary. They make my life make sense when the rest of the world doesn't. Our families—both immediate and extended—have also been a continued source of support both in Hong Kong and in the United States. Finally, this book is dedicated to my mother, Jill Michaels. When we were growing up, she made sure that my sister and I knew that a life devoted to the fight for justice and equality was a life well spent.

ARMED CITIZENS

INTRODUCTION

The Long Road to the Second Amendment

THE SECOND Amendment to the US Constitution no longer makes sense.

It no longer makes sense not because today's weapons are more powerful or because American gun violence is out of control (although both of those statements are true). The Second Amendment no longer makes sense in a much more basic way: people no longer understand what it means. Nor do they understand what it meant to the generation that created it. The first half of the amendment—"A well regulated militia, being necessary to the security of a free state"—has become a cryptic phrase, waving at us across the centuries.

The amendment's second half still makes sense. "The right of the people to keep and bear arms, shall not be infringed." Some Americans like that phrase more than others, but everyone understands what the words mean. In 1791, though, when the states ratified the Bill of Rights, the entire amendment made sense. Contemporaries understood what the framers of the Constitution meant by a "militia," and they knew how important it was that those militias be regulated. And they knew why, for eighteenth-century republicans, a state without such a militia could never be truly free.

They knew about militias because Britain's North American colonies had militias. Of the thirteen colonies that fought for their independence, all but one had maintained a militia since their founding. As a result, the militia was a familiar institution to the inhabitants of the United States. These were not the voluntary associations that call themselves militias today—far from it. The colonial militias were official institutions, governed—sometimes effectively, sometimes less so—by colonial laws and regulations that required most citizens to participate. As a result, those citizens were accustomed to mandatory militia service of one sort or another. (Most of the people who lived in the colonies were not citizens—more on that below.) Since the 1607 arrival of English colonists in what would become Jamestown, Virginia, settlers had been expected to provide their own security. The Jamestown colonists were responsible for planting their own crops and fighting their own battles. And as Virginia grew, that remained true. The other colonies developed along mostly similar lines, with citizens required to participate in the militia and with relatively few professional soldiers.

What, then, were these colonial militias? They were official military forces under the command of the colonial government and acting on its behalf. Their duties included both internal and external matters—in other words, they could act either as an army or as an internal police force. Such overlap in tasks was not unusual at the time: in Europe, which had a much larger population, the distinction between soldiers and police officers was only just emerging in the eighteenth century. What differentiated a militia from other armed forces was that its members were only part-time soldiers. They had careers to attend to, homes to maintain, and, ideally, families to lead. These militias had their own lines of command, as in the army, though in many colonies the officers were elected by the militiamen themselves. Peacetime duties were relatively light: the men would muster on several Sundays over the course of the year. Sometimes these musters were serious affairs with rigorous training and exercises. At other times, musters were little more than excuses for gathering and drinking. When colonists decided the situation demanded it, these militias sprang into action—which, again, amounted to the colonists' looking after their own military needs. For most of the colonies' existence, the militias were not just the colonies' first line of defense but their only one.

When full-scale war broke out between France and England, the militia system was not enough for the colonies' military needs. During the French and Indian War (1756–63), the British government sent professional soldiers to do most of the fighting—aided, though not always effectively, by colonists who had experience in the militia.[1] In that war's aftermath, Britain stationed far more soldiers in North America than it ever had before. Eventually, those troops' presence began to rile the colonists. The citizens of Boston, especially, began to bristle at the presence of so many "redcoats" stationed among them. The tensions between the New Englanders and the British soldiers would lead to the two sides fighting each other in Lexington and Concord in April 1775. After that, the war was on.

Britain would send far more professional soldiers to its North American colonies during the American Revolution, this time to fight against those same colonial militias—their former comrades in arms. In response, the Continental

Congress authorized the creation of the Continental army, which became the United States' main fighting force. For the first time, the Americans had their own professional army.

Once the War of Independence ended, everyone accepted that the states would revert to having citizens meet their own military needs. The Articles of Confederation, which the Continental Congress wrote during the fighting, required each state to "always keep up a well-regulated and disciplined militia." Most of the states wrote constitutions during the Revolution that included some mention of a militia. And the US Constitution—as ratified in 1787, before the Bill of Rights was included—not only called for a militia; it devoted more words to the militia than it did to the army and navy combined.[2]

So the leading men of the day agreed on the need for a militia. They did not agree on how the militia should be run or who should run it. During the debates about the Constitution and its ratification, Federalists and Anti-Federalists would fight quite viciously over the national government's authority of "calling forth" the militia. But both sides agreed on the militia's importance.

Familiarity and continuity, then, guaranteed the militia a place in the young republic. Economics provided another guarantee. "We are too poor to maintain a standing army adequate to our defence," George Washington noted, and few people—neither his contemporaries nor historians—would take issue with the notion.[3] France maintained such an army, but it was a larger and richer nation. And whereas the United States gratefully accepted French aid during the Revolution, British citizens on both sides of the Atlantic had for decades seen the French army's existence as proof that the English were a freer people than their French rivals. The founders of the new republic were not about to abandon that belief. France's military spending would also bankrupt the French government by the late 1780s. The new United States, all but buried beneath its war debts, was in no position to hire a large professional army. Nor did it need or desire one. Come peacetime, citizens would again be expected to handle their own military needs and their own policing.

The Second Amendment gave a stamp of approval to an institution that the colonists, as much for practical and economic reasons as for ideological and philosophical ones, had come to know. But the language of the Second Amendment showed that the founders' attachment to the militia went beyond familiarity, continuity, and the need to economize. When the authors of the Bill of Rights declared that a well-regulated militia was necessary for the security of a free state, they also endorsed a tradition of republican thought that had elevated militias to a place of honor and glory well above what their lackluster military achievements would suggest.

During the seventeenth and eighteenth centuries, writers and politicians—mostly, though not only, in Great Britain and the British Empire—developed a view of militias, and of human society and history, that placed militias at the center of all that was good, just, and manly. These writers claimed that militias could outfight any other army because citizens who were part-time soldiers fought better than professional, full-time soldiers. They also claimed that the time those men spent training as part-time soldiers would mold them into better citizens. In these pro-militia theories, a state with no armed forces could never be secure, and a state with a professional army could never be free. Only a state in which the citizens were part-time soldiers—and in which all soldiers were also citizens—could be both. Hence the militia's necessity to the security of a free state. By the time of the American Revolution, the basics of these theories had become part of the nation's guiding assumptions, accepted even by those who, through personal experience, were aware of the militias' shortcomings.

George Washington wrote *Sentiments on a Peace Establishment* in 1783, after the fighting against England had ended. It was his way of sharing his thoughts on the sort of defense force the new nation would need. The United States had raised a professional army during the Revolution, and Washington had led that army, but the war was over, and everyone knew that the thirteen states would go back to having citizens protect themselves. Most soldiers would be returning to civilian life; the question was what sort of force would continue to exist. By the standards of his day, Washington was not an enthusiastic proponent of the militia. His experiences with colonial militias during the French and Indian War (and the superiority of the British professional soldiers) had left him skeptical of the likelihood that relatively untrained citizens would shine on a battlefield. "To place any dependence upon Militia," he wrote in 1776, "is assuredly resting upon a broken staff."[4] His experiences in the War of Independence mostly confirmed those views. Yet in his plans for a peacetime force, Washington introduced his discussion of the militia by declaring it a "great Bulwark of our Liberties and independence."[5]

Washington knew his readers well. He knew he did not need to convince them that the militia was needed. Washington spent most of his section on the militia discussing how to ensure that the militia would be strong enough and ready enough. Much of that material was of a fairly technical nature ("it appears to me extremely necessary that there be an Adjutant General appointed in each state"), leading Washington to ask of his readers "the indulgence of suggesting whatever general observations may occur from experience and reflection."[6]

If Washington's advice on the militia was more technical than ideological, that was because he found it "unnecessary and superfluous to adduce arguments to prove what is conceded on all hands"—namely, that the nation's protection depended upon a "respectable and well established Militia." Should a justification of citizens' militias be needed, though, Washington reminded his readers that

> we might have recourse to the Histories of Greece and Rome in their most virtuous and Patriotic ages to demonstrate the Utility of such Establishments. Then passing by the Mercinary Armies, which have at one time or another subverted the liberties of all most all the Countries they have been raised to defend, we might see, with admiration, the Freedom and Independence of Switzerland supported for Centuries, in the midst of powerful and jealous neighbours, by means of a hardy and well organized Militia. We might also derive useful lessons of a similar kind from other Nations of Europe, but I believe it will be found, the People of this Continent are too well acquainted with the Merits of the subject to require information or example.[7]

The nation that George Washington helped found has changed. The citizens of today's United States are no longer so well acquainted with the subject of the militia. To understand why Washington insisted on the militia's importance in 1783—or why, eight years later, the Bill of Rights declared those militias necessary for the security of a free state—Americans now do in fact require information and examples.

That Washington would turn to the lessons of history for proof of the militia's necessity likewise typified the thinking of the era. Writers and politicians alike could count on their readers to know about the history of the Roman Republic and how it became an empire. They could count on readers to know the histories of Cincinnatus and Hannibal, of Louis XIV and Oliver Cromwell. Militia advocates had not only created a theory that saw in citizens' militias the key to the security of a free state; they had also assembled a series of historical examples to support their points. This theory and these examples were a major component of the knowledge that the educated men of the eighteenth century shared, to the point where Washington could declare any further explanation "unnecessary and superfluous." That common knowledge has since become the domain of specialists and academics. What was once superfluous has become necessary. Providing that information, and explaining those examples, is the first task of this book.

At the center of these theories lay two basic points. The first was about how good militias were. The second was about the monstrous evils that were standing armies. The two points mirrored each other. The most devoted advocates of the citizens' militia believed that military training prepared citizens for any hardships they might encounter. Spared that training—as would happen in a society with a professional army—men would become soft and undisciplined, tempted by all the vices eighteenth-century society had to offer.

By contrast, these same writers and politicians believed that a standing army—an army of professional, full-time soldiers—could destroy a society's freedom. The logic: because soldiers' livelihood hinged on the continued existence of an army, their primary loyalty would be to their general—or even to a king or a dictator. Whoever commanded the army could even take the earth-shattering step of ordering his army to march on the citizens themselves. This was the fundamental lesson of Julius Caesar crossing the Rubicon (the subject of chapter 1). There was also a practical consideration: the costs of a standing army could bankrupt a nation, while a militia's costs were minimal. Above all, though, a militia could guarantee a society's freedom.

There was a question at the heart of all of the militia theorists' projects: How can a society defend itself without being threatened by its defenders? Any society that hired soldiers to do its fighting for it could, in turn, be attacked by those very soldiers. Or, as the Scottish writer Andrew Fletcher of Saltoun (chapter 6) would put it, "What security can the nations have that these standing forces shall not at some time or other be made use of to suppress the liberties of the people?"[8] Thus a standing army became a sure-fire path to an oppressed and emasculated citizenry. This fear of the standing army stood at the center of everything that militia advocates wrote during seventeenth and eighteenth centuries. Any nation with a standing army could never be free. Generals could order the army to march on the people; kings could order the army to destroy any parliament, any legislative body. When Washington wrote his *Sentiments on a Peace Establishment,* he made no attempt to go against this view. "A large standing army in time of Peace," he wrote, "hath ever been considered dangerous to the liberties of a Country."[9] If the advantages of a militia were one of the early republic's guiding assumptions, the other side of that coin was the fear of standing armies. It was a point on which Federalists and Anti-Federalists, as well as northerners and southerners, agreed.

This book's first task, then, requires not only explaining why and how the men of the eighteenth century came to consider militias so necessary for a free people; it also requires explaining why and how those same men came to consider standing armies to be such a threat to freedom. The second task of this book is to show the role that militias played in the societies of the eighteenth-century Atlantic World—especially in England's North American colonies. Again, from the time of their first arrival, European settlers had looked after their own military and police affairs. As Virginia's settlers became more established and set down the rules for their colonies, they put this reliance on citizen-soldiers into law, establishing an official Virginia militia. All of the other colonies, save Quaker-run Pennsylvania, would follow suit. Studying these militias in action shows them in a different light. There was a gap between the militias that writers described in their books and the ones that mustered on Sundays in the towns of colonial North America—or, for that matter, in Great Britain. When it came to their performance on the battlefield, the militias of the eighteenth century were something less than the citizens' army of the Roman Republic. Eighteenth-century militias were inconsistent and unpredictable forces, capable of great heroism, capable of inflicting enormous violence at times, but also likely to evade their responsibilities and even, on some occasions, to cause more troubles than they resolved.

Militias and militiamen were at the heart of every case of insurrection and domestic unrest of colonial America. Sometimes they were the force that put down the insurrection; at other times, militiamen started insurrections, as in the 1676 Bacon's Rebellion (chapter 5). This ambiguity came with the territory of the citizen-soldier, men who were at once soldiers and citizens. The belief among writers at the time—and it was not without merit—was that soldier-citizens were less likely to blindly follow orders than were paid soldiers. But the choice of whether to participate in an insurrection or to suppress one was rarely random. The most important thing to remember about eighteenth-century citizen-soldiers is that by the laws at the time, most people were not citizens. Even among citizens, some were more equal than others, and not all were eligible to take part in the militias.

There's a useful contrast to be made here between the 1676 Bacon's Rebellion and the Stono Rebellion, which occurred sixty-three years later several hundred miles to the south. When Virginia's colonial governor William Berkeley found himself facing an uprising in the western part of his colony, it took him months (and some lucky breaks) before he could put down the rebellion. Disgruntled fellow colonists had rallied around newcomer Nathaniel Bacon, who in turn declared Berkeley and his allies "Trayters to the King and Country" and began a war that was in part an insurrection against Berkeley's government and in part a violent incursion into neighboring Indian lands. Berkeley's recourse as colonial governor was to call out the militia to put down the insurrection. When he did so, though, the men he called out had no interest in fighting their fellow colonists. Berkeley would prevail in the end, but only after Bacon and his men had burned Jamestown to the ground—and after Bacon himself died of natural causes. The Stono Rebellion of 1739 (chapter 7) played out much differently. When the lieutenant governor stumbled upon the rebellion of enslaved Africans, he rushed to call out the militia—"raised the Countrey," as one description later put it.[10] And the country responded. The South Carolina militia jumped into action, tracked the insurgents down, and defeated them in a firefight, all before a full day had gone by. This contrast between the two rebellions showed what these militias were and were not good at. They were best at being repressive domestic forces.

North America's colonial militias were not unique in being repressive forces. The seventeenth- and eighteenth-century societies discussed in this book all found one way or another to keep much of the population out of the militia; these societies also made sure that those they excluded from the militia were unarmed and unable to organize themselves. That had been the rule back in the early days of the Roman Republic, where all soldiers were citizens but only citizens who could afford to arm themselves were soldiers. In England, poor Englishmen were deemed too much of a threat if allowed to carry weapons or participate in the militia. The English added restrictions on Catholics, on Scots, and, above all, on Irish Catholics. When the French began their revolution in 1789, they too began to arm citizens who had property—all while keeping poorer citizens unarmed.[11]

One quirk of the English colonies in North America was that from their start, richer English colonists were willing to include poorer colonists in their militia. This was a change from the English traditional militia, which had been limited to men of means. While back in England the government was passing laws keeping guns out of the hands of poorer Englishmen, the North American colonies were encouraging poorer settlers to own their own weapons. The colonies' decision to include poorer citizens in their militias does not mean that these militias were more inclusive than their British counterparts. The American militias let poor citizens in, but only white settlers could be citizens. Native Americans could not be citizens and, for the most part, were not included in the colonial militias. There were exceptions; colonial militias often used men from allied tribes as scouts, for instance. The limitations on African Americans were even stricter. Those living in slavery were forbidden from taking part in the militia or from owning weapons without their owners' permission; even for free blacks, there were few possibilities for being in the militia or owning weapons. In all of these places the militia was an all-male affair, one more reminder of the proper roles for women and men. Well before the Second Amendment came along, the question was never whether or not there was a right to bear arms but, rather, who had the right to bear arms.

Deciding what to include in a book like this one is never easy, and some readers will have their own views about which events should or should not be here. Some notes, therefore, about the logic behind the choices made. Some of the events in this book are here because of the obvious importance they had at the time. The chapter on Lexington and Concord is about the "shot heard round the world"—and while that phrase dates to the nineteenth century, the importance of Lexington and Concord was clear from the start, in the Old World and the New. Other chapters focus on events or developments that only became important well after they occurred. When Niccolò Machiavelli died, for instance, most of his writings were still unpublished. Their eventual publication and spread, however, would provide the framework for subsequent writing about republicanism and citizen-soldiers. Some of the other events in this book are included less for what happened, or for any changes they brought about, than for what they revealed about the working of the militia system. The 1739 Stono Rebellion, for instance, did not much change the evolution of colonial South Carolina where it occurred. But the way that rebellion played out, and the role that the militia played in suppressing it, showed the role that the militias had come to play in the colonies of Virginia, the Carolinas, and Georgia. Together, these events explain why, during the eighteenth century, the idea of citizen-soldiers became so popular.

All of which is to say that the goal of this book is to tell the story of ten events that, together, explain how and why the men who wrote the US Constitution came to embrace citizens' militias and distrust professional armies and why they preferred citizen-soldiers to professional soldiers. These chapters will show why those men believed that these militias were necessary to the security of a free state and why, in the words of several state bills of rights also from that era, peacetime standing armies "should be avoided as dangerous to liberty." It is a history of why so many leaders of the founders' generation believed that citizens had an obligation to bear arms on behalf of their society. It is a history of both ideas and actions, of both books and institutions. These ten events are included here in chronological order. At the risk of overexplaining, this is why the account connecting them can be thought of as a "road" leading to the Second Amendment.

It was not, however, the only such road. Imagine a trip from, say, Los Angeles to Washington, DC. There is more than one route to take. Some are more direct, some more scenic. Some spots on the itinerary are more important than others. Tortured though this metaphor may be, it can help explain why some events are included in this book and others are not. Because the goal of driving from Los Angeles to Washington, DC, is to see the country, to learn more about its people and its places—but eventually you have to get to DC. So you make choices. Phoenix or Las Vegas, but not both. The Grand Canyon or Arches National Park but, again, probably not both. St. Louis or Atlanta. And if you've got a lot of people on the trip, they won't all like every one of your decisions.

So it will surely be with this book—not all readers will agree with the choice of events. Chapter 6, about the Scottish writer Andrew Fletcher of Saltoun, could also have been about the English writer John Trenchard. The chapter devoted to the battles of Lexington and Concord will seem like a classic topic to some, cliché to others. And academics familiar with the history of civic republicanism might question including a chapter on Niccolò Machiavelli's work, in the same way that well-seasoned travelers might hope to avoid a stop at Wall Drug or Little America. But the idea—again, as with a sightseeing road trip—is to balance out the well-known landmarks with some that are more obscure and to include some that have received less attention than they warrant. This "itinerary" is also based on the principle that, faced with a choice between several similar sites, it is better to visit just one, but with the leisure to take one's time and see it well, than to rush through shorter visits to each of them.

There is a method to this madness. The goal is to bring together the different elements that together made it inevitable that once the United States decided to attach the Bill of Rights to the Constitution, the Second Amendment, *or something very similar to it,* would be included in those rights. So while the chapters are in chronological order, the lessons from each chapter build on each other in ways that are less linear. Some chapters, particularly those dealing with colonial North America, are about the institutional history of militias. Others, including the chapters on Machiavelli, Fletcher, and *The Federalist,* are about the intellectual history of citizen-soldiers. The chapter on Bacon's Rebellion shows how the colonial militias could cause trouble for local governments—a story that could also be told with the Regulators or the Green Mountain Boys. That chapter also shows how the colonial context reshaped the militias' role—or, to put it more directly, how militias' main task became fighting Native Americans and how brutal, violent, and indiscriminate those militias could be when fighting against Indians. The chapter on the Stono Rebellion tells the next phase in the story of the colonial militias, as the frontier between English settlement and the indigenous population shifted west, while the coastal areas of the southern colonies became slave societies. Here, too, the role of the militias changed, and policing the enslaved population became the militia's main task. Here, too, the militias could be brutal, violent, and indiscriminate.

Meanwhile, the ideas that would provide the intellectual scaffolding for the militia system were coming to their full development in England in the aftermath of the Glorious Revolution of 1688. These were ideas that the leaders of the American Revolution would know intimately but that had only a passing influence on the militias that existed in the colonies. When South Carolina's militiamen put down the Stono Rebellion, they were not focused on the dangers of a standing army. During the century or so leading up to the American Revolution, it was almost as if the colonial militias and English theoretical writings on the militia existed in two separate worlds. Yet both strands—the militias' institutional history in the colonies and the republican ideas that supported it—came together in the Second Amendment.

It was this mutual history of institutions and ideas, along with the colonists' military situation in relation to neighboring tribes and their need to police the enslaved population, that made the Second Amendment possible. Without the history of republican thought and militia advocacy, without Machiavelli and Fletcher of Saltoun and all of their fellow travelers, there might still have been militias in the colonies. There would have been no Second Amendment, though, at least not one phrased anything like the one that still exists. Without the racial divisions of colonial North America, the militia, as an institution in that society, would not have had the same importance in people's lives. This confluence of theory and practice, of ideology and institution, of race and republicanism, is the key to understanding the road to the Second Amendment.

This approach differs from that taken by other books on the Second Amendment in a number of ways. The most basic, of course, is that this book ends where the others begin. Beyond that, this book takes a view of the Second Amendment that is not only more long term, but also more big picture, than other books on the topic. In a field dominated by legal historians and historically minded legal scholars, this book uses a decidedly less legally oriented methodology. Again, the goal of this book is to explain why, once the United States decided to attach the Bill of Rights to the Constitution, it was inevitable that the Second Amendment, or something similar to it, would be included in those rights. This big-picture approach necessarily means that some details fade out of focus. This book therefore includes no discussion about how many commas the amendment has. (This debate does exist; there are at least two commas, but there are probably three.) There is no attempt to determine where "regulated" ended and "infringed" began. Nor is there an attempt to determine whether or not the founders intended to create an "individual" right to bear arms. The existence or nonexistence of that individual right is an important political question for the twenty-first century. It was not, however, an important question during the eighteenth century, and as much as possible, this book is focused on the questions that were important at the time of the events described.

This book is also not about the relationship between the amendment's two clauses. The question of that relationship has been key to all debates Second Amendment for some time now, in popular discussions, among politicians, and in the courts. Focusing on the relationship between the two phrases risks overlooking the obvious: it is one amendment. It is twenty-seven words long. The whole thing matters. The working assumption going into the process of researching this book was that both clauses are important and that the two clauses were related to each other; nothing discovered during the research phase challenged that assumption. To be sure, this book pays more attention to the first half of the amendment than the second. The second half is more straightforward, but the first half is more interesting. For historians, it has more meat on the bone: there is more history behind it, there is more to explain, there is more to understand, and yet, ironically, less has been written about it. Hence the focus throughout this book on explaining why these men believed that a well-regulated militia would be necessary to the security of a free state. This emphasis is an attempt neither to somehow deny that the second half exists nor to minimize its importance. Or, to reassure gun rights advocates: yes, I have read the amendment all the way to the end.

Above all, this is a work of historical research and historical writing. It is history with political stakes and political implications, but the methods used here are historical, and the message is also historical. The Second Amendment was and remains an eighteenth-century text. The best way to understand it is to come as close as possible to understanding it in the conditions and terms in which it first appeared. The most fundamental message is that the men who wrote it lived in a very different world than our own, and they had very different concerns than we do. To those men, the Second Amendment made sense.

ONE

Julius Caesar Crosses the Rubicon

49 BC

NOT LONG after his presidency ended, Thomas Jefferson told a story of a conversation he had had with Alexander Hamilton in the early 1790s. Hamilton had asked Jefferson, the host that day, about the paintings of three men hanging on the walls. Jefferson identified them as John Locke, Francis Bacon, and Isaac Newton, "the three greatest men the world has produced." To this Hamilton replied, "The greatest man that ever lived was Julius Caesar."[1]

For a republican like Jefferson, few names could have been more shocking.

Julius Caesar did have a collection of lifetime achievements that, from other perspectives, merit his discussion among history's great men. He was a brilliant military leader who conquered huge swaths of territory for Rome. He defeated his rivals in Rome's civil war, became Rome's ruler, and helped end a long period of chaos and instability. He instituted an impressive number of reforms. It was a lifetime full of accomplishments, and Julius Caesar did it all with a certain flair and a knack for the dramatic. When he was twenty-five years old, a group of Sicilian pirates kidnapped him and held him for ransom; Caesar laughed at them and told them they had set their price far too low. Though from one of Rome's richest families, he won the love and support of Rome's poorest citizens. He even wrote his own memoirs. "Caesar was both genius and demon," wrote historian Barry Strauss, "excelling at politics, war, and writing—a triple crown that no one has ever worn so well."[2] But to republicans none of that mattered. To them, Julius Caesar was first and foremost the man who had killed history's greatest republic. For men like Jefferson, that made Caesar a villain, not a hero, let alone one of history's greatest men. In Jefferson's recounting, then, Hamilton's choice of a hero showed that the former secretary of the treasury had never been a true republican.[3]

Hamilton had probably revealed less about himself than Jefferson suspected. There is plenty to ask about the extent of Hamilton's commitment to republicanism, but scholars have combed through Hamilton's writings and found no other praise of Caesar—and much criticism. It seems unlikely that he idolized Caesar. Hamilton was in all likelihood just giving his fellow founder (and rival) a hard time. Jefferson had many positive attributes of his own, but a sense of humor was not one of them.

Hamilton's insincere praise for Julius Caesar might not reveal much about Hamilton himself, but it does point to a larger point about the lessons of the ancient world. Those hoping to draw lessons from the ancient writings of Greece and Rome had—and still have—quite a bit of flexibility about which lessons to draw. Lovers of philosophy, literature, and art can revel in the ancients' achievements, but so too can lovers of armies, war, and military discipline. And while that flexibility remains to this day, the ancients' relevance has faded. Few people still study Latin or Greek, and premodern history is a small part of today's education system. Not so during the eighteenth century, when the classics were the cornerstone of any formal education. Those who went to school learned Latin and Greek and studied ancient writers intensively, and this education created a common set of references. Events from the ancient world provided lessons for the eighteenth century. The heroes of the ancient world were examples to emulate, while the names of the ancient world's villains became insults to hurl at one's opponents. Likening someone to a Cato or a Brutus, a Leonidas or a Cincinnatus was among the highest of compliments. Calling someone a Catiline, a Tarquin, or a Caesar, remained a powerful insult.[4]

More substantively, eighteenth-century societies looked to the ancient world for measuring sticks with which to assess their own societies. Would they have the austere virtues of the Roman Republic? Or, perhaps, the wealth and splendor of the Roman Empire during its first centuries? Would they have the wisdom of ancient Athens? The courage of ancient Sparta? The ancients cast a long shadow over what scholars now call the early modern Atlantic World—the British Isles, Western Europe, and the European colonies of the West Indies and North America during the seventeenth and eighteenth centuries. This was why George Washington referred to "the Histories of Greece and Rome in their most virtuous and Patriotic ages." It was also why the eighteenth-century French author Montesquieu, a man whom the founding fathers held in high esteem, described Rome before its decline as "a city whose people had but a single spirit, a single love of liberty, a single hatred of tyranny."[5] To live up to the examples that antiquity had left remained a worthy challenge for all early modern nations, but those early modern nations still got to choose which example. As Jefferson's horror at Hamilton showed, everyone took lessons from the ancient world but not the same lessons.

The long road to the Second Amendment began in the ancient world. It began there because the key lessons that led the founders of the United States to embrace militias and citizen-soldiers began there; it began in the ancient world because the events that led those founders to fear permanent armies and mistrust mercenaries were lessons that they had learned from the ancient world and then applied to their own. Above all, the ancient world is where this story began because the ancient world is where the men of the eighteenth century thought the story began.

What follows in the rest of this chapter, then, is a guide to three of the lessons that the eighteenth century took from the ancient world. All three came from the Roman Republic, but this chapter is not a full history of that republic. Rather, it is an explanation of the lessons that men later took from the Roman Republic. Understanding these lessons will show why George Washington emulated a minor early Roman politician named Cincinnatus and why men of the eighteenth century saw the Second Punic War as one more reason to put their trust in citizen-soldiers. It will also show not only why Jefferson so disliked Caesar but why Caesar's march across the Rubicon in 49 BC became the most important lesson that the ancient world had to give to the eighteenth century, paving the way to a society where, as James Madison would later write, "the liberties of Rome proved the final victim to her military triumphs."[6]

Lucius Quintius Cincinnatus was not the towering figure Julius Caesar would later be. In some ways he was little more than a footnote in the Roman Republic's long history; had he not existed, Rome would in all likelihood have turned out just like it did. But Cincinnatus's story became a popular and inspirational one during the eighteenth century and eventually the namesake for the Society of the Cincinnati, a fraternal organization of officers who had fought on the Americans' side during the Revolution. When the officers formed the society in the 1780s, they chose as its motto *Omnia reliquit servare rempublicam* (He gave all to serve the Republic), a message that indicated the virtues that the officers sought to promote in the young republic, as well as the belief that Americans could achieve these virtues by emulating the ancient Romans, as long as they chose the right ones to emulate.

Cincinnatus lived during the fifth century BC, when Rome was but one power among many on the Italian peninsula. He had been born into Rome's elite "patrician" class but was not particularly wealthy. During his early adulthood he had established himself as a trustworthy if traditional patrician politician. He had earned the respect of his peers and the enmity of many in Rome's lower "plebian" class. A series of events involving his son had led Cincinnatus to leave public life while still relatively young. He retired to his fields to support himself and his family.[7]

The main historical source for Rome's early history, and therefore most of what we know about Cincinnatus, is Livy's *Ad Urbe Condita Libri,* written during the first decades after the fall of the Roman Republic. Livy wrote that in 458 BC Rome was "struck with terror" and "panic and alarm" spread. Rome's wars against two neighboring tribes, the Sabines and the Aequi, were going badly. Rome's poorer citizens were agitating for a larger role in Roman political life and were not always eager to support the patrician-led government's policies. The crisis grew great enough that Rome's existence was under threat, and the unwieldy political life of the republic made it difficult for Rome to adequately respond to the crisis. Rome had been a republic since the sixth century, when the previously existing monarchy was abolished. Replacing the monarchy with a republic had gone well for Rome; the new political system allowed more men to take part, and Rome had continued to expand and thrive. The Romans believed, though, that in times of crisis it was useful to return to one-man rule until the crisis had passed. They therefore had created the office of "dictator," a man who would wield unlimited power for a limited time. It was this position that Rome's Senate offered to Cincinnatus, which he accepted, with his tenure to last for half a year.

Once he took office, Cincinnatus sprang into action. He reorganized the army and led it to victory against the Aequi and the Sabines. The Romans destroyed the Sabines' fields. Cincinnatus made the Aequi surrender their weapons and leave "with only their shirts on." He also required each Aequian soldier to "pass under the yoke," a ritual act of submission and humiliation. Cincinnatus's actions on the battlefield intimidated the plebeians, who, for the time being, stopped their agitations against the patricians. After fifteen days Cincinnatus declared that the crisis had passed. Seeing no more need for a dictator, Cincinnatus resigned the position, with all of the power it possessed, and returned to his farm. The same story would play out again twenty years later, when Cincinnatus would again restore order to Rome and then relinquish his power as soon as he deemed the crisis over.

That's the story of Cincinnatus. Livy adds a few more details but not many—when it comes to the very early history of Rome, we simply do not have much to go on. Livy did add one editorial note about Cincinnatus's lifestyle that helped bring this brief episode to the attention of later readers, though. For Livy, whose own life spanned the last years of the republic and the first years of the empire, Cincinnatus's actions served as a useful message for "those who despise all human qualities in comparison with riches, and think there is no room for great honours or for worth but amidst a profusion of wealth." Livy made a point of emphasizing Cincinnatus's humble life and disdain for riches. When the Roman Senate's deputation found Cincinnatus, the retired politician was "either digging out a ditch or ploughing, at all events, as is generally agreed, intent on his husbandry." Asking the deputation "if all was well," Cincinnatus asked his wife to bring him his toga. "Wiping off the dust and perspiration, he put it on and came forward, on which the deputation saluted him as Dictator and congratulated him, invited him to the City and explained the state of apprehension in which the army were."

For Livy, then, Cincinnatus was a welcome contrast to the more wealth-oriented Rome of his day—and this interpretation would resonate among eighteenth-century readers as well. Several elements made Cincinnatus's story key for later republicans. He walked away from power and glory. He resisted the temptation to enrich himself. He acted on behalf of his fatherland instead of himself. In short, he embodied a selfless virtue to which all Romans were supposed to aspire. Cincinnatus was the perfect leader because he was first and foremost a citizen. When George Washington finished his second term as president of the United States and returned to his estate at Mount Vernon, he knew—and his contemporaries knew—that he was doing what Cincinnatus had done so many centuries earlier.[8]

Again, Cincinnatus lived at a time when Rome was just a regional power, sharing the Italian peninsula with its neighbors. The republic itself was still less than a century old. According to the myths, Rome had abandoned monarchy after too many kings had abused their authority. In the king's place, Rome's leading citizens set up a system that let them rule collectively. The defining characteristic of Roman politics remained the limits of any one man's power. The republic—the Latin is *res publica,* which literally means the "public thing" and is best translated as "commonwealth"—was born as a rejection of monarchy, and the Romans took this origin seriously. The citizens themselves would rule Rome. In times of crisis, the institution of the dictator allowed Rome to return to one-man rule, but only for a limited time. And if Cincinnatus provided the perfect example of why rulers had to be citizens, the events of the Second Punic War provided the perfect example of why soldiers, too, had to be citizens.

The Second Punic War began three centuries after Cincinnatus's lifetime. By that time Rome was no longer the small bellicose society Cincinnatus had rescued; Rome had begun its transformation into a much larger, but just as bellicose, Mediterranean power. It had taken over the entire Italian peninsula and showed no signs that it would stop expanding. This growth had put it into conflict with the Carthaginian Empire, a Mediterranean empire based in Northern Africa. The two powers first fought in the middle of the third century BC in the First Punic War, when Carthage's military forces, led by Hamilcar Barca, proved no match for the Romans. Unfortunately for the Romans, Hamilcar Barca's son Hannibal would come out of the war with a burning desire to avenge his father's defeat. Hannibal would go on to give Rome all that it could handle.[9]

To speak in the most basic terms, the Europe of the third century BC was a violent world. Tribal peoples dominated most of Europe; their societies tended to have strong warrior cultures but little in the way of political structures or higher cultural developments. They did not have written languages or large cities. In small battles, these peoples could easily be the equals of a Roman force of similar size. What they lacked compared to Rome was the ability to organize large-scale armies and to communicate across long distances. These tribes sometimes made alliances with other powers, though, and the men in these societies were often willing to hire themselves out to other forces.[10]

Mercenaries—soldiers for hire—were a major factor in the ancient World, and the Carthaginians made full use of them. This was one of the major differences between Rome and Carthage: Rome relied on its citizens' army, while Carthage relied on hired soldiers.[11] As Hannibal began his attack on Italy, this system seemed to work fine for the Carthaginian army. The tribes whom he had brought into his army fought well. The early battles all went Hannibal's way, with his armies defeating Rome and killing tens of thousands of Rome's soldiers. In response, the Roman Senate put together the largest Roman army to date in the hopes that a decisive battle would defeat Hannibal once and for all. This decision would instead set the stage for the Battle of Cannae in 216 BC, one of Rome's worst defeats.

Ancient sources vary on the size of the two armies that met at Cannae, with numbers ranging between forty thousand and ninety thousand troops on the Roman side. The Carthaginian army was smaller but probably not by more than ten thousand men or so. Rome had the superior numbers and was ready to fight, but Hannibal used the Romans' aggressiveness against them, putting his weakest fighters at the center of the battle, where the Roman troops began to slaughter them and to advance on the Carthaginians—or so they thought. "As the Romans rushed incautiously in between," Livy wrote, Hannibal's soldiers "enveloped them, and presently, extending their wings, crescent-wise, even closed in on their rear." From that point on, the Romans "were at a twofold disadvantage: they were shut in, while their enemies ranged on every side of them; they were tired and faced troops that were fresh and strong."[12] As another ancient account put it, "The result was exactly what Hannibal had planned."[13] Hannibal's men killed most of Rome's soldiers that day and took perhaps eight thousand more as prisoners.[14]

When news reached Rome, the city panicked. Women wailed in the streets. Some of the younger men in the Senate were seen "looking to the sea and the ships, proposing to abandon Italy and flee for refuge to some king."[15] The city was sure that Hannibal's forces would be arriving any time to take the city itself. Hannibal, though, was in no hurry, focusing on the prisoners he had taken and trying to figure out what kind of ransom he could demand. One of the other Carthaginian generals told him, "'In very truth the gods bestow not on the same man all gifts; you know how to gain a victory, Hannibal: you do not know how to use one.'" Added Livy: "That day's delay is generally believed to have saved the city and the empire."[16]

Rome's leaders took advantage of this brief respite. They prohibited women from crying in public and commanded human sacrifices. Roman men made oaths to never abandon the republic. And Rome set about reconstituting its army. The republic named a new dictator, the previously unpopular Fabius. Rome also temporarily eliminated its property restrictions on allowing soldiers to be citizens. Rome's requirements that citizens also be soldiers usually only applied to citizens with a certain amount of property—a topic that will become central later in this chapter. But this was a time of crisis, and the Roman Senate decided to arm all the men it could, even arming eight thousand slaves, and was able to put a new army into the field. Rome was no longer defenseless, though Fabius was not eager to engage Hannibal in a direct battle. Instead, by avoiding direct fights, he was able to turn the fight against Hannibal into a war of attrition where Hannibal's tactical genius would be less of an advantage. The Romans had disapproved of this strategy earlier in the war, but in the aftermath of Cannae it began to make more sense. Hannibal, after all, was the invader; Rome was in a better position to wait him out.

One more detail from Cannae's aftermath is worth noting. Hannibal sent a delegation of the prisoners he had taken back to Rome to propose a ransom. Rome, despite being desperate for soldiers, said no. In fact, simply proposing the trade turned out to be Hannibal's first major miscalculation. Rome had a tradition of giving little account to its own prisoners of war—it was far nobler to die on the battlefield. Rome was also in some financial straits, having just paid to rebuild and reequip the army. Beyond that, Livy wrote, "They were also moved by the greatness of the sum required, not wishing either to exhaust the treasury . . . or to furnish Hannibal with money—the one thing of which he was rumored to stand most in need."[17]

Fabius never did fully defeat Hannibal on the battlefield—that honor would go to another Roman general, Scipio Africanus—but he guided Rome through its darkest hour. There was a lesson here to be learned about battle tactics, for anyone interested in finding it. Fabius had shown that it was not a dramatic large-scale confrontation that Rome needed and that the need to prove one's self on the battlefield could be self-destructive. Few, however, chose to take that lesson from the Second Punic War. It was Scipio Africanus who emerged as the hero, not Fabius, and "Fabian tactics"—delaying confrontations in the hopes of wearing the opponent down—are still looked down on. George Washington himself faced criticism during the American Revolution that he was too hesitant, too much like an American Fabius.[18]

But there was another lesson that later writers took from the aftermath of the Battle of Cannae: citizen-soldiers could be counted on, but mercenaries could not. Had Hannibal marched on Rome with an army of his own countrymen, fighting for Carthage's glory and their own, they would have been successful. Had Rome relied on mercenaries, those mercenaries would have abandoned Rome in that dark hour. Citizens, though, could be trusted to fight as long and as hard as they could because they were not fighting for money. They were not even fighting just for their lives. They were fighting for their homes, their families, and their fatherland. This difference between the Carthaginian and the Roman armies gave Rome an advantage that even a military genius like Hannibal could not overcome.

This analysis, that the key to Rome's victories was its reliance on citizen-soldiers, has not earned the universal support of subsequent commentators. It is an old analysis, though, one that predates even Livy. It dates at least to the Greek historian Polybius, who wrote in the third century BC. "The Carthaginians," Polybius wrote,

> employ foreign mercenaries, the Romans native and citizen levies. It is in this point that the latter polity is preferable to the former. They have their hopes of freedom ever resting on the courage of mercenary troops: the Romans on the valour of their own citizens and the aid of their allies. The result is that even if the Romans have suffered a defeat at first, they renew the war with undiminished forces, which the Carthaginians cannot do. For, as the Romans are fighting for country and children, it is impossible for them to relax the fury of their struggle; but they persist with obstinate resolution until they have overcome their enemies.[19]

The Second Punic War would be a major turning point in the history of both Rome and Carthage. Carthage never fully recovered; one century later it no longer existed. Rome emerged from the war richer, larger, and well on its way to becoming the Mediterranean's dominant power. But this newfound power would lead to other changes as well. It was after the Second Punic War that Rome's growth began to strain at the limits of the republic. Poorer Roman citizens began a descent into deeper poverty; richer citizens became wealthy beyond previous measure. Rome had never been an egalitarian society, but the extent of inequality between its citizens created strains that Rome had not seen before.

Rome went through cultural changes as well. It conquered Greece during the second century BC. Greece, like other conquered regions, would provide Rome with its share of slaves. Some of these enslaved Greeks were different, though. Ancient Greece's cultural accomplishments loomed far higher than Rome's, and some of the new Greek arrivals were well-versed in the classical Greek culture that had emerged in Athens during the fourth century BC with Plato and Aristotle and began teaching their Roman masters about Greek philosophy and drama. *Graecia capta ferum victorem cepit et artes intulit agresti Latio,* the Roman poet Horace would later claim (Greece, the captive, made her savage victor captive, and brought the arts into rustic Latium).[20] While some might look at this and see a certain refinement and sophistication, others saw a softening, even a weakening of a traditionally violent and virile Roman culture. The Romans, critics would claim, were no longer the men they once were. The virtues of the early republic were military virtues: they trained hard and they fought hard. When they were not fighting, they worked hard. They lived as they could and did not require wealth. It was this lifestyle that had allowed Rome to grow from the small bellicose society Cincinnatus had rescued into the much larger but just as bellicose society that defeated Hannibal. But with the Carthaginians defeated, with new wealth streaming into the empire, with the arrival of Greek learning and culture, the average Roman citizen might finally start appreciating the finer things in life and leaving behind the exclusive focus on the glory of the battlefield.[21]

To clarify: a society is bellicose when war animates all, or at least most, of that society. It does not mean that that society's army will be particularly powerful: many warlike societies lacked the organization for a large-scale army. Similarly, a well-organized society could have a large and effective army that lived in relative isolation from the rest of society, as is the case with most large armies today. The Roman Republic had been a bellicose society because there was such a high level of integration between its army and the rest of the society. All citizens who met the property requirements served in the army, and all of the soldiers Rome sent to the battlefield were Roman citizens.

This was always an idealized, mythical view of Rome during the first centuries of the republic.[22] Still, in the century and a half or so between the Battle of Cannae and the rise of Julius Caesar, Rome did change, and those changes would lead Rome to reshape the relationship between citizenship and being a soldier. There were new ways of being a leading citizen, based more in culture and learning than in fighting. In the years before Julius Caesar took power, one of Rome's leading politicians was a man named Cicero who built his reputation on his writing and his oratory rather than his military prowess. For later writers this newer version of Rome, with its drama and its philosophy and its great wealth, began looking like it was in decline. For the poorer citizens, though, the influence of Greek philosophy was not their problem. They were not the ones with Greek slaves or the ones learning to read Plato. They were the ones displaced by the new enslaved population. They needed land and they needed work.[23]

To relieve those social strains, in 107 BC the Roman leader Marius changed the requirements of the Roman army. Poor citizens could now be soldiers.

This reform was not a temporary emergency reform, as the Romans had done after the Battle of Cannae; it was a permanent change that gave citizens a way to earn their livelihood. Victorious soldiers would be able to earn enough booty or land to carve out a livelihood for themselves. The possibility to make a career of sorts in the army came as a welcome change for those citizens with fewer options open to them and no land of their own. This seemed like a way to handle the same sorts of social strains and fights between patricians and plebeians that Rome had struggled with since before the time of Cincinnatus. In the process, though, the nature of the Roman army changed. The traditional ideal of the Roman soldier was a man who, in his own way, resembled Cincinnatus: when his country needed him, he picked up his weapons and went out to fight; once the danger was over, he returned to his fields.[24]

Whether this ideal had ever really existed in Rome was a moot point, at least to the men of the eighteenth century; they saw in the early republic a model of citizen-soldiers to emulate, and they saw in Marius's reforms the beginning of the end of that ideal. "The soldiers then began to recognize no one but their general," Montesquieu would later write, "to base all their hopes on him, and to feel more remote from the city. They were no longer the soldiers of the republic but those of Sulla, Marius, Pompey, and Caesar."[25] To be sure, there was one sense in which Marius's reforms made the link between soldier and citizen even stronger. The reforms allowed all citizens to be part of Rome's army, not only the wealthy ones. But the ideal of a citizen-soldier was that the soldier was only a part-time soldier and that when he was not needed on the battlefield he would return to his home. For such a man, at least as the eighteenth century would come to understand him, being a soldier was only a part of who he was, and the duties of citizenship did not end with his military service—he was expected to participate in political life, to help his neighbors, to be a part of the community. His allegiance was to his family and, beyond that, to Rome itself. Marius's reforms created something new to Rome: the permanent soldier, a man who, once the fighting was over, did not necessarily have a home or a career to which he could return. His ties to the community were broken. His allegiance was now to their generals. And no Roman general was as successful in winning his soldiers' allegiance as Julius Caesar.

Winning people's allegiance was one of Caesar's great talents. As noted above, Rome's poorer citizens loved him, despite his enormous wealth. He embraced the population and made his cause their own, bypassing the Senate to pass land reform laws that aided poorer citizens. (Caesar's fellow nobles were less keen on this populist approach to politics.) And while Marius's reforms had created a situation that fostered soldiers' allegiance to their generals, Caesar's own charisma helped too. He fought alongside his soldiers, and in his accounts of his wars he sang his soldiers' praises. He shared their risks and their sacrifices, and the soldiers appreciated that. But during the civil war, Caesar had to divide his troops up and spread them across the empire; he also fell behind in their pay. Some of his soldiers, missing both their leader and their money, began to mutiny. Caesar was able to resolve the crisis with one speech—with one word, even. When he addressed the mutineers, he referred to them as "citizens" rather than "soldiers," as he usually did. He was telling them that their time in his service had come to an end. Hearing this, the men renounced their complaints and recommitted themselves to his service. "By this single word," the historian Suetonius would write roughly 150 years later, Caesar "so thoroughly brought them round and changed their determination, that they immediately cried out, they were his soldiers."[26]

Caesar also made a point of being gracious with his enemies, especially those whom he had defeated. After conquering Gaul he made the men of that region citizens; despite the carnage and death of those wars, the surviving inhabitants viewed Caesar as their hero. He sought out the praise of Cicero and returned it in kind, even though he knew that Cicero stood for everything Roman that Caesar had destroyed. When the republican hardliner Cato committed suicide rather than live in a Rome that no longer functioned as a republic, Caesar regretted the lost opportunity of pardoning one more enemy. His graciousness with enemies may have been what eventually led to Caesar's downfall. Brutus had long been an ally of Cato's until Caesar welcomed Brutus into his ranks.[27]

Caesar had his quirks as well. He was known as a womanizer, something less common among early Roman leaders and not particularly approved of in republican Rome. He was probably an epileptic and suffered fits and dizzy spells. In Suetonius's portrayal, Julius Caesar was bold and decisive—though a bit vain as well. Caesar was "so nice in the care of his person," he wrote, "that he not only kept the hair of his head closely cut and had his face smoothly shaved, but even caused the hair on other parts of the body to be plucked out by the roots. . . . His baldness gave him much uneasiness, having often found himself upon that account exposed to the jibes of his enemies. He therefore used to bring forward the hair from the crown of his head."[28] Julius Caesar, shaper of history, wore a comb-over.

Like Cincinnatus—and, for that matter, like all the other Roman generals mentioned in this chapter—Caesar was born into Rome's patrician class. Caesar's early career was successful in an unspectacular way. When he was in his thirties, he is said to have passed by a statue of Alexander the Great and to have "heaved a sigh, and as if out of patience with his own incapacity in having as yet done nothing noteworthy at a time of life when Alexander had already brought the world to his feet."[29] Still, Caesar took the positions that came open to him and cultivated friendships and alliances among powerful Romans. It was a time when an ambitious young Roman man could rise to the top but only if he was willing to take some risks, and Caesar did not want for bravery. Nor did Caesar hesistate when he was given command of an army despite having little military experience. He took that army and conquered all of Gaul, even traveling with his men across the English Channel and becoming one of the first Romans to visit Britain.[30]

The Rome into which Julius Caesar was born was still a republic, but it was not a healthy one. Civil wars had been tearing it apart for most of the previous century. There had been wars between the different classes of Roman citizens, and there had been civil wars between rival leaders. In 82 BC the Senate appointed Rome's first dictator since the Second Punic War. The man they chose, Sulla, was already a military hero, and given the difficulties Rome was facing, appointing a dictator made some sense. The Senate broke with tradition by not limiting the duration for that position, though Sulla would voluntarily resign the position later that year. Then from 73 BC until 71 BC, Spartacus led the largest revolt of enslaved people Rome had seen. The Roman Republic had always thrived on a certain level of boisterous instability, but things had moved beyond that. During his dictatorship Sulla had ordered the execution of thousands of Rome's leading citizens, something unprecedented in Roman political life. A rough-and-tumble political world had become a kill-or-be-killed political world. But for Julius Caesar, this world might as well have been created just for him.

The crucial turning point for Caesar's life—and the one that would echo across the centuries—came in 49 BC. Caesar and his soldiers had completed their conquest of Gaul. This was one of Rome's greatest military accomplishments to date, adding an enormous (if not particularly wealthy) territory to the growing empire. Caesar and his armies began the trip back to Rome. But he knew that it was not a hero's welcome that awaited him. The politics and intrigues had not stopped, and his absence from Rome had given Caesar's rivals an advantage. In all likelihood there was an arrest waiting for him upon his return.

Rome, for all of its integration between military leaders and political leaders, between being a soldier and being a citizen, still had laws meant to keep the armies and the government physically separated. Generals could not just march their armies anywhere they saw fit. They could not march their armies into territories controlled by other Roman generals, and they could not march their armies into Rome itself unless the Senate had invited them to do so. Specifically, in Julius Caesar's case, this meant that in returning from Gaul, to Rome's north, he could not march his army across the Rubicon River, which was Rome's northern boundary at the time.

Marius's reforms helped paved the way for Caesar's invasion of Rome, but it still took some chutzpah on Caesar's part to even contemplate it. Julius Caesar showed no lack of bravery during his fifty-five years, but when it came to crossing that border with his troops, even the normally decisive general hesitated. Plutarch, writing in the following century, described it best:

> When he came to the river which separates Cisalpine Gaul from the rest of Italy (it is called the Rubicon), and began to reflect, now that he drew nearer to the fearful step and was agitated by the magnitude of his ventures, he checked his speed. Then, halting in his course, he communed with himself a long time in silence as his resolution wavered back and forth, and his purpose then suffered change after change. . . . But finally, with a sort of passion, as if abandoning calculation and casting himself upon the future, and uttering the phrase with which men usually prelude their plunge into desperate and daring fortunes, "Let the die be cast," he hastened to cross the river.[31]

Other ancient writers differed in their details but gave the same overall story: Caesar and his troops arrived at the Rubicon and paused as Caesar weighed the consequences, showing an uncharacteristic moment of thoughtful prudence before reverting to form. According to the writer Appian, Caesar said to his soldiers, "My friends, to leave this stream uncrossed will breed manifold distress for me; to cross it, for all mankind."[32] Suetonius claimed that when Caesar reached the banks of the Rubicon he halted and told his troops that "even yet we may draw back; but once cross yon little bridge, and the whole issue is with the sword."[33]

Caesar knew that by crossing it with his troops under arms he was breaking Roman law. Breaking such a fundamental law warranted an appropriate reaction—such an infraction seemed to necessitate a severe punishment, but who would be able to impose it? Caesar's army could only be stopped by another, stronger army. Caesar had started a civil war. He also finished it. His military power was stronger than the law that he broke, and it was stronger than any other force capable of punishing him for his transgressions. The republic did not disappear that day, but it never did recover. Of course, it had been ailing for quite some time.

The civil war that followed Caesar's march on Rome would last for several years, but from the start, Caesar and his troops were in the dominant position. Recognizing the political and military realities, not long after he marched his troops across the Rubicon the Senate named Julius Caesar dictator. He would soon resign the position, but then the Senate again named him dictator the following year—first for a term of one year, then for a term of ten years. By 44 BC, five years after he had marched his troops on Rome, the Senate named him dictator for life. He would hold the position until he died, though that would come soon. Only one month after being appointed dictator for life (though having already held the position of dictator for the better part of five years), a group of Roman politicians who resented Caesar's rise to power assassinated him.[34]

In a sense, the characteristics that had helped Caesar rise to power—his bravery, his graciousness with his enemies—brought about his downfall. He was unique among leading Roman men in not having bodyguards with him. And among the assassins was Brutus, the former enemy whom Caesar had pardoned and welcomed into his ranks, just to have him turn enemy again. There was more than just personal animosity involved in the assassination, though. The Roman Republic was based in a rejection of one-man rule. In the myths of Rome's origins, the city had begun as a monarchy but thrived once it overthrew the last king. Caesar himself had paid at least some respect to this tradition—he became dictator for life but refused to become king. Plutarch wrote of a festival Caesar attended not long before his death. Caesar watched from a "golden throne" as young men from the nobility ran naked through the streets of Rome, "striking those they met with shaggy thongs." That was the traditional celebration of the festival, but one of the participants decided to introduce a new element. Marc Antony took a break from running to approach Caesar and offer him a crown—"a diadem, round which a wreath of laurel was tied." In Plutarch's telling, when Caesar pushed it away, "all the people applauded; and when Antony offered it again, few, and when Caesar declined it again, all, applauded."[35] It was a symbolic rejection of monarchy. In this case, though, a symbolic rejection of kingship was not enough to cover the reality of one-man rule.

Dictators like Cincinnatus were a necessary measure but a temporary one. By becoming dictator for life, and by the way he was ignoring the Senate and Roman traditions, Julius Caesar seemed to be ending a centuries-long tradition of republican rule. It was this threat to the tradition of republican rule that led Caesar's assassins to act. Those men were able to kill Caesar, but they were not able to save the republic. Again, the republic into which Julius Caesar had been born was an ailing one. Civil strife had become the norm, and many Romans were ready to see that come to an end even if it meant a reversion to one-man rule. Soon after Julius Caesar's assassination, his great-nephew Augustus rose to the top of Rome's political ladder. In 27 BC Augustus officially became Rome's first emperor.[36]

This was the end of the Roman Republic. Rome, though, was far from dead.

During the first years of the Roman Empire, Rome's expansion sped up. Rome became richer, and organization within the empire improved. Literature and the arts flourished (indeed, most of what we know about the Roman Republic comes from writers who lived during the early years of the empire; the republic produced far fewer writers). The needs of a large empire had outstripped the capabilities of republican rule, but the conversion to an empire allowed Rome to thrive. Even the rule of several subpar emperors did not stop the empire's growth during its first century. There is, then, no inherent need to mourn the passing of the Roman Republic. Nor is there any inherent need to regret Julius Caesar's own actions. Rome became more stable after he became dictator, and the reforms he passed helped modernize Roman society. He was popular with the people of Rome. And Julius Caesar's military success, his ability to reform Roman politics, and even his literary contributions, meant that he had many admirers in later centuries, even if Hamilton turned out not to be one of them.[37]

Again, this chapter is not a history of Rome but rather a history of the lessons that eighteenth-century republicans took from Rome. What really happened during Rome's first centuries is less important here than what the men of the eighteenth century believed had happened. The early modern period saw the emergence of a sort of "core curriculum" of republican lessons. Understanding the histories of Cincinnatus, Hannibal, and Julius Caesar goes a long way toward understanding those lessons.

Cincinnatus represented the virtue required of a republican leader. He represented the ideal leader who acted on behalf of his fatherland and not on behalf of himself. He became the model to emulate for future leaders. Hannibal and Julius Caesar left different lessons, and theirs were more specific to the issues that concern this book. Both men's stories represented the advantages of relying on citizen-soldiers. Hannibal's failure to conquer Rome showed the advantages of citizen-soldiers over mercenaries. Citizen-soldiers would fight for their homes and their families, so they could be counted on more than mercenaries, fighting for money, could be. Julius Caesar's lesson too showed the advantages of citizen-soldiers over professional soldiers. Here the lesson lay not in the professional soldiers' reliability but in their allegiances. Citizen soldiers were loyal to their fatherland; professional soldiers were loyal to their generals.

Julius Caesar represented another danger as well—and one more reason for Jefferson to have been so aghast at Hamilton's comment. For all of their belief in the importance of military virtue, later republicans believed that military power had to be under civil control. Politicians gave orders to generals, not the other way around. But what happened when military leaders thumbed their noses at the law, as Caesar did when he crossed the Rubicon? That event came to represent the danger that any military leader posed to civilian authority. "The most inviolable of all the laws of nature," Jean-Jacques Rousseau would later write, "is the law of the strongest. No legislation, no constitution can exempt anyone from that law."[38] If no one in civilian power was stronger than the military leaders, then civilian authority would exist only at the whim of the strongest generals. The problem of a Caesar, then, loomed over any discussion of political and military power. Supporters of the Roman Republic could hope for a Cincinnatus; they could emulate Cincinnatus in their own actions. But they had to plan for a Caesar.

These were the lessons that the eighteenth century took from the ancient world. They were not the only lessons that could have been taken, nor were they the lessons that earlier centuries had taken. During the millennium that followed Rome's downfall, the lessons of the Roman Republic were less important. The republican emphasis on virtue, active participation in public life, and belief in the dangers of mercenaries and permanent armies was relatively unknown. Medieval Europe had had little sympathy for the republic, and some of its greatest leaders sought out the title of emperor. Leaders of Russia and Germany would choose titles derived from Caesar's name—"kaiser" in Germany, "czar" in Russia. Then came a period that called itself the Renaissance—a term that means rebirth and refers to the return of the values of the ancient world. This rebirth would cover many aspects of ancient culture, including philosophy, literature, and science. It would also include a rebirth of European republicanism—what scholars now refer to as "classical" or "civic" republicanism—which returned in the works of a failed politician, playwright, and political theorist named Niccolò Machiavelli. Machiavelli did as much as anyone to help shape the lessons that early modern republicans took from the ancient world. In doing so, he lay the groundwork for a republicanism based on active participation in public life. He emphasized a point that would become one of the founding blocks of early modern republicanism: a society could only succeed if, like in the first centuries of the Roman Republic, its citizens were soldiers and its soldiers were citizens.

TWO

Niccolò Machiavelli Retires to His Estate

1513

CESARE BORGIA was a Renaissance prince, a military leader, and the illegitimate son of a future pope. He was also a central figure in Niccolò Machiavelli's *The Prince,* which included several stories of Borgia's exploits. None was quite as memorable as that of the 1502 assassination of Ramiro d'Orco, the man Borgia had chosen to bring order to Italy's Romagna region. Borgia had taken over Romagna but found it full of "robberies, quarrels, and every other kind of insolence" and, as such, quite difficult to govern. So Borgia delegated—he hired d'Orco and authorized him to take whatever steps were necessary to bring order to the region. D'Orco turned out to be just the man Borgia needed. Ruling harshly but efficiently, torturing and killing when he saw fit, d'Orco brought peace and stability to Romagna. The problem, though, was that the people hated d'Orco, and it was only a matter of time before they would start hating Borgia himself. So one night Borgia had d'Orco cut in half and left his corpse laid out on the main square. Next to him were a chopping board and a bloody knife. "The ferocity of this spectacle," Machiavelli wrote, "left the people at once satisfied and stupefied."[1]

It was this sort of story that made the term "Machiavellian" stand for a willingness to lie, cheat, or steal in order to get ahead. Borgia looks like a sadistic killer to modern eyes, but from Machiavelli's perspective, Borgia had "made use of every deed and did all those things that should be done by a prudent and virtuous man."[2] And while the story of d'Orco's assassination was the most memorable account of Borgia's exploits, it was by no means the only violent account that Machiavelli chose to include. Machiavelli filled *The Prince* with stories about rulers willing to kill and lie and men who made sure to sow fear throughout the population. Along with those stories, Machiavelli mixed in advice for rulers about the proactive steps they should take to secure their power from their rivals, such as "In taking hold of a state, he who seizes it should examine all the offenses necessary for him to commit, and do them all at a stroke,"[3] or "Men . . . avenge themselves for light offenses but cannot do so for grave ones; so the offense one does to a man should be such that one does not fear revenge for it."[4]

That sort of rhetoric can be hard to square with the life that the man who wrote them led. To put it mildly, Niccolò Machiavelli was no Cesare Borgia; much as he praised Borgia's actions, those were the actions of a leader and a ruler, and all Machiavelli hoped for was to be an advisor. Niccolò Machiavelli was also no Julius Caesar. Caesar was a leader and a soldier who succeeded in his endeavors. Machiavelli was an advisor and a writer, and even at those tasks he was a failure during his lifetime. Caesar conquered all of Gaul, defeated his Roman rivals, and became dictator for life; Machiavelli advised some rulers, went on several diplomatic missions, lost his position, then spent the rest of his life trying to regain it. The books he wrote were not well known during his lifetime, and most remained unpublished when he died. Those books became famous later on, however. What he wrote in those books warrants his place in this one. In a nutshell, Julius Caesar played an important role in the history of citizens' militias because of what he did; Machiavelli played an important role in that history because of what he wrote. As it turns out, not everything Machiavelli wrote was as evil as *The Prince* seemed to be.[5]

Over the past several decades, scholars have shown that there was more to Machiavelli's writings than the disturbing violence of *The Prince.* To be sure, there is more than enough material in *The Prince* to warrant Machiavelli's reputation as an advocate for evil. But there was also a lesser-known Machiavelli, who was still quite rough around the edges but was less focused on violence and treachery and more focused on reforming his native Italy so that it might recapture the glory of its ancient past—a glory that, in his view, Julius Caesar had helped destroy. In other words, as strange as it might sound for a writer who believed that leaders should kill their citizens when needed, Machiavelli was a republican. He believed that citizens should play an active role in a boisterous public life. It was a vision of society that he found through his study of the Roman Republic. This strain of republicanism was present in all of Machiavelli's works—even *The Prince,* for those who know where to look. It took center stage in his 1517 *Discourses on Livy,* which focused less on rulers killing rivals and betraying allies and more on what had made the

Roman Republic successful. Those keys to success included the wisdom of Rome's laws, the virtue of its people, and its citizens' army.[6]

Alongside his less savory advice for rulers, then, Machiavelli also put together a cluster of ideas that would become the foundation for eighteenth-century ideas about the citizen-soldier. With these ideas Machiavelli began an intellectual tradition that brought him no fortune and that his native Italy had little interest in, but that would later flourish elsewhere, including in England and its North American colonies. When the Scottish writer Andrew Fletcher of Saltoun wrote at the end of the seventeenth century that it was a mistake to put any trust in mercenary soldiers "who had no interest in the commonwealth than their pay," he was giving the same warnings that Machiavelli had made back at the start of the sixteenth century.[7] When George Washington wrote in his 1783 *Sentiments on a Peace Establishment* that he hoped to make it "universally reputable to bear Arms and disgraceful to decline having a share in the performance of Military duties,"[8] he was giving the same advice to the United States that Machiavelli had given to his native Florence. And when Patrick Henry told his fellow delegates to Virginia's 1788 Ratifying Convention, "The great object is, that every man be armed," he was echoing Machiavelli's call for rulers to arm their own subjects.[9] The later authors did not usually cite or credit Machiavelli. But the cluster of ideas that Machiavelli put together was one that later militia advocates would embrace: that citizens should be armed, that mercenaries could not be trusted, and that all soldiers should be citizens.

Machiavelli's life can be divided into three phases. Of the first, which lasted from his birth in 1469 until 1498, there is almost no information available. (There are a few random notes from his father, but nothing of substance.) The second phase left more traces. In 1498, at the age of twenty-nine, Machiavelli entered the government of his native Florence. He would remain in that government until 1512, rising in both status and responsibilities. From what evidence is available, he seems to have been a conscientious and competent civil servant, trusted enough to be sent on diplomatic missions, including negotiations with the pope and with the French court. Certain aspects of his government service showed hints of the political philosophy he would later develop (though not, it should be noted, its more amoral aspects). Florence at the time was a republic. It was not necessarily a state that modern readers would recognize as a republic; standards for a republic were different in the sixteenth century. Florentine political power was in the hands of a wealthy oligarchy, and even Machiavelli, born into a middle-class family and well educated, was not a full citizen. But it is nevertheless easy to see the dedication to republics that Machiavelli would later show as a continued attachment to the Florence of his formative years, a city he would later declare he loved "more than my soul." Machiavelli also tried raising his own militia at this time. During the first decade of the sixteenth century he set out to organize the people of the countryside into an armed citizens' force. The idea had been floated in earlier decades, but it was Machiavelli who got the project moving.[10]

In the grand scheme of western military history, the Florentine militia would not merit any attention were it not for its organizer's later writings. Machiavelli put together a moderately successful military force that lasted a few years—but nothing more. It was gone in less than a decade and had no concrete legacy. Still, it showed a bit about what was going on in Machiavelli's mind at the time. Florence was struggling militarily against other Italian city-states. Florence, like its Italian neighbors, relied on hiring mercenary armies and on forging alliances with larger kingdoms for its protection.[11] Machiavelli apparently felt that he could do better. So he organized the rural population into a militia, believing that although the peasants had grown lazy, these were the same people who "in times gone by made Italy flourish"[12] and that they could again bring glory to Italy, if they experienced military discipline. His militia even had some early success on the battlefield. It could not, however, prevent Florence's fall to the Medici in 1512. Florence's fall, in turn, would also be Machiavelli's own. Success in the government of a Renaissance Italian city was fleeting; for all of its cultural glory, sixteenth-century Italy was a mess, politically, diplomatically, and militarily. Italy's major cities—Florence, Venice, Naples, etc.—were their own political entities, often at war with each other, seeking favor and protection from the larger powers nearby like France, Spain, or Austria, even when seeking that support meant risking any sense of independence. This context of instability and regional rivalries had allowed Machiavelli to have some level of political and even military success early in his career, but when the Medici family took over Florence, they had no use for him.[13]

Machiavelli took his fall from power hard. In the immediate aftermath of the Medici's victory, Machiavelli was implicated in a conspiracy against them. In all likelihood, Machiavelli took no part in the plot—the Medici found no evidence he had, nor have historians. Still, the Medici had him tortured in the hopes of getting him to make a confession. He did not, and the Medici released him after several weeks. There would be no quick return to public life, however. Instead, Machiavelli returned to his family estate in the Italian countryside. This was not the proud retirement of a Cincinnatus. Failure, not success, preceded Machiavelli's retreat from public life. As he wrote to a friend in March 1513, "As you must have learned . . . I got out of prison, amid this city's universal rejoicing. . . . I shall not repeat the long story of my disgrace to you but shall merely say that Fate has done everything to cause me this abuse." That sense of bitterness, and a belief that "fortune" had conspired against him, would never leave him. He sought eagerly to return to his position in the government. He wrote to the same friend one week later, "If these new masters of ours see fit not to leave me lying on the ground, I shall be happy and believe that I shall act in such a way that they too will have reason to be proud of me. And if they should not, I shall get on as I did when I came here: I was born in poverty and at an early age learned how to scrimp rather than to thrive."[14]

The Medici did, indeed, leave Machiavelli "lying on the ground" for the rest of the decade. He quickly settled into a routine, however. In a letter he wrote to the same friend on 10 December 1513, he recounted how he spent his time. That letter is quoted quite often, and deservedly so, for in it Machiavelli gave an excellent description of his daily life during that era. He spent his days gathering food and tending to the demands of his meagre estate. "I am living on my farm," he wrote, "and since my latest disasters, I have not spent a total of twenty days in Florence. Until now, I have been catching thrushes with my own hands. . . . With my household I eat what food this poor farm and my minuscule patrimony yield." He tried to manage his forests and sell off the wood, haggled with local merchants, and, in general, kept himself busy and kept himself alive, though not in anything approaching material comfort. "I am wasting away," he wrote toward the end of the letter, "and cannot continue on like this much longer without becoming contemptible because of my poverty." Still, the end of the day brought him respite from the tasks of his farm. "When evening comes, I return home and enter my study; on the threshold I take off my workday clothes, covered with mud and dirt, and put on the garments of court and palace. Fitted out appropriately, I step inside the venerable courts of the ancients, where, solicitously received by them, I nourish myself on that food that alone is mine and for which I was born. . . . For four hours at a time I feel no boredom, I forget all my troubles, I do not dread poverty, and I am not terrified by death. I absorb myself into them completely."[15]

This time spent in the company of ancient writers was the most intellectually productive phase of Machiavelli's life, during which he produced the texts that would make him famous—and infamous—for later generations. Already in that letter he mentioned having written a "study" on being a prince, "in which I delve as deeply as I can into the ideas concerning this topic, discussing the definition of a princedom, the categories of princedoms, how they are acquired, how they are retained, and why they are lost." That study would later be published as *The Prince* and would shape Machiavelli's legacy as an advocate of ruthlessness and deception. For Machiavelli at the time, it was a job application of sorts. He dedicated it to Florence's new Medici leaders in the hopes that his torturers would see fit to hire him as an advisor. He was desperate to return to public life and to the sort of civil servant position he had held before 1512. As he wrote in his letter, he was hoping that the Medici "should begin to engage my services, even if they should start out by having me roll along a stone."[16]

The book failed to achieve that goal, though. Machiavelli had to remain on the family farm. This exile from public life left Machiavelli the time—unwanted time, to be sure—to continue writing. This spurt of productivity included a number of histories, plays, and poems. For the purposes of this book, three of the books Machiavelli wrote during his exile from public life are of primary importance: *Discourses on Livy,* which he wrote in 1517, but which remained unpublished during his lifetime; *The Art of War,* written during 1519–20 and published in 1521; and *The Prince,* also published after Machiavelli's death. These three books complemented each other in some ways, but they also contradicted each other. After all, Machiavelli praised strongman rulership in *The Prince* and then emerged as a republican in *Discourses on Livy.* When it came to militias, citizen-soldiers, and mercenaries, though, Machiavelli was a consistent thinker. It was here, in these three books, that his theories of militias and citizen-soldiers took shape.

To write about Livy is to write about the Roman Republic, particularly its earliest years, and in his *Discourses on Livy,* that is what Machiavelli did.[17] Livy—his full Roman name was Titus Livius—was the greatest chronicler of Rome's earliest years. Livy was born during the last years of the Roman Republic and died several decades into the empire. His major accomplishment was *Ad Urbe Condita Libri,* which literally translates as "Books from the Foundation of the City," but which is best known in English as *The History of Rome.* It is the most detailed history of Rome's first centuries, and for many events of early Roman history it is the only remaining source. Most of what is known about Cincinnatus, for instance, comes from there. Such detail came at a cost: to a modern reader, Livy is long and dry. (The definitive English-language edition clocks in at fourteen volumes, even though approximately three quarters of Livy's original work has been lost.) It was not Livy's literary quality that attracted Machiavelli, though: it was the lessons to be learned from the Roman Republic and the potential of applying those lessons to his own Italy.[18]

For centuries, ancient Rome had ruled the Mediterranean and much of Europe; Renaissance Italy could not even rule itself. What was it, Machiavelli asked, that kept Italy from recapturing its greatness? During his time as a Florentine diplomat, Machiavelli had seen firsthand that Florence's independence existed only at the mercy of the larger powers. Ancient Rome had been "far from all external servitude and [its people] were at once governed by their own will."[19] Yet despite "how much honor is awarded to antiquity"[20] and despite ample evidence from history books about how the ancients had governed themselves, Machiavelli's fellow Italians ignored those lessons and continued in their self-destructive tendencies. The people of Italy had grown lazy, and "neither prince nor republic may be found that has recourse to the examples of the ancients."[21] Machiavelli's goal in writing *Discourses on Livy,* then, was to provide the lessons that his own Italy could use to regain its past greatness.

Seeking those lessons in Livy, though, meant not only that Machiavelli looking for lessons from ancient Rome but that he was specifically looking for them in the Roman *Republic*—the Rome that existed before Julius Caesar. This choice was not self-evident. As the dialogue between Thomas Jefferson and Alexander Hamilton quoted at the start of chapter 1 shows, there were valid reasons to prefer the empire. From many standpoints, the high point of Rome's success came after Julius Caesar's march across the Rubicon. Decades of civil war had preceded Julius Caesar's rule; under his successors Rome was relatively stable. The early empire also saw Rome's expansion increase. The empire was far richer than the republic had ever been; literature and the arts flourished. There was much to appreciate about the Roman Empire.

Machiavelli, though, was clear on this topic: the republic was the superior era. The empire, he wrote, was an "atrocious" time of "new misfortunes."[22] The wealth of the empire made Rome's men grow soft, weak, even effeminate.[23] Life in the republic's early centuries had prevented that. Poverty, it turned out, was good. Or, as Machiavelli put it himself, "The most useful thing that may be ordered in a free way of life is that the citizens be kept poor."[24] Machiavelli endorsed Livy's account of Cincinnatus, which had showed that while it was a time of poverty, people "were content with it, and that it was enough to those citizens to get honor from war, and everything useful they left to the public."[25] The resulting society was one where the citizens looked after the public good and not only their own personal benefit.

Machiavelli makes a curious comment, though, about the relative hardship of the early Roman Republic. The region, he wrote, was *not* a difficult place in which to live. Life there could be comparatively easy, given its soil and its proximity to the sea. And for Machiavelli "very fertile countries" were "apt to produce men who are idle and unfit for any virtuous exercise." Rome's early leaders, though, "had the wisdom to prevent the harms that the agreeableness of the country would have caused through idleness by imposing a necessity to exercise on those who had to be soldiers, so that through such an order they became better soldiers there than in other countries that have naturally been harsh and sterile."[26] The result of this forced military practice, of course, was that Rome wound up with a formidable army. The strength of its military made its expansion possible; no society could go from one small village to the domination of the Mediterranean without a strong military. But for Machiavelli, this experience seems to have also made the Romans into better citizens as well. In these passages, then, it becomes clear just how closely the military and the citizenry were tied together in Machiavelli's thought. He believed that Rome's accomplishments were possible because their army was a *citizens'* army. Motivating soldiers with money, or with fear of punishment, simply did not work as well as motivating them through glory and a sense of ownership of the army's accomplishments. There was a major difference, according to Machiavelli, "between an army that is content and engages in combat for its own glory and one that is ill disposed and engages in combat for the ambition of someone else."[27]

Machiavelli would come back to this theme quite often, that the mentality of the soldiers mattered as much as their numbers or their equipment, if not more. "In those armies in which there is no affection toward him for whom they engage in combat that makes them become his partisans," he wrote, "there can never be enough virtue to resist an enemy who is a little virtuous."[28] Warriors needed to be motivated in order to reach their potential. And while the rulers of Machiavelli's Italy paid mercenaries to fight their battles, the Roman Republic had had a far better solution. "Because neither this love nor this rivalry arises except from your subjects," he wrote, "it is necessary to arm one's subjects for oneself, if one wishes to hold a state . . . as one sees those have done who have made great profit with armies."[29]

There was another idea lurking in Machiavelli's thoughts on the relationship between citizens and soldiers, though. It was probably less central to his views, and he returned to it less often, but by saying that Roman citizens benefited from their military service by becoming stronger and more disciplined—benefits that remained, even when these citizens were no longer on the battlefield—Machiavelli was saying not only that citizens made better soldiers but that soldiers made better citizens. The idleness and soft lives of a society would make citizens unwilling to make the sacrifices necessary for their society to thrive. Poverty, not wealth, made a society strong; an easy life made people lazy and soft.

Discourses on Livy covered more than just Rome's military. Machiavelli discussed Rome's political system, the role of religion in the society, the office of dictator, and many other issues. He wanted to show his readers—and Italy's rulers—what they would need to do in order to recapture Rome's greatness. None of that would be possible, though, without a strong military. The army was the foundation of Rome's greatness during the republican era. And the foundation of Machiavelli's military thinking was there as well: citizens make better soldiers.[30]

Citizen-soldiers played an even more central role in Machiavelli's *The Art of War,* which he wrote in 1519–20.[31] That book has not had as prominent a legacy as *The Prince* or *Discourses on Livy,* but of the three it was the only one Machiavelli published during his lifetime. His views there were consistent with those he had advocated in *Discourses on Livy.* He reiterated the need "to seek to be like the ancients in things strong and rough"[32] and his complaint that "military customs are wholly corrupted and have greatly diverged from ancient methods."[33] He also made it clear that the ancient society to be emulated was the Roman Republic—and even ancient Sparta—but *not* the Roman Empire. It was during the republic that Romans learned to "honor and reward excellence, not to despise poverty, to esteem the methods and regulations of military discipline," and "to esteem private less than public good."[34] Under the empire, though, leaders began "thinking more about their own power than about the public advantage."[35] Citizens began to delight in things "delicate and soft," and "as soon as activities of this sort satisfied my Romans, my native land went to ruin."[36]

The Art of War, then, was in many ways an expansion of the views Machiavelli had expressed in *Discourses on Livy.* Again, Machiavelli was not always a consistent writer from one book to the next, but on the topic of citizen-soldiers, his inconsistencies tended to be matters of details rather than his overall philosophy. In both books, he identified the republic as the height of Rome's glory. In *The Art of War* he claims that Rome's decline began when the army's leaders stopped caring about the public good and started seeking their own personal gain. In the republic, as Machiavelli described it, "generals, satisfied with their triumph, eagerly returned to private life."[37] The generals' new selfish spirit went against the ethos of the republic's armies and set a bad example for the republic's rank-and-file soldiers. The sort of selfless dedication Cincinnatus had shown was the rule during the republic, as Machiavelli saw it. The republic's citizen-soldiers "did not practice war as their profession." They sought fame and glory on the battlefield, but once the fighting was over, "they wished to come home and live by their profession." It was a truly dual lifestyle, where every eligible citizen, "when he was not soldiering, was willing to be soldier, and when he was soldiering, wanted to be dismissed."[38]

The army of the Roman Republic thrived when filled with citizen-soldiers, Machiavelli believed. But Rome itself also thrived. In writing this, Machiavelli seemed to sense that he was going against the beliefs of his day. "Many have held and now still hold this opinion: that no two things are more out of harmony with one another or differ more from one another than civilian life and military life," he wrote, "but if we consider ancient ways, we shall not find things that are more closely united, more in conformity, and of which one, necessarily, so much loves the other as do these."[39] In *Discourses on Livy,* Machiavelli had acknowledged that "if you wish to make a people numerous and armed so as to be able to make a great empire, you make it of such a quality that you cannot manage it in your mode."[40] In *The Art of War,* though, he backtracked on this, writing that "weapons borne by citizens or subjects, given by the laws and well regulated, never do damage; on the contrary they are always an advantage, and cities keep themselves uncorrupted longer by means of those weapons than without them. So Rome was free four hundred years and was armed; Sparta, eight hundred; many other cities have been unarmed and have been free less than forty years."[41] It was when the early Roman emperors "began to disarm the Roman people in order to command them more easily"[42] that Rome's decline really got going. Rome's citizens became used to an easy life of enjoyment and entertainment; they lost their virtue and their discipline.

This discussion of Machiavelli's views of the Roman Republic, and of citizen-soldiers, has veered quite far from the popular understanding of what it means to be "Machiavellian." The author who revered the Roman Republic and called for greater citizen participation in public life does not sound like the same man who applauded Cesare Borgia for chopping his lieutenant in half. Among academic studies of Machiavelli, though, this "good" Machiavelli is well established and has been for several decades. The key text here was J. G. A. Pocock's 1975 book *The Machiavellian Moment.* Pocock wanted to reshape how people understood the origins of modern democratic society. In his account, the key traditions began with Machiavelli, before being adopted by political writers in seventeenth-century England and then, later, by the American revolutionaries. Pocock, along with American historians Gordon Wood and Bernard Bailyn, argued that the ideological origins of the American Revolution did not come from John Locke and the liberal tradition, as had long been believed, but rather from a republican tradition—referred to as either "classical" or "civic" republicanism. This interpretation has had a huge influence among historians of the American Revolution and also helped cement Machiavelli's place as major political thinker of the Renaissance, in part by shifting attention away from *The Prince* toward *Discourses on Livy* (and, to a lesser extent, Machiavelli's other works, including *The Art of War*). In doing so, it brought on a debate about what Machiavelli really meant when he was writing *The Prince,* with some scholars claiming that, despite appearances, *The Prince* was itself also a republican text.[43]

The full debate about *The Prince*'s republicanism is too far afield for this book; what can be said here, though, is that when it came to citizen-soldiers, Machiavelli wrote the same thing in *The Prince* as he did in his other works. Despite his emphasis there on having a strong ruler, as opposed to his emphasis in *Discourses on Livy* on citizen participation in public life, *The Prince* still advocated armies of part-time citizen-soldiers. Arming citizens, he wrote, made rulers stronger, not weaker:

> There has never been, then, a new prince who has disarmed his subjects; on the contrary, whenever he has found them unarmed, he has always armed them. For when they are armed, those arms become yours; those whom you suspected become faithful, and those who were faithful

> remain so; and from subjects they are made into your partisans. . . . But, when you disarm them, you begin to offend them, you show that you distrust them either for cowardice or for lack of faith, both of which opinions generate hatred against you.[44]

Here, then, he made his point even more strongly than in *Discourses on Livy,* where he acknowledged the limits to which a ruler could command armed citizens. Counterintuitively, perhaps, an armed citizenry would be more loyal than an unarmed one.

The biggest difference between Machiavelli's discussions of citizen-soldiers in *The Prince,* as opposed to his other works, lay in the amount of time he spent attacking mercenary soldiers. As much praise as he gave to citizen-soldiers, he gave that much scorn for paid soldiers. In Machiavelli's view, "The present ruin of Italy is caused by nothing other than its having relied for a period of many years on mercenary arms."[45] He also criticized "auxiliary" soldiers—soldiers whom states hired and paid but whose primary allegiance was to another state. Both kinds of troops were "useless and dangerous,"[46] Machiavelli wrote. Though most Italian states used mercenary troops during Machiavelli's time, rulers who relied on those troops could never be secure. "They have no love nor cause to keep them in the field other than a small stipend, which is not sufficient to make them want to die for you."[47] It was a claim that would spread in the following centuries: mercenaries were expensive during peacetime and useless during wartime. This was one more reason, then, to fill the army with citizens, who would fight harder than paid mercenaries.

Beneath the violence and treachery of *The Prince* and the republicanism of *Discourses on Livy,* then, Machiavelli's writing included a generally consistent view on citizen-soldiers. Mercenaries could not be trusted. Citizens would fight harder. Military discipline even made these men better citizens. Such citizens could handle hardships and overcome obstacles; they were not soft and, certainly, not effeminate. So states, whether republics or ruled by a prince, should arm their citizens. The proof of these statements could be found in the histories of Switzerland, of ancient Sparta, and, especially, the Roman Republic. In the writings of this "evil" political strategist lie the most basic foundational building block for later militia advocates: citizens make better soldiers.

In the following centuries, republican writers and other fans of militias would expand upon Machiavelli's ideas. Some of those writers acknowledged Machiavelli's influence; others were probably unaware of *Discourses on Livy* or of anything about Machiavelli other than his scandalous reputation. But a core set of ideas began to emerge, and Machiavelli's beliefs formed the foundation. Later writers would attribute preternatural powers to men fighting for their own nations; Machiavelli's fascination with the forces of "fortune" would be replaced by an obsession with the dangers of corruption. These later writers would also elaborate far more specific plans for how to organize a militia and how to integrate a citizens' army into civil society. Some would even get to participate in the formation or reformation of citizens' armies far larger than Machiavelli's own Florentine militia. But they never moved away from Machiavelli's foundation. These writers preferred the republic to the empire. They believed, as Machiavelli had, that citizens made better soldiers. They believed even more strongly than did Machiavelli that soldiers made better citizens. They saw wealth and idleness as a path to weakness and effeminacy and military discipline as a key to making men into true citizens. Machiavelli's ideas formed the foundation for why people who wanted militias *said* they wanted militias.

There was more to the subsequent militias, though, than their advocates often let on. Machiavelli made one other point in *The Prince* that also turned out to be a building block of later militia advocacy. After writing that no prince should disarm his subjects, he added, "And because all subjects cannot be armed, if those whom you arm are benefited, one can act with more security toward the others. The difference of treatment that they recognize regarding themselves makes them obliged to you; the others excuse you, judging it necessary that those who have more danger and more obligation deserve more."[48] In other words: yes, the people should be armed. Just not all of them.

There was nothing new about arming only part of the population. As shown in chapter 1, during the first centuries of the Roman Republic only citizens with enough property had been allowed to be soldiers. So while all Roman soldiers had also been Roman citizens, not all Roman citizens were soldiers—only the wealthy ones were. Eventually, Marius's reforms had changed that. He had allowed poorer citizens to become soldiers. His reforms, though—at least in the eyes of later British writers—had hastened the end of the republic. After Marius, Rome's army was still an army of citizens, but it was no longer an army of part-time soldiers whose only allegiance was to Rome; it was now an army of full-time soldiers whose allegiance was to their generals. Rome's soldiers became professional soldiers, career soldiers, even if those are anachronistic terms. So Marius's changes had paved the way for Julius Caesar's crossing of the Rubicon. The wisdom of only including a part of the society in the army seemed to be vindicated.

Caesar's rise was not the justification Machiavelli gave, though, for only arming part of the population. Machiavelli wrote surprisingly little about Julius Caesar. To be sure, he was no fan—Machiavelli was a fan of the Roman Republic. Caesar was the man who brought down the republic and that made him, for Machiavelli, the man who had "completely" spoiled Rome.[49] What Machiavelli did write about Julius Caesar was critical, but it was not a topic on which Machiavelli would dwell in the way that later writers would. Meanwhile, while Machiavelli was critical of Julius Caesar himself, he was not concerned about "a Caesar" the way later writers would be. Machiavelli took it for granted that military leaders would gain power, and he feared foreign mercenaries more than he feared other professional armies. So while Julius Caesar's success may have vindicated the early republic's laws keeping the poor out of the army, this was not why Machiavelli had advocated only arming a portion of the population. In *The Prince* Machiavelli gave few details on which factions to arm, and he gave no warnings against arming the poor. He had filled his own Florentine militia with peasants, who were presumably not that well off. The line he drew, then, was not between rich and poor but between urban and rural. (He would also later suggest keeping "falconers, fishermen, cooks, pimps, and whoever makes a business of providing pleasure" out of any militias.)[50] There was a line, though. And there always would be.

This is perhaps a very basic point to make, but it is still one worth making: most societies arm a portion of their population, but no societies arm their entire population. Some modern societies divide this by profession and arm their soldiers and their police but not their civilians. Medieval Europe, with its warrior nobility, tended to do as Rome had done and arm the rich but not the poor. Most societies keep women unarmed and out of their militaries, though there are exceptions. But no societies, including those that claim to have a right to bear arms or an armed citizenry, allow everyone to have weapons, whether as private weapons or as part of the military. Societies have divisions, and while those divisions vary, those in power tend to be quite wary about arming those over whom they rule. In one sense, Machiavelli's comment about only arming one part of the population was only describing a commonplace truth about any society. In another sense, however, this would turn out to be the most prophetic part of his discussions of militias and citizen-soldiers.

Those societies that would later embrace the idea of arming their citizens still made careful decisions about who counted as a citizen.

By 1520 there were signs that Machiavelli's political exile might come to an end. Lorenzo di Piero de' Medici, the man who had taken power in Florence in 1512, died in 1519. His successor, Giulio de Medici, granted Machiavelli an audience soon after taking power. Machiavelli would never regain the responsibilities of his earlier position, but he did secure a position as an official historian for Florence and for the Medici. He continued in that position until 1527. That May, following a defeat for the Medici in Rome, Florence rose up and expelled the Medici, declaring itself again a republic. Ironically, Machiavelli the republican was once more out of a position. His retirement was not long this time. He died the following month.

To say that his works would live on would imply that they were alive and well when Machiavelli died. His works had not remained completely unknown, as several people had copied them, and those close to Machiavelli had read *The Prince* and *The Discourses on Livy* before their author's death. But publication did not take long: *Discourses on Livy* was first published in 1532, and *The Prince* was published the following year. *Discourses on Livy* received an enthusiastic reception from Francesco Guicciardini, a friend of Machiavelli's who had led a more prominent life. Such attention from Guicciardini helped spread word of Machiavelli's writings but did not prevent most readers of *The Prince* from being appalled at the book's contents. In 1559, the pope placed *The Prince* on the church's index of prohibited books. The index was only relevant in Catholic countries, however—and even France, though Catholic, chose to ignore it. Still, the prospects for a positive reception of Machiavelli's thought were slim. Several authors took the time to write books and pamphlets denouncing Machiavelli for the wickedness of his views. He was soon known as the man who thought rulers should be evil. It was a hard reputation to shake.

"Influence" and "reception" are tricky topics for historians. In the ensuing centuries, few writers would openly call themselves "Machiavellians." The basics of Machiavelli's thought would live on, though. In general terms, Machiavelli had set the agenda for a strand of thought that would go on to thrive in England during the late seventeenth century and then become influential in England's North American colonies during the eighteenth century. Adherents to the civic republican (or "neo-Roman") tradition avoided the more

"Machiavellian" aspects of Machiavelli's thought but otherwise stayed true to the general outlines of Machiavelli's writings, starting with the call to emulate the Roman Republic and the insistence on an active citizenry that participated in public life. English writers would mix Machiavelli's concerns with their own—they added ideas about the importance of property ownership, their fear of England's poor, their sense of decorum and order. Most importantly, though, they retained Machiavelli's belief in citizen-soldiers, along with the whole cluster of ideas that would make later writers want to do away with professional armies and instead rely on citizens for protection. Later writers would go to some lengths to justify these views and to specify what these citizens' militias would look like, and in doing so, they would go well past anything Machiavelli had asserted. At the basis of all of them, though, lay the message that Machiavelli had found in ancient Rome: that the best soldiers were also citizens.

None of this would happen right away. It would be more than a century before British writers began making use of Machiavelli's ideas. By the time they did, they were less concerned than Machiavelli had been about mercenary armies. Their focus instead would be on large national "standing armies." Specifically, their focus was on France's army, something that Machiavelli had rarely had to worry about. In *The Prince* Machiavelli discussed France several times, usually describing it as a kingdom that squandered its opportunities and, therefore, was a less powerful force than it might have been.[51] During the decades following Machiavelli's death, France would be engulfed in civil wars and, therefore, even less of a factor in European politics. Then things began to change. Over the course of the seventeenth century, France ended its civil wars and emerged as a major European power with a strong monarchy and an enormous standing army, all at a time when England was going through its own internal strife. As England emerged from its civil wars, it found itself outgunned and outmanned by its rivals across the channel. France had developed an army with which the English, it seemed, had little hope of competing. It was at that point in the story that Machiavelli's ideas about citizen-soldiers became relevant for British writers—and so it will be at that point that this book will return to them. Before then, the following chapters will explain in more depth the broader context in which those ideas about citizen-soldiers eventually became so necessary, and so useful, to British writers of the late seventeenth century, by exploring France's rise as a European power at a time when the English were turning against each other.

THREE

The Fall of La Rochelle

1628

November 1, 1628. France's King Louis XIII entered the city of La Rochelle, riding atop his horse. Walking in front of him was his minister Armand Jean du Plessis, better known as Cardinal Richelieu. Behind the king and the cardinal marched several hundred French soldiers. Their entrance marked the end of a siege that had begun the year before and had brought what had been a fiercely independent city to its knees. They were entering what had become a ghost town. When the siege began, La Rochelle had been a wealthy city of twenty-seven thousand or so inhabitants. By the time the city surrendered, only around five thousand remained. Roughly that many had managed to flee the city before then. The rest had died during the siege, mostly from starvation or disease. It was a bitter end for a city that had emerged during the previous century as the strongest bastion of resistance to France's monarchy.[1]

La Rochelle's defeat was an early sign in what would become the main story of seventeenth-century France: the monarchy was getting stronger, and those regions of France that had enjoyed some level of autonomy no longer did. Specifically, the king's army was becoming more powerful, and it was doing so at the expense of France's nobility, which was losing its military autonomy.[2]

The rise of the monarchy was not the only story; La Rochelle was also a stronghold for France's Huguenots—the largest Protestant community in a kingdom with a Catholic monarchy. In a very direct way, La Rochelle's fall was a victory of Catholics over Protestants. That the king chose All Saints' Day to make his entrance into the city reinforced the message that France would again be a Catholic kingdom. But it was not the religious aspects of this fighting that makes the fall of La Rochelle warrant a place in this book, nor was it the city's Protestantism that led the king to besiege it. Louis XIII attacked La Rochelle because he wanted to strengthen his control over the kingdom. The city's fall was a victory for France's royal army over a rebellious portion of the French nobility and for French unity and centralization over regional autonomy.[3] According to an anonymous 1625 memorandum often attributed to Richelieu—and, in any case, consistent with his views—"As long as the Huguenot party subsists in France, the King will not be absolute in his kingdom. . . . It is also necessary to destroy the pride of the great nobles, who regard La Rochelle as a citadel in whose shadow they can demonstrate their discontent with impunity."[4] In other words, the fall of La Rochelle was a step for France away from the kind of feudal military system that had thrived in the Middle Ages and had survived into the sixteenth century. In its place would rise a more powerful and centralizing monarchy, one that controlled the kingdom's military in a way that French kings never had before.[5]

The rest of Europe took note. The pope, focused on religious matters, was happy to learn of the Protestants' defeat. Europe's other Catholic powers, though, were not. Spain and Austria, both Catholic (and both ruled by branches of the Habsburg dynasty) had been fine with knowing that France was weakened by its own internal divisions; they knew that a powerful France would be a threat to their own interests.[6] It was one sign—and many others were to come—that even as Protestants and Catholics were still fighting each other in Germany, Europe was starting to turn away from the violence of the Reformation and moving toward the system of nation-states and policies based on national interest that would dominate after midcentury.[7]

England had tried to help the people in La Rochelle during the siege. England's legacy of helping France's Protestants went back to the time of Queen Elizabeth, and that traditional role was still popular among the English public.[8] Beyond that, English kings from past eras had a tradition of raiding France, of fighting French armies on the continent, and even of claiming large portions of France for themselves.[9] But at La Rochelle, the English troops failed dismally. At the start of the seventeenth century, as European powers were growing stronger, England was not keeping up. It was one more way in which the siege at La Rochelle provided an excellent vantage point to see the dynamics at work in Europe at the start of the seventeenth century and how they would shape the world that was starting to emerge.[10]

The siege of La Rochelle was not a world-changing event along the lines of Caesar ordering his soldiers across the Rubicon had been or like the 1649 execution of England's King Charles I would be. But while some of the events in this book are included because of their importance, others, including the fall of La Rochelle, are here for what they revealed. Before the siege of La Rochelle lay the entire history of post-Roman Europe, the remnants of a medieval society of fragmented authority, little government presence, a nobility with its own military power, and a Europe more closed off from the rest of the world than it had been under the Romans or than it would be after the discovery of the New World.[11] But the changes that had begun, as the medieval world gave way to early modern Europe, also showed their impact in La Rochelle. First among these was the Protestant Reformation, which had divided a Catholic Europe into Protestant and Catholic camps. Second was the growth of the Atlantic World, which provided new economic opportunities for port cities like La Rochelle. Also showing its impact was a phenomenon that historians call the "military revolution," which had brought an end to the style of fighting that had taken place throughout the medieval era, replacing it with larger armies—themselves made possible by larger administrative states capable of funding those armies. And then there was the rise of "absolutism": during the seventeenth century, in a number of European countries, but especially in France, central governments became stronger, monarchs became more powerful, and nobilities lost much of the autonomy that they had enjoyed since the medieval era.[12] At La Rochelle, then, it was not just Protestants and Catholics who were fighting; it was one vision of society against another and one version of military authority against another.

This is not to say that the siege of La Rochelle was unimportant in and of itself; tens of thousands of soldiers fought there, and thousands of people—mostly the inhabitants of La Rochelle—died there. It would be a turning point in the political careers of many of the men involved as well. For Richelieu, it helped cement his leading role in the kingdom; for the Duke of Buckingham, who led the English forces there, it helped cement the already negative opinion that many English people already held of him. But while other events were as important in shaping seventeenth-century Europe, few events were as revealing in understanding the rise of absolutism in France as the siege of La Rochelle and its eventual fall. It was an event situated between the France of the late sixteenth century, where religious fighting and autonomous military units led by noblemen tore the kingdom apart, and the France of the late seventeenth century, where reason of state took precedence in religious matters, and where any noble who wanted any part in the military had to join the royal army.[13] That the two key players from the era were there, in King Louis XIII and Richelieu, made it all the more useful as a window into the forces and dynamics that would make France into a powerhouse in European politics. England would have to respond, one way or another.

The rise of absolutism in France might seem like an odd detour on the road to the Second Amendment. The most direct roots of the Second Amendment, like the roots of the rest of the US Constitution, lay in English history.[14] Nor were Richelieu and Louis XIII putting Machiavelli's ideas about citizen-soldiers into practice—quite the contrary. But as this book will show, France held a unique place in the story of why militias became so important in English political life. England's attempts to reject standing armies and embrace citizens' militias during the seventeenth and eighteenth centuries occurred in the context of—and as a reaction to—France's growing strength and particularly France's growing army. One thing that will become clear in the coming chapters is that there is no way to understand the Second Amendment without understanding what it was that the amendment was meant to prevent, and key among those was the "standing army"—a full-time army made up of professional soldiers.[15] Those armies came to represent everything that England disliked about France, at a time when dislike of France was becoming central to English identity.

In other words, the differences between England and France that emerged during the seventeenth century were not only a matter of two nations who happened to choose different paths. As Linda Colley writes, by the eighteenth century, the women and men of Great Britain came to identify themselves as "Britons" because their "circumstances impressed them with the belief that they were different from those beyond their shores, and in particular different from their prime enemy, the French." By the eighteenth century, for the British, "imagining the French as their vile opposites, as Hyde to their Jekyll, became a way for Britons—particularly the poorer and less privileged—to contrive for themselves a converse and flattering identity. The French wallowed in superstition: therefore, the British, by contrast, must enjoy true religion. The French were oppressed by a bloated army and by absolute monarchy; consequently, the British were manifestly free. . . . That many of these assumptions about French disadvantages and British benefits were wrong was immaterial."[16] As England's Parliament grew stronger, France's monarchy grew stronger; as England prided itself in its liberties, France prided itself in its stability. As France prided itself in its military glory, won primarily through its conquests on the European continent, England prided itself in its independence from all things continental. And as France's armed forces grew, England prided itself on its militias and its citizen-soldiers.[17]

Understanding why England came to embrace militias and citizen-soldiers to the extent that it did—and why its North American colonies came to embrace that legacy—therefore requires understanding the developments in France against which English writers were reacting. They were opposing France's move toward an absolutist state with a powerful monarch and a large professional army. That army would peak during the reign of Louis XIV and would be at its height during the final decades of the seventeenth century. Its seeds were planted, though, at the start of that century, under the reign of Louis XIII and with guidance and direction from Cardinal Richelieu. When those two men led the siege and capture of La Rochelle, there were two visions of society fighting against each other: on one side, a vision of decentered authority, where the nobility's authority grew out of its military autonomy; on the other, a vision of centralized authority and a strong monarchy that could dictate terms to the nobility—where the king would, indeed, be "absolute in his kingdom." It was a battle that played out during the seventeenth century in both England and France, though with dramatically different outcomes.[18]

Surrounded by marshes on three sides and the ocean on the fourth, La Rochelle's position made it easy to defend and hard to attack. To these natural advantages the city's leaders had added some of the highest and strongest fortifications in all of France.[19] This setting was how La Rochelle had managed to survive the civil wars that had torn France apart during the sixteenth century and why it emerged from those wars as the main stronghold for France's Protestant minority. The combination of the city's military strength and its differences with the rest of the kingdom had led La Rochelle, in the first quarter of the seventeenth century, to be like a state within a state, a city that could set its own rules and that the king of France could not control. The 1598 Edict of Nantes had written La Rochelle's autonomy into French law. But it was La Rochelle's military strength that guaranteed the city's "privileges"—the Edict of Nantes had only formalized that.[20]

The fighting between France's Huguenots and the king's forces resumed earlier in the 1620s, and the king's army defeated Protestant forces elsewhere in France. By 1627, La Rochelle was no longer the most important and best protected of a number of Protestant strongholds; it had become an isolated outpost of Protestantism.[21] The Huguenots still had nobles on their side, and those nobles still had men fighting for them—but their numbers and their status were not what they had been sixty years earlier.[22] Still, Louis XIII and Richelieu had their work cut out for them in trying to take over La Rochelle. The city had its fortifications; the monarchy had more soldiers and more resources. Time, too, was on the monarchy's side. For the king and his forces, an immediate frontal attack would be a disaster. Instead, they decided to surround La Rochelle and isolate the city until it gave up. It was a sound strategy, though one that could not hold Louis XIII's attention for very long. "I am here in the middle of winter," the king wrote in November 1627, "having just recovered from a great and perilous illness, acting personally in all matters, sparing neither my person nor my health, and all this to bring back into obedience my subjects of La Rochelle."[23] In February he left the region and returned to Paris. Richelieu was now in charge of the thirty thousand royal troops in the region. The most important activity that Richelieu directed, though, was not fighting but building.

On the inland side, it was easy enough to isolate La Rochelle; the same attributes that made it hard to invade made it easy to isolate. The royal troops did not allow anyone to walk out of the city during the siege.[24] Cutting off the sea was another matter. The key to the siege wound up being the construction of a bulwark that closed off La Rochelle's bay. The construction began late in 1627. It was an enormous project, which took months to complete.[25] Once it was done, only one boat was able to make it through from the sea into La Rochelle during the remainder of the siege. The people of La Rochelle were indeed cut off. Their only hope had been to get help from outside, and the most likely such source of help was England. This was not an idle wish on the part of the citizens of La Rochelle—or at least, it hadn't been, until the construction of the bulwark—given England's legacy of both helping France's Protestants and waging war in France.[26] As both of these traditions were still popular among much of the English population, that population was generally pleased when their military operations began, even if they did not like the man whom King Charles I had chosen to lead those operations.

That man was England's George Villier, Duke of Buckingham. In July of 1627, before the construction of the bulwark began, Buckingham led seven thousand soldiers to help the Huguenots and La Rochelle.[27] He began his attack just west of La Rochelle, at the Ile de Ré. He and his men quickly established a foothold there but were never able to get further. Aside from the one English ship that later managed to get past the bulwark, Buckingham's arrival on the Ile de Ré was the closest the English were able to get to La Rochelle itself.

Whether any leader could have led the English to success here was questionable, but Buckingham had no military experience and showed no sign of being able to learn on the job. During the reign of England's James I, Buckingham had established himself as the king's main advisor and confidant. He was also by all accounts an impressively attractive man, and while that may or may not have helped bring him James's favor, it did not put Buckingham in good stead with other leading Englishmen. After James I died in 1625 and his son Charles I became king, much to the chagrin of the rest of England's leaders, Charles continued to place his trust in Buckingham.[28] Buckingham's actions at the Ile de Ré would prove his critics correct.

The duke's first approach was to surround the Ile de Ré's main citadel and starve it out. He was never able to fully cut off that citadel, though; resupplies got through, and the failed siege was far harder on the besiegers than it was on the besieged. Eventually Buckingham ran out of patience. He ordered his men to attack the citadel. It was an ill-advised move, against the advice of his war council; his soldiers were forced to attack by scaling ladders to reach the top of the citadel's walls. It would be a dangerous mission in the best of conditions; these, however, were not good conditions at all. The ladders the English used were shorter than the citadel's walls.[29] As one of the participants wrote, the soldiers "reared some fourty ladders against the outworks and Cittadell, but finding them not came near the toppe by almost a 5th part. . . . When they almost attained the height of their ladders and had no futher means to go on, casting their threatening eies about they remained unmoveable till they were shott and tumbled doune."[30] When it came to military interventions in continental Europe, the English, in 1627, quite literally did not measure up.

Some five thousand of Buckingham's men died in the expedition. Soon the duke himself gave up. He and his surviving troops returned to England. A few months later one of his officers assassinated him.[31]

The English would return to La Rochelle the following year with fewer casualties but with little success, aside from the one supply ship that reached La Rochelle in March 1628. That ship may have delayed the fall of the city; it was not enough to prevent it. Toward the end of the siege, the people in La Rochelle were eating dogs and rats; bodies piled up at the cemeteries.[32] In May 1628, Jean Guiton had become mayor of La Rochelle and announced that he would never talk of surrendering. Then, in late October, La Rochelle surrendered.[33] The king's entrance came a few days later. Louis XIII had won this battle, thanks in large part to Richelieu's help. France was on its way to becoming an absolutist monarchy, and France's army was on its way to becoming a force to be reckoned with for all of Europe.

France was hardly unique in building a larger army in this period. For some time now, historians have looked at the period from the late Middle Ages into the seventeenth century as the time of a "military revolution." The theory goes back to the historian Michael Roberts, who coined the term in the 1950s, and whose interpretation has proved surprisingly enduring.[34] Roberts focused on the changes between the mid-sixteenth and mid-seventieth centuries, the period during which knights on horseback disappeared and when large national armies replaced them. Roberts attributed these changes to new military tactics and strategies, which required large numbers of well-trained and disciplined soldiers. Given the training required, meanwhile, it made more sense for soldiers to remain on active duty during peacetime. Hence the "new tactics . . . gave rise inexorably to the emergence of the standing army," while the new strategies allowed states to be more ambitious, coordinating multiple simultaneous campaigns. All of this required more men to be soldiers, leading to an increased scale of warfare and a larger burden for civilian populations who supported those armies through taxes and who would bear the brunt of any military activities in their region. Coordinating these armies, collecting those taxes, and paying those soldiers in turn mean that the state itself had to be bigger.[35]

The relationship between the growth of the army and that of the administrative state is a bit of a chicken-and-egg puzzle; the two needed each other, and there was more behind the rise of state power than just an inevitable effect of new military tactics. Still, as Geoffrey Parker would write in the 1970s, there was "absolutely no doubt about . . . growth in army size. Between 1530 and 1710 there was a ten-fold increase both in the total numbers of armed forces paid by the major European states and in the total numbers involved in the major European battles."[36] Scholars have reduced some of these numbers a bit—estimating army sizes for the seventeenth century is not easy—but not the overall story. During the seventeenth century, national armies grew and national governments grew. Private armies were disappearing; large armies under more direct state control were taking their place. France, having moved past its own religious wars, was becoming the dominant power on the continent.[37]

Again, France was not the only nation in Europe that was building up its army at this time, nor was it the only place in Europe dealing with religious divisions. Four years after the Medici exiled Machiavelli from the world of Florentine politics, the German monk Martin Luther wrote his Ninety-Five Theses, criticizing many of the Catholic practices of the time. Europeans' reaction to Luther—especially in his native Germany—was massive and fast. Within a few years, much of the German-speaking population left the Catholic Church. The Protestant Reformation had begun. The relative unity of Catholic Christendom—and it had always been relative—would never return. From that point on western and central Europe would be divided between Protestants and Catholics. In the first century of the Reformation, both sides still hoped for a total victory of their version of Christianity. Thoughts of toleration and peaceful coexistence would have to wait.[38]

In Germany, Lutheranism quickly became the most important branch of Protestantism. In France, it would be the "Huguenots"—a term of perhaps dubious value, but one that has stood the test of time, much like the equivalent term "Puritans" for their English counterparts.[39] Though religious writers produced text after text justifying their side, and though religiously minded people devoted their lives to proselytizing, the Reformation's most important fights were won on the battlefield. The Reformation, in other words, was not only a religious event; it was also a military one whose violence grew out of the kind of military forces that were already in place before the Reformation began. Powerful aristocratic families of the day owed their power not only to their wealth but to the retinues of armed men whom they commanded. The largest of these retinues could stand up to any other forces around. When a powerful nobility chose their allegiance to one of their churches, they brought their retinues with them.

When the Reformation reached France, much of its nobility was still a warrior nobility; violence and warfare were still an integral aspect of the lives of nobles. Their homes—the châteaus that still dot the landscape of rural France—were fortified residences that also served as safe places for inhabitants in the region, as gathering places for troops, and as weapons depots. They would stockpile food there in case of a siege. Men born into the nobility grew up with military training and a familiarity with horses, weapons, and violence. This was part of the code of honor code that guided nobles' behavior and also contributed to a "culture of revolt."[40] A king might have had the largest army in his kingdom; he would not have had its only army. Into the seventeenth century, a nobleman could raise an army of several thousand soldiers and conduct independent campaigns—either in support of or against the king's army.[41]

Through the sixteenth century, then, royal power was weak. It was weak in England, where the king had long shared power with Parliament. It was weak in the German-speaking lands, which would remain a patchwork of kingdoms and principalities well into the nineteenth century. And royal power was weak in France as well. The representative institutions had less of a pedigree there than they had in England, which makes the eventual victory of French absolutism seem inevitable in retrospect. During most of the sixteenth century, however, royal power was stronger in England than it was in France; no king controlled France during the century the way that Henry VIII and Queen Elizabeth controlled England. The 1570s saw several important books that argued for the limits on the power of French kings and even advocated resisting the king in certain situations.[42] France's nobles also still maintained their own military forces and, therefore, retained much of their autonomy. As the Reformation spread through France, it gained the allegiance of a fair number of these noble families. Having members of France's high nobility on the Huguenot side meant more than just respectability or status for French Calvinists; it meant that there would be soldiers on the Huguenot side as well.[43] A king might wish to declare France a Catholic kingdom. To enforce that declaration, though, he would have to defeat the Protestant nobility on the battlefield.

During the first decades of France's religious wars, the kings had come close. They defeated France's Huguenot nobility more often than not. But the fighting took its toll on Protestants and Catholics alike.[44] The lack of stability of the throne did not help, either. France had four different kings from 1547 to 1589; then when Henry III died in 1589 without a direct heir, the crown fell to Henry of Navarre, the most powerful of France's noble Protestants. Henry of Navarre would rule as a Catholic—Henry IV—but never fully earn the trust of France's Catholics. He did bring an end to the worst phase of the fighting with the 1598 Edict of Nantes, which established a means of mostly peaceful coexistence for Huguenots and Catholics in the kingdom. This edict guaranteed Protestants some level of protection. It also made official what was already a military reality: Protestants would have several safe zones, including La Rochelle.

A Catholic zealot assassinated Henry IV in 1610.[45] Henry IV's death made his son king, as Louis XIII—not yet nine years old. Power fell to his mother,

Marie de Medici, who took control of the kingdom for the next several years. This period would also be Richelieu's first taste of power and court intrigues. The queen mother had noticed Richelieu and brought him in as an advisor, saving him from the remote diocese in western France where he was serving as bishop. In doing so, she brought Richelieu into a world of court politics and drama not all that different from the kinds of scenarios Machiavelli had described. Marie de Medici would not give her power up voluntarily, including to her own son. When the king was old enough to rule, he would have to banish his mother from the capital a number of times. Throughout the early years of his reign Louis XIII would also have to fight off various attempted power grabs from his own brother.[46] Richelieu had to keep in mind the fate of one of his predecessors as advisor to the queen, the Italian Concino Concini. In 1617, as Concini crossed Paris's Seine River, the king's men closed the gate after him, separating Concini from his guards. As he reached for his sword, the king's men shot him. After that, crowds outside of the king's palace cheered him from below. Louis XIII's reply to the crowd was, "Thank you! I really am the king now."[47]

This, then, was the world in which Richelieu had to survive: one of chaos at court, where a wrong step could get a minister like himself killed; one of different factions of the royal family vying for power and a weak royal authority in the kingdom. To thrive within those court circles, Richelieu would have to show all of those tactical skills that Machiavelli had praised in *The Prince*, especially as he entered the story as a protégé of the queen mother, before switching his allegiance to her son. This was also the world that Louis XIII was inheriting, and it was no foregone conclusion that he would be able to rule successfully, or even for very long. And yet together, Louis XIII and Richelieu put France on the path away from the violence of the sixteenth century and toward the France over which Louis XIV would rule, where the king had control over the nobility, and over his army, in a way that no earlier French king had.[48]

As a man, Cardinal Richelieu was a collection of contradictions, so strong in some ways yet so weak in others. He was a small, frail man, sensitive to slights. He was a hypochondriac, and not without cause: he suffered various recurring illnesses throughout his life, including migraines and insomnia, before dying at age fifty-seven. He surrounded himself with doctors at a time when medical care was not always reliable. (The doctors, for instance, would often bleed him.)[49] Yet he was also a man who inspired fear in others. Above all, he was able to win the trust and allegiance of Louis XIII, even though, at a personal level, Louis XIII never did like his first minister. As the historian John Elliott wrote, the king had "an intense personal antipathy towards a man whose naturally authoritarian manner he feared and mistrusted."[50] But Louis XIII liked Richelieu's vision for what France could be, and for the stronger role that a French king should have.

There is no need to guess at Richelieu's personal views or beliefs; like Machiavelli, he took the time to write them down. In his *Political Testament,* Richelieu spelled out clearly what he wanted to see out of the king, out of France's government, and out of France's armies.[51] He wrote that book as if talking directly to Louis XIII himself. Thus he began: "When *Your Majesty* was first pleas'd to admit me into your Councils . . . the *Huguenots* shar'd the State with you . . . the Grandees behav'd themselves as if they had not been your Subjects; and the most powerful Governours of Provinces, as if they had been Soveraigns in their Imployments."[52]

Richelieu's first goal was to consolidate the king's power. Unlike the writers of the 1570s who had argued for limits on what a French king could do, or even advocating resisting royal power under certain conditions, Richelieu wanted to see royal power become the dominant force throughout the entire kingdom. That meant weakening those forces that most stood in the way of the king's ability to exert his authority. So Richelieu's promise to the king was "to ruine the *Huguenot* Party, to abate the Pride of the Grandees, to reduce all your Subjects to their Duty, and to raise your Name again in Foreign Nations, to the Degree it ought to be." And soon enough, Richelieu had helped the king do just that—taking over the lands where the Huguenots enjoyed autonomy, after which they "reduc'd the rest of the *Huguenot* Party throughout your Kingdom to Obedience."[53]

For Richelieu, it was not enough to weaken the nobility's military autonomy; he also wanted to build up the king's own military power. To achieve this, France needed a permanent army, especially along the borders. Previously, France's armies had disbanded between wars—something Richelieu wanted to change.[54] "It is necessary to keep at least four thousand Horse, and forty thousand Foot actually in Arms at all times, and it is easie without burthening the State, to keep ten thousand Gentlemen, and fifty thousand Foot listed, ready to be rais'd on all Emergencies."[55] Any other arrangement would leave the kingdom unprotected. And as Richelieu noted, "The most potent State in the World cannot boast of enjoying a certain Peace, unless it be in a condition to secure itself at all times, against an unexpected Invasion, or Surprise. In order thereunto it is necessary that so great a Kingdom as this is, should always keep a sufficient Army on Foot to prevent the designs which hatred and envy might form against its Prosperity and Grandeur."[56] Rejecting the vision of a nation only called to arms when needed, Richelieu replied that "as a Souldier who do's not always wear his Sword is lyable to many inconveniences; that Kingdom which do's not always stand on its Guard, and keep it self in a condition to prevent a sudden surprise, is in great danger."[57]

This army, moreover, should be precisely what Machiavelli had warned against: an army full of mercenaries and auxiliary forces. "One half of the *French* Armys were formerly Compos'd of Foreigners, and we have experienc'd how advantageous it is to use them, to supply the defect of our Nation," he claimed, adding that "it is almost impossible to undertake great Wars with Success with the *French* alone" and "Foreigners are absolutely necessary to maintain the Body of Armies."[58] Part of this cause lay in Richelieu's view of the French themselves—a topic on which he was almost as critical as his cross-channel counterparts. "There is no Nation in the World so unfit for War as ours; their Levity and Impatience in the least hardships, are two Principles which are but too well known." Though the French were at times "Valiant, full of Courage and Humanity; their Heart is void of Cruelty, and so free from Rankor, that they are easily reconcil'd." Richelieu described these traits as "the Ornaments of Civil Society." When it came to those traits needed for war, the French were lacking: they were "inconstant, impatient, and little inur'd to Fatigues," and, even worse, "have no great Affection for their Country." French people who did fight often fought on the other side—"There are few who wage War against *France,* without having *French* Men in their Army"—and those who did fight on the French side did so for their own reasons, not for patriotic ones; French soldiers on the French side, in other words, "are so indifferent in what relates to its Interest."[59]

Richelieu's vision for France, then, was that of a kingdom with a strong monarchy and a strong army—and, more specifically, a strong monarch with *his own* strong army upon which he could call. France had, at the time, more of a martial culture than Richelieu would have cared to admit. It was a martial culture, though, that had at best a limited attachment to "France" and where a desire for glory on the battlefield could lead Frenchmen—especially men from the nobility—to "sometimes to take Arms against their King."[60]

In order for Richelieu's vision for France, for its king, and for its army, to come to fruition, the nobility would have to change. And they were not going to change themselves. The monarchy would have to impose change on a nobility that was at best recalcitrant, but that could easily become insurrectionary. What Richelieu wanted, though, was not an end to the nobility; he wanted a more orderly nobility, one that would support the king, and one that would devote its military strength to the service of the king. "The Nobility which does not serve you in the War," Richelieu wrote, "is not only useless, but a Burthen to the State; which in that Case may be compar'd to the Body which supports an Arm which is troubled with the Palsie, as a Load which burthens it, instead of affording it any ease."[61] Those nobles who did not serve in the army should be deprived of their privileges, and "reduc'd to bear part of the Burthen of the People."[62] As for those noblemen who would serve in the king's army, though, "the Nobility must be Respected, as one of the principal Sinews of the State, capable to contribute much towards its Preservation and Settlement."[63] It would best accomplish this by serving as the officer corps of an army that served the king.

After La Rochelle fell, there were still members of the nobility willing to fight against the Crown. But under Richelieu, the tide was turning against those nobles and their private forces. In 1633, a local administrator wrote to one of Richelieu's chief lieutenants, telling him that "I have issued decrees for the arrest of 34 gentlemen and others who have levied troops against the King, and I am ready to issue decrees against eight more, who cause much trouble in this province." As he would write later, these were "gentlemen of good birth"—often of higher birth than the men who were arresting them—but who had "carried arms against His Majesty."[64] And more and more members of the nobility wanted to fight on the same side as the king, not against him. Even Guiton, the leader of La Rochelle who had vowed never to surrender, went on to serve for fifteen years in France's royal navy.[65]

With the private armies disappearing, Richelieu was able to build up the national army. The total troop size of France's army probably reached around seventy to eighty thousand soldiers during the 1630s and 1640s when it was fighting in the Thirty Years' War.[66] The real growth of France's national army would take place after Richelieu and Louis XIII had died. By the 1690s, France was maintaining a permanent standing army of 300,000–350,000 soldiers.[67] To field an army that size, Louis XIV and his ministers had to build up a financing system capable of raising and distributing enough tax revenue to keep that army fed and paid. In doing so, they would also sideline most of the traditional institutions that had provided France's nobility with a way to participate in France's political life. The nobility was not only losing its military autonomy; it was also losing its political influence.[68] Viewed from England, this was a clear sign that the French were losing their liberties, but it was just as clear a sign that French military strength was growing. Already in the 1620s, England had not measured up to the French militarily. As the century went on, the gap between the two nations' armies would grow even more and, in the process, help reshape the nature of the rivalry between the two kingdoms.

Competition between England and France was nothing new. The Hundred Years' War during the fourteenth and fifteenth centuries was but the longest in a long series of conflicts between the two kingdoms. But the rivalry between the two nations that emerged during the seventeenth century was different from conflicts of the medieval era. For centuries, armies loyal to England's king had fought against armies loyal to France's king, but the two kingdoms had been fairly similar in many ways. Until the sixteenth century, they had both been faithful to the Catholic Church. They were both feudal monarchies, where the king relied on its nobility for any major military efforts. Their nobilities overlapped and intermarried. It was not always a given that a noble in France would support France's king; medieval laws specified that nobles with fiefs in both kingdoms had to choose which of the kings he would pay homage to.[69]

The Protestant Reformation changed the two kingdoms' relationship. During the sixteenth century, England's King Henry VIII took England out of the Catholic Church. From that point on, the rivalry was between Catholic France and Protestant England. During the seventeenth century, that process of mutual differentiation became even stronger. By the turn of the eighteenth century, France would come to represent everything that England was not: not just a Catholic state but an absolutist state with a standing army of professional soldiers. By the end of the seventeenth century, British writers would be re-creating histories of both France and England that showed the nations as each other's opposites—in ways quite favorable to England. Or in the words of one of the most influential British critics of professional armies, "It is the fashion of the French king to have a standing army, and it is the fashion of his subjects to be slaves under that standing army. . . . For in Lewis the 11ths

Time, the French gave up their liberties for fear of England, and now we must give up ours for fear of France."[70]

In that context ideas about citizen-soldiers—including Machiavelli's views—became relevant to English writers. As will be shown in chapter 6, for English republicans, any movement toward strengthening the monarchy risked making England more French. Should England's king become more powerful, he would become more like France's absolutist monarch; should the Parliament falter, it would become as irrelevant as France's own representative institutions. This kind of thinking was especially prominent when it came to professional soldiers—of which France had many—versus citizens' militias. To embrace professional armies became an embrace of absolutist monarchy and therefore something to be avoided at all costs.

This desire on the part of the English to differentiate themselves from their continental counterparts remains an underappreciated aspect of the rise of eighteenth-century militias and of the growing numbers of men who wrote book after book, pamphlet after pamphlet praising citizens' militias and warning of professional armies and their evils. Historians who have searched for the more distant origins of militias have looked mostly at earlier militias and earlier laws that encouraged either militia obligations or the rights of citizens to own their own weapons. Those searches, meanwhile, have been focused on England and its history and have stretched back deep into the Middle Ages. Such research makes sense: during the eighteenth century, militias would be strongest in England's colonies, and militia advocacy would be strongest in the Anglophone world. Trying to find its earliest traces in previous English laws and institutions was the logical first step in understanding the background of the militias that would emerge during the eighteenth century and understanding the earlier precedents for the rights of citizens to keep and bear arms.[71]

The question to be asked, though, is not whether or not medieval England had had some version of citizens' militias. In medieval central and western Europe, most societies placed some sort of military obligations on a portion of its population.[72] The question to ask is, Why, during the seventeenth and eighteenth centuries, were militias more popular in Great Britain than they were elsewhere in Europe? And specifically, Why were militias so popular among British writers and politicians, as the criticism of professional armies became so dominant in the Anglophone world, compared to elsewhere? Similarly, all over Europe, there were laws that governed who could or could not have their own weapons and why. Why were the leaders of England's Parliament the first to formulate something approaching a modern right to bear arms and a limit on the government's ability to field a professional army?

Any answer to those questions must be, at the very least, a comparative one. A certain amount of this can be attributed to chance—to who wound up inheriting England's throne and to the extent to which the British Isles had different military needs than their continental rivals.[73] But there is also a perspective that takes this beyond a question of comparison and asks how nations, rather than simply evolving independently, defined themselves in distinction to their neighbors. The road to the Second Amendment did not pass through France; it lurched to avoid France. The British writers who did the most to popularize the ideal of the citizen-soldier were explicit about the dangers that France posed—particularly to those nations who tried to emulate it.[74]

FOUR

England's Parliament Debates the Militia Act

1642

IN JANUARY 1649, the Parliament of England put King Charles I on trial for high treason. Charles had been king since 1625, ruling over Scotland and Ireland as well as England. He had been king during the Duke of Buckingham's disastrous attack on the Isle of Ré. In retrospect, that was far from the worst disaster of his reign. The English public had supported the idea of helping French Protestants at La Rochelle. They were less supportive of Charles's attempts to rule as if he was an absolute monarch. Yet time and again, Charles had attempted to do just that. Over the course of the 1640s, Charles's dismissive attitude toward Parliament would catch up with him—first with the outbreak of civil war in 1642, then with his defeat and capture in the fighting that ensued.[1]

The king's trial was a chance for Parliament to state its case against Charles I. It was also a chance for the leaders of Parliament to state their views on the monarchy itself. According to the prosecutor, when "Charles Stuart" became king, he was "trusted with a limited power to govern by and according to the laws of the land." He had been given that power not to benefit himself but in order to "use the power committed to him for the good and benefit of the people, and for the preservation of their rights and liberties." Instead, the prosecution claimed, Charles had tried to seize for himself "unlimited and tyrannical power to rule according to his will, and to overthrow the rights and liberties of the people."[2] It was a claim that went to the heart of the ongoing battle between Parliament and Charles I but also a claim that went to the heart of a battle that had been going on for centuries.

Kings and other nobles had been fighting each other for centuries throughout the British Isles and on the continent as well. As shown in the last chapter, in seventeenth-century France, the balance of power had shifted toward the king. This had been Richelieu's project, and thus far in France, it was paying off for the monarchy. France's nobility was losing much of the autonomy it had had over the previous centuries.[3] Things were playing out differently in England, though, where Parliament gave England's nobility a more consistent forum in which to air their grievances.[4] The Parliament of England, in the seventeenth century as in the medieval era, had long represented the interests of England's nobility. Charles had done what he could to ignore that nobility and to rule without Parliament. The Parliament and its leaders had fought back, though—first with pamphlets, claims. and remonstrances and then, when those failed, with soldiers.[5]

During the trial, the prosecution blamed Charles I for all of the problems the war had caused, telling him that the "cruel and unnatural wars" had been his fault, and as a result "much innocent blood of the free people of this nation hath been spilt."[6] Whether they were indeed Charles's fault is a moot point. There had been much blood spilled during the war, though; according to one recent estimate, the death toll in England itself was probably around 180,000 men, or around 3 percent of the population.[7]

According to the minutes of the trial, "The prisoner, while the charge was reading, sat down on his chair . . . looking very sternly, and with a countenance not at all moved, till these words, viz., Charles Stuart to be a Tyrant, Traitor, &c., were read, at which point he laughed, as he sat, in the face of the court."[8] In defending himself, Charles did not dwell on any of the prosecution's specifics. He asked instead, "by what lawful Authority I am seated here"—claiming that as the king, he did not need to answer to Parliament for anything that he had done. "Remember," he told them, "I am your King, your lawful King, and what sins you bring upon your heads, and the Judgment of God upon this Land."[9]

Charles I could question Parliament's authority all he wanted, but in 1649, like it or not, he was their prisoner, and Parliament decided that "the said Charles Stuart" was "a tyrant, traitor, murderer, and public enemy to the good people of this nation." As a result, he "shall be put to death by the severing of his head from his body."[10] Fifty-nine members of Parliament then signed the king's death warrant. One of the signers was Oliver Cromwell, the military leader of Parliament's forces. As for the execution itself, an anonymous account described Charles I's last moments: "After a very short pause, his Majesty stretching forth his hands, the executioner at one blow severed his head from his body; which, being held up and showed to the people, was with his body put into a coffin covered with black velvet and carried into his lodging."[11] It was not new for England's nobility to fight with the monarchy over their respective powers. Those fights had gone on over centuries, and over those centuries, the nobility had succeeded in establishing Parliament as a permanent institution. The idea that the British people had certain "rights and liberties" was also an old one, even if those liberties rarely extended to the common people. And the nobility had fought back against a number of monarchs who, in the views of enough of the nobility, had exceeded the proper role for a king. But Parliament had never put a king on trial and executed him before. This was new ground.[12] Charles I could say what he wanted to deny that Parliament had the authority to try him; the two sides had fought a war. Charles lost.

Back in December 1648, with Charles I in custody and Parliament not quite sure what to do about him, Cromwell wrote, "We will cut off his head with the crown on it."[13] In other words, the goal was not only to execute Charles I but to do away with the monarchy altogether. In March 1649 Parliament declared that "it is and hath been found by experience that the office of a king in his nation and Ireland . . . is unnecessary, burdensome, and dangerous to the liberty, safety and public interest of the people."[14] New ground, indeed.

To describe England's seventeenth century as "tumultuous" would be an understatement. Yet as tumultuous as England's seventeenth century was, it was equally formative. Between 1642 and 1688, England would see one king executed and another sent into exile; the people of England experienced almost a decade of civil war during the 1640s, and then in 1688 were invaded by armies from the Netherlands. They would have their first experience as a republic, after which Parliament would invite the son of the king they had executed to return to the throne his father had held. England went from having no professional armies in the 1630s to having two armies fighting against each other in the 1640s until, by the 1650s, only one of those armies was left standing.

The details of England's seventeenth century were confusing, but the big picture was clear. In the seventeenth century England came to identify itself definitively as a nation of rights and liberties and to associate those rights and liberties with the limitations on the monarchy. Eventually, England would come to associate those rights with the lack of a standing army—even as, for the first time, it was building one.

The English self-understanding as a nation of rights-holding men was not an entirely novel development: there was a tradition of English rights that went back to the Middle Ages, back at least to the Magna Carta of 1215.[15] But England had its tradition of strong monarchs as well. Across the channel, meanwhile, France had its own traditions of rights and liberties and noble resistance to the monarchy. In the sixteenth century, it was England whose monarchy thrived under Henry VIII and then Queen Elizabeth, while France was plunged into the disorder of the Wars of Religion. By the end of the seventeenth century, though, England would be the nation with a stronger nobility and limits on the monarchy; France would be the nation with a stronger monarchy and a nobility that had been brought under control. The English came to consider themselves freer than their neighbors across the channel.

Whether England or the rest of Great Britain deserved that identity is another matter; this is the topic of the debates over "Whig history," which sees in England's development an inevitable march of progress toward liberty.[16] But this was a story the English told about themselves—and it would grow even stronger during the eighteenth century, leading the men who led the American Revolution to do so in the name of their rights as Englishmen.[17] This chapter tells the first part of that story, which starts—or claims to start—in the depths of medieval Britain. During the upheavals of the mid-seventeenth century, the first signs started to appear of a specific part of that story: that the people of England were freer than other nations because they did not have a standing army. Like the rest of the story, its accuracy is debatable, but its popularity among apologists of England was well established. In the nineteenth century, Thomas Macaulay—one of the most influential of the Whig historians—wrote that "England, protected by the sea against invasion, and rarely engaged in warlike operations on the Continent, was not, as yet, under the necessity of employing regular troops. The sixteenth century, the seventeenth century, found her still without a standing army." If England had required one, Macaulay continued, "our princes . . . must inevitably have become despots."[18]

It would take until the end of the seventeenth century for the story to take its full form. This legacy would lead England to declare in 1689 that domestic standing armies in times of peace required Parliament's consent and that some subjects had a right to "arms for their defense." This was also the start of the intellectual tradition that would lead the United States, some century and a half later, to include the Second Amendment in its Bill of Rights. Central to this legacy, and to this intellectual tradition, was the idea that England's history was the source of its liberties and, more specifically, that English people were freer than their neighbors because they did not have a standing army.[19]

Once this idea was in place, it allowed British writers to recast their own history, making England's militia into something it had never quite been.

There was nothing inevitable about this legacy. Until the seventeenth century, England's military traditions were not exceptional; its evolution was, for the most part, similar to what had taken place in the rest of western Europe. There were also several ironies about the developments that led the people of the British Empire to make the belated development of their national army such a key part of their identity. While later writers associated English liberties with the strength of Parliament and with the lack of a standing army, it was Parliament, not the monarchy, that created England's first professional army. Parliament's army, in turn, would produce its own Caesar in the person of Oliver Cromwell. As for the English militia that Charles I and Parliament fought over in 1642, and that later writers would romanticize as the source of English liberties—its record as a fighting force was spotty at best.

England's militia during the seventeenth century can be seen as a legacy of the medieval era, but this was only true in the most general sense. Medieval Europe itself had grown out of the interactions between the Roman Empire and the many warrior tribes of Europe, both those whose presence in Great Britain preceded Rome's, like the Britons, and those who arrived after Rome's fall, like the Angles and the Saxons. In both the pre-Roman and post-Roman Europe, England included, there was little that distinguished a society's leading men from its warriors; the elite was a warrior elite, and the king was a warrior king.[20] In Anglo-Saxon England, men who owned land were required to participate in the collective defense and to own weapons. The Norman Conquest of 1066 meant that there were new rules in place, but as with everything medieval, there is rarely any way to verify whether or not the people subject to those laws obeyed them. Enforcement was local, communications were minimal, and documentation was rare at the time and most would not have survived. What was clear—and what would remain clear for centuries, in England as on the continent—was that power lay in the hands of the nobility and that there was little that could be called a "national army."[21] Meanwhile, many of the distinctions of the modern age did not exist in medieval Europe. It would be centuries before the distinction between police and army would emerge or before there would be a clear distinction between military and civil authority. Meanwhile, medieval Europe was a relatively poor society. The cities were small, and trade was not what it had been during the Roman

Empire. The English monarchy had neither the financial resources to support a professional army nor the administrative state to organize and supply that army. During larger expeditions, England's king would hire mercenary troops as needed, but there, too, the king would be reliant on the cooperation of the nobles who had their own troops to call on.[22]

As in much of Europe, there were requirements for English men to do military service, though the exact nature of these requirements is hard to pin down. Several medieval English laws codified the military requirements of Englishmen. All of these required a certain amount of military participation from landowning men; they also gave local elites significant control over the use of armed force in their regions. These forces were the ones responsible for keeping order in their regions, and local barons were the ones who controlled those units. So in order to maintain order throughout his kingdom, the king had to maintain good relations with his barons. Again, the specifics of these laws varied from time to time and from place to place, and the actual practices would have varied even more. The general principles involved remained the same: the military hierarchy was supposed to represent the social hierarchy. And even beyond that, the military hierarchy was supposed to strengthen and enforce the social hierarchy. As in France, England's nobility was a warrior nobility. Those at the top of the social hierarchy, the dukes and barons and the knights below them, would be those most responsible for participating and leading any military forces, at home or abroad.[23]

There was no mystery as to why this arrangement would support the social order. These military units were commanded by nobility, and they acted in the interests of the nobility—they were not "the people in arms" in any sort of eighteenth-century sense (let alone in any sort of twenty-first century sense). In the case of any sort of peasant uprising, there would be far more peasants than nobles; the nobles, however, would be better armed, trained, and organized. This system would prove enough to get by—medieval England had its share of social unrest, but the nobles were usually able to shut down any peasant uprisings before too long.[24] The times when England had its worst domestic unrest would be when the elites themselves were divided, putting members of the nobility, along with their armed, trained, and organized supporters, on both sides of the battle.[25] For that matter, it was members of the nobility who were able to force King John to sign the Magna Carta in 1215—no peasant uprising was ever able to accomplish such a feat. Later generations of Englishmen would look back to the Magna Carta as the origin of England's tradition of liberties—again, an agreement between the monarchy and the leaders of a warrior nobility.

This system was often inefficient. Noblemen eager to prove their status by holding military rank were not necessarily good soldiers or leaders. Still, this tradition of requiring landowning men to participate in the common defense would provide English writers of the seventeenth century with a past that they could use—with a mythical past of armed citizens that forsook professional soldiers in favor of a citizens' army, with an armed elite that ruled over an unarmed populace.[26] It was a local past that, if viewed from the right angle, could look enough like the Roman Republic's tradition of citizen-soldiers, despite England never having been at all republican. They were similar enough, in any case, that Machiavelli's writings would become relevant. British writers could advocate the sort of citizens' militia Machiavelli wanted to put in place, framed not as some sort of "Italian" reform but rather as a return to an earlier version of English society. All of this would have to wait, though. In England's case, it was not a dislike of mercenaries but the fear of professional armies that first made writers embrace the militia system, and the English did not begin to truly fear standing armies until they had experienced them directly, which would happen starting in the 1640s, after the fighting between Parliament and Charles I began.

The British writers of the later seventeenth century portrayed Britain's military traditions in a positive light, but they knew that the militias that existed were not well. The start of the early modern era saw England's military system stretched to its breaking point. Queen Elizabeth I and King James I both tried to reform the militia, but neitherwas particularly successful. A 1558 militia law formalized a new system of "Lords Lieutenant" responsible for local military units. This law was, as historian Michael Braddick notes, "a move away from the dependence on the armed baronage and towards a national defence force."[27] But it was also a matter of at best incremental progress, at a time when continental powers were undergoing revolutionary changes. From a long-term perspective, the lords lieutenant represented a fair deal of continuity. The men who held the positions were still members of the nobility, upon whom the king relied in order to make the system function.[28] The lords lieutenant were in charge because of their birth. It was the class that they were born into that made them eligible for their positions, and their exercise of those positions, to the extent that it was effective, was most effective in reinforcing their status. When militias mustered, as they were now required to do, these were "special occasions, demonstrations and reaffirmations of local hierarchy and order."[29] Lords lieutenant were required to organize and muster the militia and to ensure a certain level of training. Lord lieutenant was a prestigious position, but it could easily become an unpopular one. Englishmen often disliked musters, as it took them away from their work for several days.[30]

When Queen Elizabeth found it impossible to reform the entire militia, in 1572 she attempted instead to create an elite force that would handle most of the duties of the militia, forming units known as "trained bands" who would be a "sufficient number" of the "most able." Charles I would later have a similar project, when he attempted to create an "exact militia."[31] None of these measures satisfied the rulers who put them in place. As one historian has noted, the English military under Queen Elizabeth was "unequal to the demands of post military revolution warfare." By 1588, when England prepared to face the Spanish armada, things were slightly better due to the trained bands' existence. Though the trained bands policy "was not only expensive and troublesome, but also unsanctioned by any statute," and "had been broadly resisted in the country, largely with the kind of quiet inactivity at which the English gentry excelled," they were still "a major improvement on what had gone before."[32] But things seem to have gone downhill for England's militia after Queen Elizabeth's death. In 1604 the government abrogated the 1558 law, without anything taking its place. The militia remained in place but it was problematic during the first half of the seventeenth century, even by the standards of early modern militias. This change should not be overestimated, nor should the impact of any particular law—during this era, the militia's legal status was not always clear. Still, by 1640, the militia's legal status was especially murky; the Crown devoted very little money to it, it was an inefficient system wherein service was resented by the men who had to participate, and its enforcement was uneven at best. As one historian notes, "By the 1620s the importance of proper military training had long been recognized, although in the first decade of James I's rule the dream was more evident than the reality." What followed was an attempt to reform the trained bands, though even then their importance was "more social and political than military." By 1642, "paralyzed by opposition and a lack of statutory authority, the old lieutenancy was useless."[33] Yet by 1642 this militia would be a major bone of contention between Charles I and his Parliament.

In 1641 a rebellion broke out in Ireland. Irish Catholics hoped to end the domination of a Protestant elite over the mostly Catholic population. But what Irish leaders could see as a fight for self-determination looked to English Protestant leaders like one more part of an international Catholic plot to eliminate English Protestantism. By that time, Parliament and Charles I had already been fighting with each other for years, making it more difficult for the government in London to respond to the events in Ireland. And while some crises can bring two sides together, the outbreak of rebellion in Ireland drove Parliament and Charles I further apart. In 1641, when he found himself unable to disband Parliament, the king attempted to have his men arrest five members of Parliament. Even that failed. Parliament did not trust the king to keep peace in England or Ireland and began to worry about its own safety as well. Taking matters into their own hands, the leaders of England's Parliament asserted their right to control England's militia. Though that militia was not a particularly effective institution, and its legal status was unclear, for England at the middle of the seventeenth century, it was its one permanent fighting force.[34] In their ordinance, Parliament declared,

> Whereas there hath been of late a most dangerous and desperate Design upon the House of Commons, which we have just Cause to believe to be an Effect of the bloody Counsels of Papists and other ill-affected Persons, who have already raised a Rebellion in the Kingdom of *Ireland,* and, by reason of many Discoveries, we cannot but fear they will proceed not only to stir up the like Rebellion and Insurrections in this Kingdom of *England,* but also to back them with Forces from abroad; for the Safety, therefore, of His Majesty's Person, the Parliament, and Kingdom, in this Time of imminent Danger, it is Ordained by the Lords and Commons now in Parliament assembled . . .[35]

The bulk of the ordinance after that was devoted to listing the men who would be leading the militia through the crisis, and who would be responsible "for the Suppression of all Rebellions, Insurrections, and Invasions that may happen" in their regions. In other words, Parliament's key move here was not to make a theoretical demand, insisting on the nature of English sovereignty; rather, the ordinance took the much more practical step of making sure that the men who commanded the militia would be men whom the leaders of Parliament could trust.

The king, unsurprisingly, was not pleased with this move. For all of the practical language of the ordinance, it was a major expansion of parliamentary jurisdiction in several ways, and Charles I's response focused on these implications rather than on the practical issues at hand. "Kingly power is but a shadow" without the control of the military, Charles claimed, making the debate "the Fittest Subject for a King's Quarrel."[36] For all of the ambiguities since the start of the century, it was nevertheless the case that earlier kings had commanded the militia; Parliament had not. Second, such a claim was, on any topic, an expansion of the legislative role that Parliament had previously taken. The king rejected the law. Parliament, in turn, rejected his rejection. On 15 March 1641 Parliament declared "that, in this Case of extreme Danger, and of His Majesty's Refusal, the Ordinance agreed on by both Houses for the Militia doth oblige the People, and ought to be obeyed, by the fundamental Laws of this Kingdom."[37]

With the king declaring that those who obeyed Parliament were breaking the law and Parliament declaring that those who did *not* obey the new ordinance were breaking the law, the two sides were at a point of irreconcilable difference. During 1642, each side began raising its army. The question of the respective authority of the king and Parliament would be decided on the battlefield.[38]

In May 1642, as both sides prepared for a season of warfare, Charles I again replied to Parliament's militia ordinance. Hearkening back to the militia's medieval origins, Charles claimed that it had always been up to the Crown to determine who would or would not be required to fight: "To the King it belongeth, and His part it is by his Royall Séigniority, straitly to defend wearing of Armour, and all other Force against the Peace, at all times when it shall please Him." Charles therefore declared that any men taking part in the militia under Parliament's orders, instead of under his, was in violation of the law. "We shall then call them in due time to a strict Account," he warned, "and proceed Legally against them as Violaters of the Laws, and Disturbers of the Peace of the Kingdom."[39] When the king issued that proclamation, though, he would have known that he was in no position to enforce it. By that point the king had left London, where he no longer felt safe, and set up his court in the distant city of York, some three hundred kilometers to the north. In August, with his troops in Nottingham, King Charles would raise the royal standard for the first time. It read, "Give Caesar his Due."[40]

Over the following years, an unprecedented portion of the men in the population took up arms—to fight each other or perhaps the Scots or the Irish.[41] The men fighting on Parliament's side would win that war, but this was not the golden age of the English militia. Again, there were a number of ironies in the relationship between the English Civil War and the history of the English militia. One was that, for all of the implications involved in Parliament's claim of authority over the militia, that claim did not survive. In 1662, after the civil wars had ended, Parliament declared that the king did indeed have authority over the militia.[42]

In another of the many ironies of England's seventeenth century, a dispute sparked by a debate over the control of the militia led to the creation of an English permanent standing army, which has existed ever since. In 1645, Parliament voted to create the New Model Army. A number of traits distinguished the New Model Army from England's previous forces. Historians often point to the religious devotion of many of the soldiers, who were supporters of the Puritan cause, but it stands out, too, for its organizational differences with other previous English fighting forces. It was much less tied to locality than previous forces, including the militia, which was still composed of local units under the lords lieutenant. The creation of the New Model Army meant that Parliament's forces could be more easily and quickly deployed across Great Britain. This ability to move larger distances and the deemphasis of the lords lieutenant meant that this army began breaking the traditional power of nobility. England, in 1645, found itself with a professional standing army.[43]

The creation of the New Model Army was a key part of what can best be looked at as England's belated (then accelerated) version of the military revolution. As Braddick notes, "More was achieved by way of modernising the military capacity of English government between 1642 and 1646 than had been achieved in the previous ninety years."[44] Between 1642 and 1660, a significant portion of Englishmen would serve in the armies of either the royalists or Parliament, perhaps one in ten at any given time, and a larger portion served at one point or another over the course of the fighting.[45] All of this required money, which Parliament was better at supplying than were the royalists. Parliament was better able to levy and collect taxes than were its opponents, and this kept the New Model Army better armed and better fed—but also made that army a financial burden for the English people, even when they were able to avoid the fighting.[46]

It was Parliament's forces, then, that were at the forefront of England's military centralization. Parliament was eventually unable to control the army it had created. Oliver Cromwell became the New Model Army's most successful leader and, from there, became the leader of the entire parliamentary cause. In 1653 Cromwell was sworn in as Lord Protector. Like Caesar, he had used his military strength to take power. Once in power, he used that military strength to stay in power.[47]

Cromwell was a singular figure in English history—the one man to rise to power without having been born into it. Before the English Civil War began, Cromwell had been an obscure member of England's lower nobility, perhaps a bit more hotheaded than most but otherwise unremarkable. In 1641 he became a member of Parliament, just before the definitive split between Parliament and Charles I. He was a religiously devout man who preferred the austere religious practices of England's Puritans to the more ostentatious ones of the Anglican Church. He knew, too, that he was opposed to Catholicism and its influence in England. What he did not know in 1641—what no one knew—was that he was a brilliant military leader. That would quickly become clear once the two sides started fighting, and Cromwell soon made himself indispensable in Parliament's army. In the words of the poet John Milton, Cromwell was "guided by faith and matchless fortitude."[48] This military power made Cromwell the most influential man in Parliament; from there he became the most powerful man in England, Scotland, Ireland, and England's nascent overseas empire as well. A few years after Charles's execution, his power over the army allowed Cromwell to become Lord Protector. Parliament's forces brought England its own Julius Caesar.

Cromwell reigned until his death in 1658; his son reigned for a few years, also as Lord Protector. But England had grown weary of its fighting and wearier still of the second-rate Caesar who had inherited an already dubious quasi throne. In 1660, the leaders of Parliament came to an agreement with Charles I's oldest son, who had been living in exile on the continent. Agreement made, he returned to England's throne. He would reign as Charles II until his death in 1685. Parliament had restored the Stuart dynasty to the throne. It also restored royal control over the militia.[49]

Parliament wanted to disband the New Model Army—but this was trickier. Many English people had not only grown tired of civil war; they had grown tired of the presence of so many soldiers. The experience had created a hostility toward a standing army, though it was not yet expressed as such. It was, at this point, an antimilitarism "stripped of all intellectuality."[50] It makes sense—for a society to have much of an opinion on standing armies and professional soldiers, it must first have a good sense of what they are. England was learning this during the 1650s and not much liking what it learned.

There was, then, some real momentum in 1660 to do away with the New Model Army. Charles II, however, was eager to retain as much of it as he could. Charles II wanted an army of six to eight thousand men. What he wound up with instead was an army of around thirty-five hundred men—meaning it hovered somewhere between a real army and a personal guard force. It was a pittance compared to Louis XVI's army across the channel, which by this time had over fifty thousand soldiers.[51] But this was as small as England's standing army would get. England has had a standing army since 1645.

At some level, the relationship between political and military strength is a key to any society. The quirk of early modern English history, though—and an underrated element that made even mainstream English politics so important to the development of the Second Amendment—was that this relationship between political authority and military power became a central and explicit issue in English political life. The political solutions the English chose would be fairly moderate; the implications that opposition writers proposed would be far more radical and would provide the specific ideological background for American revolutionary beliefs, but the content of the debate, and its focus on the relationship between political authority and military power, was the background that made the great debates over militias and standing armies possible. In the middle of the seventeenth century, the English people began debating the relationship between civil and military authority and asking how to guarantee civil control over the military. British writers began investigating these questions as well.

Institutional legacies are one thing; intellectual legacies are another. As discussed in chapter 1, it was less the real history of Julius Caesar that interested the founders than the morals that republicans since Machiavelli had made of Caesar's rise. That distinction between myth and history was not limited to ancient history. England's civil war not only saw the birth of England's standing army; it also saw the beginnings of an intellectual tradition that would see in citizen-soldiers everything that Machiavelli had seen in them and then some. In the writings of James Harrington, England first saw an attempt to apply the Florentine's lessons of citizen-soldiers to English political life. It happened at exactly the time when England was professionalizing its army.

In 1656 Harrington published his major work, *Oceana,* a utopian model of his ideal society. Like Machiavelli, Harrington was a major figure in Pocock's *Machiavellian Moment.* He had also played a big role in historian Caroline

Robbins's 1959 work on the "commonwealthman tradition." Still, he had been a mostly obscure writer for most of the period since he first wrote. According to Robbins, Harrington had helped shape a movement that represented "only a fraction of politically conscious Britons," and "no achievement of any consequence in England can be credited to them."[52] The intellectual movement he helped shape would prove influential in North America, though—hence Harrington's importance to this book.[53] For understanding the history of militias in the English intellectual tradition, Harrington provides a good opportunity to see the origins of the militia ideologies that would flourish at the end of the century. In Harrington's works, the main themes of the English pro-militia tradition started to come together. He began the work of applying the tradition of ancient republicanism to England's own past. As such, he was one of the earliest advocates of the kind of thinking that would eventually be part of the republican tradition of militia advocacy. Or, more succinctly: Harrington liked militias before militias were cool.

Harrington's *Oceana* stood out as a book that took Machiavelli's work seriously. Machiavelli's works were "neglected," Harrington wrote, but the Florentine was the only person who had retrieved the "ancient wisdom" needed for England to reconstruct itself. Using Machiavelli's writings and that "ancient wisdom," Harrington traced out a plan for a society that would do away with the flaws of Harrington's England. In doing so, it would bring back the "liberty of Rome," which had existed until that liberty was "extinguished" by the "arms of Caesar."[54]

The details of that plan are well beyond the scope of this book, but there are some elements worth noting. First, Harrington wanted a society with a strong nobility. "Oceana," he wrote, "or any other nation of no greater extent, must have a competent nobility."[55] England was becoming a more commercial and urban society during the seventeenth century, but Harrington's vision was still based on agriculture and landownership as the source of wealth. Those in the nobility were to be landowners. The power would be in the hands of these landowners, and those same landowners and their sons would be members of the militia. Many of England's woes, according to Harrington, came from the willingness to let the poor do the fighting while the rich sat idle.

> And this is the first point of the militia, in which modern prudence is quite contrary to the ancient; for whereas we, excusing the rich and arming the poor, become the vassals of our servants, they, by excusing

> the poor and arming such as were rich enough to be freemen, became lords of the earth. The nobility and gentry of this nation, who understand so little what it is to be the lords of the earth that they have not been able to keep their own lands, will think it a strange education for their children to be common soldiers, and obliged to all the duties of arms; nevertheless it is not for four shillings a week, but to be capable of being the best man in the field or in the city the latter part of which consideration makes the common soldier herein a better man than the general of any monarchical army.[56]

Harrington was able to combine a number of elements—Machiavelli's "ancient wisdom," and specifically the importance of relying on citizens instead of professional soldiers, a sense of England's past (albeit a different one than later English writers would hold), and a belief in the importance of a strong class structure dominated by the nobility. By bringing together these intellectual threads that supported relying on citizen-soldiers and linking them to the English notion of freedom, he was able to bring themes into English political thought that would flourish later in the century.[57] He was not able to influence the politics of his day much, however. Nor did the militia he described bear much resemblance to the militia of seventeenth-century England over which Parliament and Charles I had fought.

The English militia would continue to exist throughout the eighteenth century. It would come to thrive most, though, in other parts of the British Empire. Back in 1607, just over one hundred Englishmen had landed in North America. They would soon set up fort in an area they would call "Jamestown," after James I, located in a region they called Virginia, after Queen Elizabeth. Upon arrival these settlers found themselves in conflicts with a number of local tribes. The private company that organized the first expeditions required all men to participate in the colony's common defense. As Virginia became large enough to write its own laws, those laws also included a requirement that men participate in the militia.

Virginia's militia began out of necessity. The colony was already a questionable endeavor from a financial standpoint. It needed soldiers but did not intend to pay for them. When Virginians first mustered, the English had no tradition of seeing in their citizen-soldiers any sort of bulwark of liberty. England had, as of yet, no standing army and certainly no fear of a standing army.

Eventually, just as English writers would be able to apply Machiavelli's and Harrington's theories to the militias of England's distant history, American writers would be able to apply those same theories to England's North American colonies. By that point, though, they already had their own institutional history—one that was quite different from the experiences back in the British Isles. England's North American colonies were going to show what it meant to rely only on citizen-soldiers. It would not always be smooth sailing.

FIVE

Bacon's Rebels Burn Jamestown to the Ground

1676

JUNE 1676, Jamestown, Virginia. Two men stood facing each other outside of the colony's statehouse. On one side was Nathaniel Bacon, a twenty-eight-year-old who had arrived from England just two years earlier. Despite his youth and recent arrival, he had built up a following on Virginia's western frontier. Across from him stood William Berkeley, seventy-one years old but not about to back down. Berkeley too had come to Virginia from England, though he had arrived more than thirty years earlier. More to the point, perhaps, Berkeley was Virginia's colonial governor, the highest-ranking office in North America. He had held that position for twenty-five of the past thirty-five years. He was used to giving orders, not taking them. But this Bacon fellow, he was a problem—and the hundreds of armed men whom Bacon had brought with him were not making things any easier.[1]

The governor had men on his side, too—just not as many as Bacon did. Calling out the troops to fight Bacon was not an option. So Berkeley tried a different approach. Walking up to his adversary, Berkeley bared his chest and thrust it out toward Bacon. "Here!" he yelled. "Shoot me, fore God, fair mark, shoot!"[2]

It was an old-school approach, rooted in the habits and rituals of an England that both men had left behind. Berkeley was challenging Bacon to a duel. Bacon, though, was having none of it. "No may it please your honor," Bacon told the governor. "We will not hurt a hair on your head, nor of any other man's."[3]

Understood in that last claim, of course, was "unless." Bacon's men had surrounded the colony's statehouse. They outnumbered Berkeley's forces. They were willing to leave without fighting and hoped to do so—unless Berkeley continued to reject Bacon's demands. Specifically, they wanted Berkeley to give Bacon a "commission" authorizing him to lead his men against the neighboring

Indians. It was a military expedition that Governor Berkeley had hoped to avoid. Berkeley knew the risks of long fights against local tribes. He knew that further north up the Atlantic Coast, fighting between local tribes and English colonists—King Philip's War—was pushing the New England colonies to the brink of extinction. He also knew that there were profits to be made from trading with Indians and military benefits to alliances with certain tribes. But at this juncture Berkeley had two options: fighting Bacon and his men right there and then in Jamestown or giving Bacon the commission and letting Bacon lead his men against the Indians. Berkeley gave Bacon his commission, and Bacon led his men out of Jamestown and off to Virginia's frontier, where they could renew their campaign to "ruine and extirpate all Indians in Generall."[4]

In Jamestown, the immediate crisis passed. But the rebellion itself was just beginning. Jamestown was the capital and Berkeley was the governor, but he had no way of enforcing a law that the citizens did not support. It was one of the contradictions that any colonial government had to face: the colonial laws required citizens to participate in the militia, and the militia itself was responsible for enforcing that law, just as it enforced all the other laws. When most of the men took part, the system worked. But what happened when most of the men refused to take part in the militia? Under normal circumstances, this was an abstract sort of question. As Berkeley and Bacon stood face to face on that June day, though, the contradictions were anything but abstract. Berkeley had the legal authority, but Bacon and his men had the muscle and the firepower. As Berkeley would soon write, "How miserable that man is that Governes a People where six parts of seaven at least are Poore Endebted Discontented and Armed."[5]

This was not the first time that Bacon and Berkeley had met each other—far from it. They had first met upon Bacon's arrival. Bacon came from a wealthy background and brought considerable funds with him. This wealthy background set Bacon apart from most English settlers. Bacon's family background was similar to Berkeley's, as both were from the upper reaches of England's social ladder. Their wives, too, seem to have had ties that predated either's arrival in the New World. Bacon had served in the assembly, where he would have worked alongside Berkeley. The two men knew each other far better than historians today can know either man.[6]

Of Bacon, our knowledge is particularly limited. He left few writings other than a proclamation and his communications with Berkeley, and there is relatively little direct testimony about Bacon from his contemporaries. We can tell quite a bit about him from his actions, though, and from what little evidence and contemporary testimony exists. His father owned a fair amount of land in England, enough to put the family toward the upper edge of England's middle ranks, or even the lowest ranks of England's nobility. It was enough money to send young Nathaniel to study at Cambridge, although not enough to warrant keeping him there when his study habits proved insufficient. Bacon had not, in any case, gone through the acid test of indentured servitude upon his arrival in Virginia. He had arrived with resources, money, and a welcome from Berkeley and the rest of Virginia's elite. English society had emphasized birth and class rank, and Bacon never seems to have questioned that system, despite the potentially egalitarian aspects of his rebellion. He even seems to have been bothered by the "vile" backgrounds and "sudden advancement"[7] of the men who had come to make up Virginia's elite.

It was not his economic circumstances that drove him out of England but his temperament. He appears in retrospect as a restless spirit who had not fit in back in England. At Cambridge his tutor remarked of Bacon that he had a "quick wit" but that "his temper will not admit long study."[8] His adventure at Cambridge ended with his father withdrawing him before the end of his studies. Soon after that Nathaniel married a woman of similar status but in a match neither's parents approved of. Her father disowned her. His marriage, then, was not a sign Bacon was moving past his youthful indiscretions. Bacon was then caught trying to cheat a neighbor, at which point Bacon's father had had enough and shipped his son off to Virginia, where the family already had some connections.

Those family connections—and money from Bacon's father—meant that Nathaniel Bacon arrived in Virginia with an entry into the colonial elite waiting for him. By the standards of the England he had left behind, Bacon was "better born" than most of the men running the show in Virginia. Many of those men (though not Berkeley himself) had come from poor families back home. They had made their fortunes in the tobacco trade or by marrying wealthy Virginia widows. In the Virginia Bacon encountered, then, the old English tradition of deference for those born higher on the social scale still existed, but it existed alongside conditions that had allowed a new crop of men to become rich and powerful despite their humble beginnings.

Bacon set himself up with a house in Jamestown and purchased land out farther from Jamestown, toward the frontier in Henrico County. There, settlers' tobacco farms continued their encroachment onto Native American lands. In many ways it was less desirable land, given the risks of confrontations with Indians. But Bacon seems to have been more comfortable among frontiersmen who felt excluded than among an elite that, in Bacon's eyes, did not warrant the lofty positions they were holding. The temperament that had put him at odds with the system at Cambridge soon put him at odds with the system in Virginia as well.

His adversary, William Berkeley—*Sir* William Berkeley—was a gentleman, born into England's nobility at the start of the seventeenth century. His father had left him some land and, more importantly, the connections that would let him mix with England's elite. As a young man he hobnobbed with England's best and brightest, first while in school at Oxford, then later at the king's court, where Berkeley fell in with a group of young intellectuals and wrote several plays. He went to war with England against Scotland at the end of the 1630s and fought well enough to be knighted afterward. His upbringing in the English countryside had even taught him the basics of agriculture. He was far from the pinnacle of fame and success, but he was establishing himself as a renaissance man of sorts, dabbling in a wide range of interests. While he did not rise to the top in any of them, he did not fail in any either.[9]

Berkeley was in his mid-thirties in 1641 when King Charles I appointed him governor of Virginia. Virginia's laws at the time let Englishmen who had settled in the colony vote on their government, but that only applied to the "Burgesses," the colonial assembly. Governors were appointed by the king (and would remain so for as long as Virginia remained a colony). In other words, as soon as Berkeley arrived in Virginia, he was already the man in charge.

Berkeley had a vision for what Virginia could become—a vision that required some changes to the colony. He began experimenting with different crops. He negotiated with local Indian tribes. He began trying to put in place his vision of a Virginia that did not rely only on tobacco and that maintained friendly relations with some local tribes. He set up trading arrangements with those tribes, as one more way to diversify the colony's economy. That said, Berkeley had been a soldier and he remained one—he did not shy away from war against local tribes when he thought it appropriate. In the 1660s he ordered Virginia's militia to attack the Doeg and Potomac Indians, destroy their villages, and sell their women and children into slavery. He had no doubt about the superiority of England and English culture over that of the indigenous people. He also had no doubt about the superiority of England's elites over the rest of English society, nor the superiority of Virginia's elites, even if many of Virginia's elites were of relatively new vintage.

Berkeley embodied a way of being a Virginian, and it was a very English way indeed. He believed in learning, trade, and agriculture, and he believed in a hierarchical society ruled by the elites. He understood the importance of war and fought it when he felt it was needed. But Berkeley also valued culture, and family life. The citizens at the top of the social ladder should embody those traits; those lower on the ladder might be held to a lower standard but were still expected to respect their leaders. Berkeley was doing what he could to re-create a genteel English society in a colonial setting.[10]

Such a genteel Virginia would arrive eventually, but only in the eighteenth century, well after Berkeley had left. The Virginia of the 1670s was still a rough-and-tumble place. To be sure, Virginia had come a long way from its beginnings. Roanoke, the first English attempt at setting up a colony in the New World, had begun in 1585 and was gone by 1590. The colony at Jamestown began in 1607. It had lasted ever since—though the winter of 1609–10, when almost 90 percent of its settlers died (and some of the survivors turned to cannibalism) had brought the expedition to the brink of failure. Then, during the 1620s, Virginians started growing tobacco. Sales in Europe skyrocketed. Suddenly there was money to be made in North America, and there was no chance that the Jamestown colony would go the way of Roanoke.[11]

The influx of riches from the tobacco trade transformed Virginia.[12] It made some people rich, and it made others believe they could become rich themselves. It did not make Virginia an easy place to live, though. For the local indigenous population, it meant more arrivals, more demand for farmland, and a farther retreat into the interior. Colonists who arrived early were in a position to become rich if they survived. Survival, though, was far from a given. Local diseases led to the death of many European settlers in their first year in North America. Between 1625 and 1640, fifteen thousand people left England for Virginia, yet Virginia's population increased by only seven thousand during that time. Emigration to Virginia was an endeavor for the daring or the desperate. In the first half of the seventeenth century, England was sending both.[13]

In the early years of the tobacco boom, it was relatively easy for colonists who survived to get their own land. Finding labor to work that land was far harder. Colonists had tried enslaving the indigenous population, but they kept escaping. Virginia had its first enslaved Africans in 1619, but until the eighteenth century it had relatively few. By the 1670s there were perhaps a thousand Africans enslaved in Virginia, compared to over twenty thousand white Virginians. For the landowners, the costs of purchasing African people were too great. The wealth tobacco brought into the colony paled in comparison to the money made in the sugar-producing colonies of the West Indies. Virginians could not match the prices that West Indian slave owners were paying. The dominant form of labor became indentured servitude. In this system, people from England could exchange a boat ride to Virginia for several years of their labor. At the end of that labor—if they survived—they would be given a plot of land and a chance to make something of themselves as independent farmers and landowners.[14]

Most of the Englishmen who arrived in Virginia during the seventeenth century arrived as indentured servants. Indentured servitude in the colonies appealed only to Englishmen in dire straits, who had even fewer chances if they remained in England. Most of the English women who arrived came from similar backgrounds, but there were far fewer of them; Virginia society remained primarily male for most of the seventeenth century. Year after year, indentured servants would arrive from England; year after year, those who survived their servitude would get their plot of land and set up their farms. Year after year, these land grants would push the frontier between Native Americans and English settlers farther from Jamestown.[15]

A Virginia culture was beginning to take shape, then—though not exactly the culture Governor Berkeley had been hoping for. In Jamestown itself, and in the lands right around it, lived Jamestown's elite. These families benefited from arriving first and surviving. Surrounding it were the farms of the newer arrivals—mostly "freedmen" who had made it through their servitude. By the 1670s the economic conditions were less favorable for small farmers than they had been earlier in the century. As historian Edmund Morgan put it, during the last three or four decades of the seventeenth century, "most of the men who worked in the fields were losers and they did not much like it."[16] The emergent Virginia culture was more than a little rough around the edges. By 1661 the burgesses felt obliged to enact a law against those who would "shoote any guns att drinking or marriages (buryalls excepted)."[17] So Berkeley was probably accurate when he described these men as "poore endebted [and] discontented." He was definitely correct when he described them as "armed." Settlers—including the freedmen—were expected to have guns and to know how to use them. After all, they were now citizens of Virginia and, as such, members of the Virginia militia.[18]

Jamestown had a militia from its very beginning. When the first settlers landed there in 1607, they were as much soldiers as they were farmers. All the men who took part in the early waves of settlement—and those waves were overwhelmingly male—were expected to take part in the colony's defense. As the Virginia colony expanded and the settlement pushed farther and farther into Indian lands, the men who set up their farms in newly appropriated land were expected to defend themselves, their farms, and their families if they had them.[19] Back in 1609, when it was not even clear that the colony would last, the London-based Virginia Company told its settlers that "everie of them shall and lawfull maie" look after the colony's defense, "by force and armes."[20] As soon as Virginia started creating its own laws, those men were also required to show up periodically for training. The colony's 1641 regulations, which Berkley had brought with him from England, required four musters a year. Those regulations also stated, "To the End the Country may be the better served against all Hostil Invasions, it is requisite that all persons from the Age of 16. to be Armed."[21]

Virginia's militia was still going strong when Berkeley and Bacon faced off. Almost all of England's North American colonies relied on their militias. The one exception was Pennsylvania, whose Quaker founders rejected violence. Every other colony up and down the East Coast had militias, and a significant portion of the men who lived in those colonies were required to participate. These militias were official institutions whose regulations were set out in the colony's laws. Over the course of the colonial period, these regulations would vary some from colony to colony. There were times when some colonies kept white servants out of the militias, while others required those servants to participate; some kept Catholics out of the militias, while others did not. Overall, though, certain patterns held true from Georgia to New Hampshire: adult white men were required to participate; they were expected to have a way of arming themselves; they were also required to register their presence in the colony and, often, to register the weapons they had at their disposal as well. Officers were required to organize and train their units. Frequency varied, but men eligible for the militia could expect to spend a few Sundays per year mustering with their fellow colonists. These militias answered to the colony's government, and governors had the authority to order colonial militias out into the field. It was these militias that the colonies relied on to fight against Indian tribes. Later, these militias had to maintain control over the local enslaved populations in the southern colonies. The militias were also the colonies' first line of defense against any attack by a foreign European power such as France or Spain. The presence of these militias meant that England's colonies could be the societies that writers in Europe came to praise, with no standing armies and with a populace trained and organized in the basics of the military arts.[22]

For all of the ideas circulating in Europe about the virtues of a militia or the dangers of professional soldiers, though, it was not the fear of a standing army or a belief in military virtue that led Britain to institute militias in its North American colonies. It was much more of a practical matter. Militias were cheap. Economically, the North American colonies were already a dubious venture. Largely financed through private investments and run by private companies like the Virginia Company, the colonies turned out to be a poor investment for most who invested in them. Neither those companies nor the English government had any interest in adding the costs of stationing professional soldiers in the New World. So the colonists were to provide for their own security. Often the system worked well. But Jamestown, in 1676, was not one of those times.

Virginia's militia was involved in Bacon's Rebellion from before it was even clear that there was a rebellion—though determining its exact role is not easy, given the way that the militia and the citizenry blended into each other. The rebellion itself grew out of a conflict between an English colonist, Thomas Mathew, and a group Doeg Indians. The dispute escalated quickly: after Mathew refused to pay them, the Doegs responded by stealing some of his pigs. Mathew then led a group of colonists to catch the thieves. Mathew and his men killed some of the Indians they caught up with, and the Indians retaliated by killing one of Mathew's employees. As one eyewitness would put it, "Ffrom this Englishman's bloud did (by degrees) arise Bacons rebellion . . . which overspread all Virginia and twice endangered Maryland."[23]

The colonists responded by putting together a party of thirty or so men, led by local militia officers, and chasing the Indians. During the ensuing fighting, the colonists found and killed ten Doeg warriors. Thinking they had found a second group of Doegs, the colonists also killed fourteen Susquehannock warriors before realizing their error. "Ffor the Lords sake shoot no more, these are our friends the Susquehanoughs," the militia officer yelled at his men, but it was too late.[24]

Killing the Susquehannock was a big deal. They were a much larger tribe than the Doegs, and they were facing their own pressures. There was nowhere for them to retreat to: in the 1670s, the Susquehannock had more enemies among local tribes than they did among English colonists. As historian James Rice has noted, the Susquehannock were "the most desperate and formidable enemy that Virginians had faced in over thirty years."[25] They began retaliating against the Virginians. They killed a number of settlers, among whom were two of Bacon's own employees, including his overseer, "whom he much loved, and one of his servants, whose bloud he vowed to revenge." Virginians on the frontier began preparing for a war. Farmers on smaller estates began staying with neighbors at larger farms. Inhabitants sent word to Berkeley in Jamestown, looking for relief. It was at this point that Bacon, angry at his employees' deaths, emerged as a leader and spokesman for the Virginians living on the frontier. He began gathering people to follow him in an expedition against the Susquehannock. He even began calling himself "General."

It was at this point, too, that Governor Berkeley proved not to be the leader that the colonists of Henrico County wanted him to be. "Frequent complaints of bloodsheds were sent to S'r Wm. Berkeley (then Govern'r) from the heads of the rivers," one account noted, "which were as often answered with promises of assistance,"[26] but concrete assistance never came. This inaction, another account noted, "did not onely terefye the wholl collony, but subplanted those esteemes the people had formerly for Sr. W. B. whom they judged too remiss in applying meanes to stop the fewrye of the Heathen."[27] Berkeley made plans for forts to be built (at taxpayers' expense) and for negotiations. But what the colonists on the frontier wanted, and what Bacon himself wanted, was a war—which Berkeley wanted to avoid. By this time Bacon had several hundred men ready to follow him into battle once they had the governor's approval. But what should they do without that approval? The people hesitated at first, then eventually followed Bacon into Indian territory, where he set out to kill as many Susquehannocks as he could—and any other Indians he might come across as well. So while Berkeley sought to reassure the Susquehannocks and sought the aid of his allies among the Pamunkey tribe, Bacon and his men were trying to rid the area of as many Indians as possible. As Bacon asked at the time, "Are not the Indians all of a Colour?"[28]

To understand why so many colonists were willing to follow Bacon despite the governor's wishes, it must be noted that the question of how to respond to the Susquehannocks was not the only dispute between Berkeley and the colonists in Henrico County. The wealth that the earlier arrivals had made was not trickling down to the later arrivals; the elites in Jamestown often seemed bent on profiting off of the labor of the freedmen. Even Berkeley's proposed forts seemed to them less like a means of protection than one more way for Berkeley and his friends to get rich off of poorer colonists. The dispute over how to respond to the Susquehannocks, then, built on some existing fault lines. Together, these disagreements were enough to drive people from discontent to defiance, and eventually to rebellion. Berkeley still hoped to avoid a large-scale confrontation with the Susquehannocks. He still saw hope for diplomacy, telling his fellow Virginians, "If they had killed my grandfather and grandmother, my father and mother and all my friends, yet if they had come to treat of peace, they ought to have gone in peace and sat down."[29] This approach was not popular with the Virginians on the frontier, who found Bacon's plan to "ruin and extirpate" the local tribes more appealing.

Once Bacon started fighting the Indians, Berkeley sprang into action. He "could not bear this insolent deportment"[30] and immediately raised troops to stop Bacon's expedition. Berkeley declared Bacon a rebel, adding "I doe therefore againe declair that Bacon proceedeing against all Laws of all Nations modern and ancient." As for those men who had followed Bacon into Indian country, Berkeley wrote that "Mr. Bacon hath none about him, but the lowest of the people."[31] So Berkeley raised what he could of the Virginia militia and headed out to catch Bacon. Concerned at the prospect of facing one enemy in front of him and another behind—"It vext him to the heart (as he said) to thinke, that while he was a hunting Wolves, tigers and bears, which daly destroyd our harmless and innosscent Lambs, that hee, and those with him, should be persewed in the reare with a full cry, as more savage beasts"[32]—Bacon headed to Jamestown with a few dozen of his followers. It was one of Bacon's least successful gambits. Berkeley outmaneuvered Bacon and had him arrested. Bacon had nothing left to do but beg for Berkeley's forgiveness and, "upon my knees, most humbly begg of Almighty God and of his majesties said governour . . . he will please to grant me his gracious pardon and indemnity."[33]

To the surprise of contemporaries and historians alike, Berkeley accepted Bacon's apology. Freed and pardoned, Bacon returned to the frontier and to his expedition against the Indians. Berkeley wound up right where he had been, still hoping to stop Bacon's actions against the Indians. By this time, though, Bacon wanted to confront Berkeley head on. The disagreement was about to become a full-scale rebellion. Two weeks after begging on his knees for a pardon, Bacon returned to Jamestown, not with a few dozen followers but with a few hundred.

This, then, was how it came to pass that Bacon and Berkeley stood facing each other in Jamestown on that June day in 1676. Berkeley had little choice, then, but to give Bacon his commission then and there. But Berkeley could not ignore Bacon's actions either. By now the rebellion was a matter for the entire colony. Unfortunately for Berkeley, Bacon seemed to have more support than the governor did. When Berkeley sent out orders to raise the militia, over a thousand Virginians heeded the call. Most of them abandoned the governor when they learned that the expedition would be against Bacon. These were Virginians from counties that had not joined the rebellion, but they were hesitant to fight their fellow Virginians and perhaps even agreed with Bacon's approach.

As noted above, Virginia's militia had been involved in Bacon's Rebellion from the beginning, but determining its exact role is not easy. In a society where all soldiers were citizens and all citizens soldiers, it was not always possible to separate a military action from a civilian one. Some of the events covered in this chapter were typical militia actions that showed that Virginia's militia, during the 1670s, was capable of doing what it was meant to do. Two militia officers leading thirty men on a search for the Doeg Indians was a typical militia action. When Berkeley called up the militia to stop the progress of what he viewed as an insurrection, this too fell into the militia's official purview—even if it was a less typical occurrence. Throughout the rebellion, the men fighting on Berkeley's side were doing so as part of Virginia's militia, fulfilling their obligations as citizens. But what about the men on Bacon's side? The vast majority of these men were also members of the Virginia militia. Officers in the Virginia militia took up leadership positions under Bacon's command. Even the actions they were undertaking against the Indians, while unauthorized, were still fairly typical for the time. Bacon's expedition against the Susquehannocks in 1676 was not all that different from Berkeley's 1660 attack on local tribes. There is no easy answer as to whether or not these were actions undertaken by the militia. Berkeley, of course, would have said that they were not, as he had not commanded them; the men involved in the fighting, one suspects, would have answered differently.[34]

The limitations and unpredictability of the militia system were also very much in evidence throughout the rebellion. Again, it was one of the contradictions that any colonial government had to face: the laws required citizens to participate in the militia, but the militia itself was responsible for enforcing that law. Berkeley had done what he could to end the rebellion by calling out the militia. But when the men whom he had gathered walked away from Berkeley once they found out that he meant for them to march on their fellow Virginians, there was nothing the governor could do to stop them. As one account described that scene, once Berkeley "proposed to them to follow and suppress that rebell Bacon," the men there began "murmuring before his face 'Bacon Bacon Bacon,' and all walked out of the field, muttering as they went 'Bacon, Bacon, Bacon,' leaving the governor and those that came with him to themselves."[35]

Bacon's Rebellion continued through the summer and into the fall. Bacon had captured Jamestown in June but had little interest in holding it; Berkeley, with a few hundred men loyal to him, had retaken it in early September. Later that month, though, Bacon led his men back to Jamestown to fight Berkeley and to retake the capital. As Bacon and his men approached Jamestown, they stopped first at the homes of several members of Jamestown's elite. They seized several wives of prominent Jamestown men and put them at the front lines as human shields. Berkeley and his men had no way to fight back without harming the women. "The poor Gent: women were mightily astonished at this project; neather were their husbands voide of amazements at his subtill invention." In the ensuing battle, Bacon and his men again took the town. Berkeley had to sail away from Jamestown, leaving the houses empty "for Bacon to enter at his pleasure." With no desire to defend the town but not wishing to see Berkeley retake it again, Bacon and his men "in the most barbarous manner converts the wholl towne into flames, cinders and ashes, not so much as spareing the church, and the first that ever was in Verginia."[36] With that done, Bacon returned to the frontier, to continue fighting against any and every Indian he came across.

Then, in early October, everything changed. Nathaniel Bacon fell ill, most likely of dysentery. He died on October 12. One of Bacon's allies took over the command of the rebels, but the movement fizzled out. In January, fourteen royal ships carrying over one thousand soldiers arrived in Virginia from England to put an end to the rebellion, but even before then Berkeley and the men loyal to him had things in hand.[37] They arrested and hanged most of the leaders (and confiscated their estates for themselves). The rebellion was over. Berkeley's place at the top of Virginia's elite would turn out to be over as well. He had to return to England and answer for his actions in Virginia and his inability to prevent the rebellion. Berkeley was eager to clear his name, but he barely had a chance to do so. He died in July 1677 in England, the land he had grown up in but had not seen for more than three decades.

For anyone who wants to understand the roles that militias would come to play in North America, Bacon's Rebellion is the best place to start the story—even if, in the grand scheme of things, Bacon's Rebellion did not have the historical importance of Caesar's march across the Rubicon; nor were there any ideas developed during the rebellion that would rival Machiavelli's or Harrington's. The Virginia of 1680 wound up looking a lot like the Virginia of 1675.[38] Yet the rebellion remains remarkably illustrative. Bacon's Rebellion showed colonial Virginia in the process of deciding what it would become. It showed a society choosing where to draw the lines between the haves and the have-nots. It showed a population deciding which grievances it would prioritize and which it would ignore. And it showed that the militia was an integral part of Virginia's evolution.

Bacon's Rebellion also played a major role in one of the classic accounts of colonial Virginia, Morgan's 1975 *American Slavery, American Freedom*. Morgan's goals in that book were lofty ones: he wanted to explain why America, the land of the free, had spent so much of its existence as a slave society.[39] Morgan came to a few conclusions. One was that firearms played a big role in establishing a sense of equality among white Virginians even when, by any economic standard, they were not equal at all. Another was that later on, the large number of enslaved African Americans made this sense of solidarity among white Virginians possible. Bacon's Rebellion played a major role in Morgan's account of Virginia's evolution. In Morgan's telling, Bacon's Rebellion was a class struggle between Berkeley's planter elite and the poorer freedmen. Virginia's planter elite had pushed the freedmen too hard, and some sort of rebellion was all but inevitable. Morgan followed Berkeley in seeing seventeenth-century Virginia as a society divided by class and the rebellion as an uprising of the lower sort against the elites. In the process of re-creating English society on the other side of the Atlantic, Virginia was re-creating England's class divisions without any real way of keeping the lower classes in check. There were no professional forces at the governor's beck and call, able to maintain order over an unarmed and unorganized population. Instead, Virginia had an armed and organized population responsible for maintaining its own order—a sure recipe for unrest. Still, for Morgan, "For those with eyes to see, there was an obvious lesson in the rebellion. Resentment of an alien race might be more powerful than resentment of an upper class."[40]

Bacon's Rebellion, then, provided both a warning and an alternative. The warning was that if the colonial elites had to make a choice about what to do with the newly arrived white settlers and the poorer white settlers: they could continue to exploit them as much as possible, or they could continue to arm them and require them to serve in the militia. If they continued to do both, though, rebellions like Bacon's would keep on happening. The alternative was to focus the anger of white have-nots away from the planter elites and toward the "racial other"—which, in the 1670s, meant the local indigenous tribes. This was not a lesson that Virginia's planter elite grasped immediately, according to Morgan. It was, however, the system that would emerge in Virginia. Or, as historian Kathleen Brown puts it, the colonial government's need for an armed citizenry was "unprecedented in the military history of England and led to unprecedented political and social alignments."[41] By the time these alignments were fully formed, however, Native Americans had become less central to the story than they were in the 1670s. Instead, social hierarchies in colonial Virginia would come to revolve around the relationship between white Virginians and the enslaved African American population, of whom there were few in the 1670s but whose numbers would start to skyrocket in the eighteenth century.

Morgan's account is over forty years old, and historians have found their share of criticisms. Some have found the jump from class struggle to racial discrimination too simplistic, while others have pointed to the problems in Morgan's chronology, given the gap between Bacon's Rebellion and the arrival of large-scale plantation slavery. The division between the Bacon's side and Berkeley's side, meanwhile, did not fit neatly along objective socioeconomic lines and turned out to look more like factions than classes. Bacon's followers were not all from the "lowest of the people."[42] The most interesting criticisms concern the role of Native Americans, though. Rice has shown that from an indigenous perspective "Bacon's Rebellion," was only a part of "a multisided conflict in which most of the 'sides' lay within Indian country."[43] In this telling, the biggest difference between Bacon and Berkeley was not about taxes or access to government offices or anything along those lines. Indian policy was always the central bone of contention between Berkeley and Bacon. Berkeley, to be sure, was no advocate of equality or multiculturalism. As noted above, he had ordered his own attacks on local tribes in the past. But in Berkeley's Virginia, some tribes were both military allies and trading partners. Such alliances required a certain amount of give and take, though, and one of the biggest assets that the Virginia government had to offer was the control of Virginians themselves, including an end to what must have seemed a relentless push into Indian spaces. Bacon and his men showed that this promise was not one Berkeley could keep.

This "Indian-centric" interpretation of Bacon's Rebellion challenges some points of Morgan's interpretation, but not all of it. For Morgan, Bacon's Rebellion had grown out of a class struggle, but it had also pointed a way out of future class struggles, albeit not a particularly attractive one: racial hatred could become a substitute for class-based resentment. This helped Morgan explain why, even though Virginia society had grown out of English society and had tried to replicate much of English society, England's class divisions had never really taken root in North America. Rice's account shows that the class issues that divided Bacon's men from the Virginia elite were never particularly important. A blunter way of putting this would be that Virginia did not become racist after Bacon's Rebellion. That racism—at least, against Native Americans—was already there. Bacon and his men were trying to make sure that Virginia's elites stopped interfering with it.

The disagreements between Morgan's interpretation of the rebellion and the Indian-centric version lay mostly in the rebellion's origins. When it came to the outcome, and to the society that emerged from the rebellion, both painted similar portraits of Virginia's society as it approached the eighteenth century. Colonial Virginia became a society where rich and poor Virginians could work together, as long as they were all white, and where poor Virginians had trouble working together unless they all were of the same race. This dynamic, where racial solidarity overrode class solidarity, would become Virginia's defining characteristic—and eventually North America's as well. In the 1670s, Virginia was primarily a colony of white settlers, pushing westward into American Indian territory. There were some enslaved people in Virginia, as had been the case since 1619, but they did not yet play a central role in Virginia society. There were also free blacks in Virginia, including some who had fought alongside Bacon and his men during the rebellion.[44]

By the mid-eighteenth century, Virginia had become a slave society, and white Virginians found a new object for their hatred, derision, and violence in the rising population of Africans and African Americans.[45]

As shown in chapter 4, English society was a class-based society. The militia, by relying on local gentry and then on the lords lieutenant, reinforced that class structure. Harrington's writings also endorsed the idea of an armed nobility dominating society. English colonists brought their militia system to North America, but things there would play out much differently. The colonial militias, rather than enforcing class divisions, wound up promoting solidarity between rich and poor white colonists. In retrospect, that decision to arm poorer whites, and to rely on their participation in the militia, would play a key role in shaping life in the colonies and, eventually, the United States. It was a decision made for pragmatic reasons, not ideological ones—a colony of settlers required a military force, and the English could not afford to pay for one, so the settlers would have to do their own fighting. The wealthy settlers had neither the desire nor the capability to do this on their own, so they turned to the poorer whites to help. In doing so, the elites handed away some of the control that they had had back in England. Governor Berkeley saw the downside of the arrangement—hence his complaint about the difficulties of ruling a population that was "poore endebted discontented and armed."[46]

The rise of a leader like Bacon showed the risks of the arrangement, given the problems he caused for Berkeley and the Virginia government. Colonial America would have other movements like Bacon's Rebellion: uprisings by whites who felt excluded yet were already armed and organized due to their participation in the militias would come along periodically throughout the colonial period and into the early years of the United States. They remained, however, the exception. Arming the poor did not lead to the sort of social upheaval English writers had predicted. Throughout the colonial period, given the choice between allying their interests with poor nonwhites or with wealthier whites, poor whites tended to cast their lot with the wealthier whites. The militia system would remain a part of this process, though the typical actions of the militia would change. In Virginia and colonies to its south, militias would evolve into slave patrols (though the two institutions were not always identical). Along the frontiers, militias would continue to fight against local indigenous tribes. And in northern cities, the militias tended to become less military institutions and more of social ones. As the threat of invasion declined in the larger towns along the Atlantic Seaboard, musters became less a matter of military training and more of a community gathering.

Along the frontier, there would continue to be a place in America for men like Bacon. Along the seaboard, colonial society began to look more like the society that Berkeley had envisioned. Both in their own way helped create a British North America that retained much of the English culture that produced it yet was evolving into something distinctly its own.

SIX

Andrew Fletcher of Saltoun Publishes *A Discourse of Government with Relation to Militias*

1698

JUNE 11, 1685. A group of eighty-two men landed in three ships near the town of Lyme Regis, toward the western end of England's southern coast. Leading them was James Scott, the Duke of Monmouth. The oldest of several illegitimate sons of England's King Charles II, Monmouth had a tenuous claim to being the king's legitimate son via a secret marriage between the his mother and Charles II, and, therefore, an equally tenuous claim to the throne, which, earlier that year, had instead gone to Charles's younger brother James. Among the men accompanying him was Andrew Fletcher of Saltoun, a Scottish aristocrat in his early thirties who had been living in exile in the Netherlands. In the 1690s Fletcher would go on to produce one of the true classics of pro-militia writing, *A Discourse of Government with Relation to Militias.* On this day in 1685, though, Fletcher was just one of the more high-profile members of an undermanned and quixotic attempt to claim England's throne. The expedition was well equipped, though. In the ships were fifteen hundred muskets, armor, and other military supplies. Monmouth's plan was to gather supporters as he went and then take the Crown by force. He had some early success. After landing in England, a few thousand men joined Monmouth's forces. On several occasions they defeated local militia forces. As had happened during Bacon's Rebellion, not all of the local militiamen were eager to attack their fellow countrymen. Many local militiamen were sympathetic to the rebellion, and some wound up taking up arms alongside the rebels. James II had converted to Catholicism during the 1660s. Monmouth was a Protestant. For a significant percentage of Britons, this alone made Monmouth a better choice as a ruler.[1]

Monmouth led his troops across southwestern England for the better part of a month. But "Monmouth's Rebellion," as it came to be known, never put

England into the kind of existential crisis that Virginia had faced during Bacon's Rebellion. King James II was in a far better position than Berkeley had been. True, both had proved unable to rely on their militia to quell an uprising. But unlike in Virginia, King James II had something of an army to call on. As shown in chapter 4, when Charles II took the throne, he retained a force of around thirty-five hundred men from the New Model Army. In the years since, that had grown to an army of around nine thousand professional soldiers under the king's command. It took some time for the king to assemble that army and to march it down to the West Country, where the revolt was taking place.

The British army met up with Monmouth and his men on July 6 at the Battle of Sedgemoor. The untrained (and apparently undisciplined) rebel forces had done well against the local militias but were no match for the king's comparatively well-trained army of professional soldiers. The king's forces captured Monmouth himself two days later. He would be beheaded the following week. That fall, England's government put hundreds of participants in the rebellion on trial, sentencing over three hundred men to death for taking part in it. Another eight hundred were exiled to the West Indies. The rebellion was over.[2]

Monmouth's Rebellion strengthened a conviction James II already held that for England to move forward it needed to build up a stronger, full-time army of professional soldiers. The militia's early failures made the king's case that much more convincing. The following November James II told Parliament, "When I reflect what an inconsiderable number of Men begun it and how long they carried it on without any Opposition, I hope everyone will be convinced that the Militia . . . is not sufficient for such Occasions and that there is nothing but a good Force of well-disciplined Troops in constant pay that can defend us."[3]

That conviction set King James II on a collision course with England's Parliament and led to his downfall three years later. In 1688, leaders of Parliament initiated a series of events that would become England's Glorious Revolution—a turning point in the history of the entire British Empire, a defining moment in the Anglo-American political culture of the eighteenth century, and a turning point in the centuries-long history of the power struggle between the monarchy and the Parliament. It was also a key moment in the decades-long debates about the relationship between state power and military force—a debate between advocates of a professional army and advocates of a citizens' militia, as well as debates about who should be in charge of whatever military force existed. The phase lasting from 1685 to 1700 included two key moments on the road to Second Amendment. The first was the establishment of England's Bill of Rights in 1689, requiring parliamentary consent for a peacetime standing army and declaring that Protestant subjects "may have arms for their defence." The second was the veritable explosion of texts during the 1690s criticizing standing armies and singing the praises of citizen-soldiers, written by men who, like Andrew Fletcher, worried that England would soon have an army like France's and believed that, were that to happen, England's monarchy would become more like France's as well.

That Andrew Fletcher would live to take part in that debate was itself an odd twist of fate—due, ironically, to his own short temper. Had he participated in Monmouth's Revolt to the extent he intended, Fletcher would have been captured and executed, if not killed in battle. His conflict with another of the rebels wound up saving him. Within two days after landing, Thomas Hayward Dare, a wealthy politician from the nearby town of Taunton who had been on the ships with Monmouth and Fletcher, had rounded up forty local men willing to serve as cavalrymen for Monmouth. Dare had also rounded up one particularly impressive horse. Andrew Fletcher claimed that horse for himself, on the grounds that he would be leading Monmouth's cavalry. Dare was already on the horse and refused to give it up. Fletcher approached Dare and tried to take the horse anyway. In response, Dare used his whip to drive Fletcher away. Fletcher drew his pistol. He shot and killed Dare on the spot.[4]

Fletcher was never prosecuted for killing Dare, but it was the end of his participation in the rebellion. Monmouth dismissed Fletcher from his camp. Fletcher would go back into exile for the next three years. In 1688 he would return to Great Britain as part of the next, and far more successful, attempt to replace King James II.

The years following the Monmouth Rebellion would be adventurous ones for Fletcher—though records from this period are somewhat speculative. He spent time in a Spanish prison, then traveled to Hungary to fight the Turks. It was but one more chapter in a life of adventures and learning. By the time he died, Fletcher had participated in two rebellions, been arrested for participating in a third, been exiled more than once, but then returned to hold elected office in Scotland. He never married or started a family, though he seemed at times in his writings preoccupied with issues of masculinity and femininity. He lived in the Netherlands, in London, in Paris, and on his estates east of Edinburgh. Over the course of his lifetime he lost and regained those estates, which were confiscated and then returned to him depending on the political winds. He also published several writings, one of which he wrote in Italian, and collected the largest private library in all of Scotland. Most of the causes he supported failed, though perhaps none quite so spectacularly as the Monmouth Rebellion had. He had a vision for England, and even more so for his native Scotland, where men of property bore arms and served their nation, where the poor were kept in line, and where commerce took a back seat to traditional values. It was a perspective that led him to prefer Britain to France and to prefer Britain's past to its present.[5]

Like Machiavelli's, Fletcher's legacy lay in his writings. Yet to call Fletcher a "man of ideas" would not do him justice, given the adventurous life he led. He was a participant in the politics of his day, at a time when political participation sometimes meant holding a pen and other times meant holding a gun. Still, most importantly for this chapter, Fletcher was a key participant in the standing army controversy, which began in 1697 when King William III proposed maintaining such a force. The controversy itself was not a monumental event in English history, but it was a key turning point in the intellectual history of armed citizens, militias, standing armies, and the right to bear arms—and, therefore, a key point on the road to the Second Amendment. British writers produced an unprecedented amount of literature on these topics in a very short time. In doing so, they took the ideas that Machiavelli and Harrington, among others, had developed, but they expanded them into a far more elaborate theoretical and ideological framework in support of citizens' militias. The intellectual foundation of militia advocacy—the reasons for which Americans would later consider them necessary to the security of a free state—came from the pamphlets these men wrote during the standing army controversy.

Before discussing that controversy, though, some notes about the political and military context of 1697 are in order—including why William III, rather than James II, alive and well and living in France—was ruling England. And a few notes, too, on the Europe of the late seventeenth century, where Dutch power was waning and Spanish power was all but gone; where the Austrian Habsburgs were still a force to be reckoned with; but where, above all, French power had grown stronger than Richelieu could have dreamed. Even more than the England of the midcentury civil wars, covered in chapter 4, the England of the last decades of the seventeenth century had to adjust to a France that seemed to be growing stronger every year. England had no choice but to respond to the threat that France posed. The only question was what form that response should take. James II, king from 1685 to 1688, son of Charles I, offered one answer to that question. William of Orange, the Dutch political and military leader, grandson of Charles I, nephew of James II, son-in-law of that same James II via his marriage to James's daughter (and his own first cousin) Mary, offered a very different answer.[6]

At the time of Monmouth's Rebellion, France's Louis XIV was the most powerful king in Europe. His army had already conquered land along France's southern, eastern, and northern borders. In 1672 he began an invasion of the Netherlands, which would last until 1679. Domestically, he was also the most powerful king France had ever had. Building on the legacy of the Cardinal Richelieu and of Louis XIII, Louis XIV continued to centralize political power. France's nobility became something totally unrecognizable from the warring factions that had torn the kingdom apart during the Wars of Religion. Aristocrats no longer had their own private armies; instead, they served in the king's army. France's warrior nobility was becoming a court aristocracy.[7]

Historians of seventeenth-century France tend to push back on this vision of an all-powerful Louis XIV at the head of an equally all-powerful army, marching over the lifeless body of a once powerful warrior nobility. At the regional level, the king still had no choice but to work with local elites. Traditions died hard. The term "absolutist" also implies a level of state control that was never possible in the seventeenth century. Still, perceptions matter; in particular, English perceptions of Louis XIV would have a major impact on their own political debates, both foreign and domestic.[8]

Behind the king's success, both domestic and internationally, was France's royal army. Here, too, the project that Richelieu and Louis XIII had begun earlier in the century reached its height under their successors. During Louis XIV's reign, France's army grew to a force of around 300,000 soldiers. It became a more modern, professional fighting force; it also became a more unified national army, rather than a collection of quasi-autonomous fighting forces.[9] Here, too, historians of the era tend to emphasize the ways in which that army differed from modern notions of a strong army. Only men born into the aristocracy had any chance of becoming generals—and once those nobles became generals, their priorities could still differ from the king's. Their living standards on the battlefield, meanwhile, could become an imposition on the entire army.[10] As a result, France's royal army was not always a well-oiled machine. It was large, and it could win by outnumbering its opponents, but it was not unbeatable. As Louis XIV's reign stretched on into the late seventeenth century and the start of the eighteenth, French power began to decline. Even by the 1680s, the peak of French power had probably already come and gone; for France's rivals, though, there was no way to know that.

As the seventeenth century drew to a close, Louis XIV's army cast a shadow over the rest of Europe. It had also made quite an impression on the man who would become James II. James had spent much of the English Civil War in exile in France and during that time had served in Louis XIV's army. Understanding both the shadow that France's army cast and the impression it made on James II is a key to understanding why James II would rule as he did, why the English people would resent that approach, and why William of Orange would make sense as a replacement for James II.[11]

As Steve Pincus has shown, historians have misinterpreted England's 1688 Glorious Revolution in a number of ways, including by failing to put English politics into a larger European context. James II was not only a veteran of the French army; he was also Louis XIV's cousin—and admirer. Though it might seem impolitic in retrospect, James II "never missed an opportunity to praise 'the greatness of spirit, the virtue and the piety' of Louis XIV."[12] James II, then, was not only a Catholic king; he was a fan of French Catholicism and of French absolutism.[13] James II wanted an absolutist state with "a centralizing bureaucratic state, a professional standing army, and a world-class navy."[14] He did everything he could to modernize the English state and, specifically, the army—which he saw as a tool of both foreign and domestic policy.[15] The Monmouth Rebellion had shown that the militia could not be counted on for even the most basic military tasks. (Meaning, among other things, that by taking part in the rebellion, Fletcher indirectly helped promote the cause of a standing army.) So in the rebellion's aftermath, James II began transforming the nine-thousand-man force he inherited at the start of his reign. By 1688 he had a standing army of over forty thousand soldiers.[16]

Such a major transformation could hardly go unnoticed. In a nation unaccustomed to fielding such a large army, the burden of the force weighed heavily on civilians' daily lives. Bureaucrats (many also new) spread across England looking for space in which to quarter the soldiers. They requisitioned homes, inns, and coffeehouses. The army lacked discipline in its interactions with civilians, leading to complaints across the kingdom about the soldiers' behavior. These complaints dated back to the Monmouth Rebellion, during which one soldier noted, "We have been hitherto much their greater enemies than the rebels."[17] These complaints could be phrased in the sort of philosophical or ideological terms of a Machiavelli or a Harrington. They were also phrased in the more practical, concrete terms of an angry neighbor or publican.[18]

James II's attempts to build up a standing army and to Catholicize England overlapped in his attempt to fill England's army with as many Catholic officers as he could. This process went furthest in Ireland, under the leadership of Richard Talbot, Earl of Tyrconnell, who served as James II's commander in chief of Ireland's military forces. Traditionally, English rule of Ireland had meant that a Protestant elite ruled over a population that was majority Catholic. That domination, moreover, was enforced by a Protestant militia that in 1672 was able to muster twenty-four thousand militiamen.[19] But with James II on the throne, those policies were no longer in line with the king's priorities. Tyrconnell set out to disarm the Protestant militia, to arm Catholic citizens, and to replace Protestant officers and soldiers with Catholics. As he wrote in 1686, "The king, who is a Roman Catholic, is resolved to employ his subjects of that religion."[20]

The tension between the king and his people—and, most notably, the entire Protestant elite, including most members of Parliament—came to a head in the summer of 1688, when James's second wife gave birth to a son. Until then, the reign of a Catholic king looked like a one-time anomaly. James was already fifty-five years old. His two daughters from his first marriage had been raised as Protestants. Until his son's birth, his elder daughter Mary had been the presumptive heir to England's throne. A daughter would only inherit the throne if there were no sons, though; now there was a son, and he would be raised a Catholic. For the first time since Henry VIII broke with Rome and England first became a Protestant nation in the sixteenth century, England was facing the possibility of being ruled not just by a Catholic king but by a Catholic dynasty. At this point, England's Protestant leaders were willing to act. Seven leading Protestant aristocrats sent a letter to William of Orange, inviting him to come to England with an army to help free them from James II. In their invitation they wrote that "the people are so generally dissatisfied with the present conduct of the government in relation to their religion, liberties and properties . . . there are nineteen parts of twenty of the people throughout the kingdom who are desirous of a change, and who, we believe, would willingly contribute to it, if they had such a protection to countenance their rising as would secure them from being destroyed before they could get to be in a posture able to defend themselves." Making implicit contrast with the Monmouth Rebellion, the letter went on to say that should William land with his forces, people would rally to him and "that strength would quickly be increased to a number double to the army here." As for that army, it "would be very much divided among themselves, many of the officers being so discontented that they continue in their service only for a subsistence (besides that some of their minds are known already), and very many of the common soldiers do daily shew such an aversion to the popish religion that there is the greatest probability imaginable of great numbers of deserters which would come from them should there be such an occasion."[21]

William of Orange had several attributes that made him the best option for English Protestants. As mentioned earlier, he was the grandson of Charles I and the nephew of James II. Beyond that, he was King James II's son-in-law, via his marriage to James's daughter Mary—that is, James II's Protestant daughter Mary, the presumptive heir to the throne until her half-brother's recent birth. These claims to the throne were an important factor: given recent experience, Parliament's leaders were not eager to return to the republican experiment of midcentury. If they were going to do away with James II, they were going to replace him with another monarch with a strong claim to the throne.

As it turned out, Mary would rule alongside William. The initial invitation to William, though, made no explicit promise of the throne. Nor was it clear whom exactly the Protestant leaders would offer the Crown to, should they have the opportunity. What was clear even before the invitation—and this too made him an ideal option for English Protestants—was that William of Orange was already the leader of the fight against Louis XIV and had been since the 1670s. William was a "stadtholder" in the Netherlands, which made him a military leader there but not a political one. Louis XIV's France invaded the Netherlands in 1672. The fighting would last for six years. Only twenty-one years old when the war started, William was one of the leaders of the Dutch resistance to France's invasion. The Dutch were eventually able to fight off the French army, but the peace that ended the invasion seemed more of a cease-fire than a lasting settlement. It was William's goal, after that, to oppose Louis XIV's attempts to expand France's territory. Replacing James II with William of Orange, then, was part of a complete turnaround in English kings' policies toward France. His invasion of England was his way to become, as the historian Charles-Edouard Levillain puts it, "the leader of an international confederacy against Louis XIV."[22]

In early November 1688 William landed on England's southern coast, not that far from where Monmouth had landed. But William brought more men, more ships, and more weapons. He may well have brought enough men with him to face James II's army, but he never had that chance. Upon William's arrival, events unrolled largely as the invitation had promised: soldiers deserted the army; civilians and soldiers alike rallied to William's cause. James II fled to France.[23]

This was England's Glorious Revolution. The fighting would go on for some time, especially in Scotland and Ireland, but it was clear quickly that James had lost England. The revolution's resolution, though, still had some question marks. Most important: How could the English be sure to prevent future kings from abusing their authority, as James II had? It is worth noting here that William of Orange, as a military leader, had shown some Caesar-esque qualities back in the Netherlands, using the military situation to increase his influence.[24] And while William announced that he "had no other Intention in coming hither, than to preserve your Religion, Laws, and Liberties,"[25] no one thought he and Mary were simply going to return to the Netherlands afterward. In the revolutionary settlement, England's Parliament would crown William and Mary as king and queen, to rule together. That rule was conditioned on their endorsement of a new set of restrictions on the king's power. Parliament wrote up those restrictions in the final months of 1688. They became law the following year. This act of Parliament setting limits on royal power became known as the Bill of Rights. Paving the way for the United States' later decision to amend its Constitution, England's 1689 Bill of Rights set a legal framework between the monarchy, Parliament, and the citizens and established limits on what the government—especially the monarchy—could do.

Scholars of the Second Amendment give England's 1689 Bill of Rights a seminal role in the history of the American right to bear arms. They have described its passage as the moment that "the right of ordinary citizens to possess weapons . . . was born" and the "climax in the development of England's domestic gun culture" and have even called 16 December 1689 "one of the most important dates in American history" because of its role in the development of the right to bear arms.[26] That importance lies in its declaration "That the subjects which are Protestants may have arms for their defence suitable to their conditions and as allowed by law." Subsequent debates have centered on the nature of the relationship between England's right and the one Americans would declare a century later. But there is a broader story to tell here, both about England's Bill of Rights and about the debates of the 1690s, when British writers expanded on what it meant to have an armed citizenry. When later writers and politicians looked back on the 1689 Bill of Rights, they saw it through the interpretive lens that the writers of the 1690s had constructed.

The official name of England's Bill of Rights was "An Act Declaring the Rights and Liberties of the Subject and Settling the Succession of the Crown." This broader scope explains in part why it was a far longer document than the US Bill of Rights would be. (The 1689 bill clocks in at over twenty-eight hundred words; the US Bill of Rights is under five hundred.) Much of the act was devoted to the specifics of the 1688 revolution and to making the case that William and Mary were the proper people to rule the nation rather than James II. It was also structured differently; the first section of the document detailed James II's crimes against "the Protestant religion and the laws and liberties of this kingdom." (Thomas Jefferson would adopt a similar approach when writing the Declaration of Independence, the bulk of which was devoted to a list of King George III's "repeated injuries and usurpations.") This was followed by a section "vindicating and asserting their ancient rights and liberties," declaring rights that would remedy the abuses detailed in the preceding section.[27]

Most of those abuses and remedies fall outside of this book's scope. Four items, though—two of James II's abuses and the two related remedies—deserve to be quoted in full. James II was accused of "raising and keeping a standing army within this kingdom in time of peace without consent of Parliament, and quartering soldiers contrary to law," and of "causing several good subjects being Protestants to be disarmed at the same time when papists were both armed and employed contrary to law." To prevent a repeat of these "abuses," the bill declared "That the raising or keeping a standing army within the kingdom in time of peace, unless it be with consent of Parliament, is against law," and, as noted earlier, "That the subjects which are Protestants may have arms for their defence suitable to their conditions and as allowed by law."

The similarities and differences between the English 1689 right to bear arms and the American version of a century later is a frequent focus of Second Amendment scholarship.[28] Some of the continuities are clearer than others, but there is no point in looking past the obvious: the English included the right to bear arms in their list of rights that Englishmen enjoyed. Just as important, if a bit less obvious, was that the English declaration also declared an opposition to standing armies. In this sense, the two texts mirrored each other, with the Second Amendment mentioning militias but not standing armies, while the English mentioned standing armies but not militias. In each case, though, both the men writing the laws and the general public understood that this was a choice: either a society relied on its militia or it employed a professional army. And just as proposed wordings of the Second Amendment mentioned standing armies, so, too, earlier drafts of the English declaration mentioned the militia.[29]

The most obvious difference between the two lay in the three restrictions the English put on their right to bear arms. The right was limited to Protestants, weapons had to be "suitable to their condition," and they also had to be "allowed by law." In practice, these last two meant that nothing in the 1689 declaration eliminated any of previous legal restrictions on gun ownership—of which the English had many.[30]

Limiting the right to bear arms to Protestants of means was at once the smallest and largest difference between the two documents. It was smallest because both documents were, in practice, restricted. As will be seen in the next chapter, the right to bear arms was limited on both sides of the Atlantic.[31] It was the biggest difference because it pointed out the most fundamental difference between the two documents: England's 1689 Bill of Rights was a fundamentally, essentially, and explicitly Protestant text. Chief among James II's crimes was his "endeavour to subvert and extirpate the Protestant religion," leading the bill's authors to declare that "it hath been found by experience that it is inconsistent with the safety and welfare of this Protestant kingdom to be governed by a popish prince."[32] The United States would become a predominantly Protestant nation. The First Amendment ensured that it would never be an officially Protestant nation.

The most important continuity between the two bills of rights lay not in the specifics of any one of those rights but in a more basic understanding of the relationship between the government and its citizens. The 1689 Bill of Rights reinforced an English tradition—albeit, a far from unchallenged one—that a citizen had both rights that the government could not infringe upon and responsibilities toward his society, and even toward his state. It also reinforced the practice that while England was a monarchy, it was a constitutional monarchy. This was a tradition the English liked to trace back to the Magna Carta of 1215 and a subsequent English tradition of limited monarchy.[33] The 1689 Bill of Rights also continued the practices of employing differing degrees of citizenship and denying citizenship to a large portion of its inhabitants. This view of the relationship between a government, its citizens, and the rest of the nation's inhabitants would be the most fundamental legacy of the English Bill of Rights to the Americans, even if, within that framework, Americans felt free to pick and choose what they wished.

Nor did the colonists need to wait for independence before seeking inspiration from the 1689 Bill of Rights. As Saul Cornell points out, in the buildup to the American Revolution, colonists "invoked the authority of the English Declaration of Rights of 1689, one of the most influential statements of constitutional principles," particularly the right to have "Arms for their Defenses."[34] This conception of rights, of militias and standing armies and citizen-soldiers, would be key to the unfolding of the early Revolution (discussed further in chapter 8). Cornell's claim is worth analyzing carefully, though, because it focuses on how Americans, one hundred years later, recognized the Glorious Revolution as a turning point. Looking back at 1689 from 1775 means looking back through everything that had happened since then. When it came to the question of arming citizens or arming professional soldiers, the most important steps taken by the British came *after* they issued their Bill of Rights.

The importance of the events of 1688 and 1689 for subsequent American history, then, came from the meanings the colonists would make of those events. And while that is true of every event, the subsequent history of the importance of the 1689 Bill of Rights' decrees on arming citizens came from a very specific time in British history: the standing army controversy of the late 1690s. Just as the meanings of the history of the Roman Republic passed through the writings of Machiavelli and other authors before they would inspire the republicanism of the early modern era, so too the passage of the 1689 Bill of Rights would pass through the writings of another group of men—including John Trenchard, Walter Moyle, John Toland, and Andrew Fletcher of Saltoun—before they would inspire the authors of the US Bill of Rights.

James II's insistence on building up a standing army had helped bring about his downfall. But William III, upon becoming king, was in no hurry to get rid of that army. As long as England was at war, this was not an issue. England's Bill of Rights had not prohibited all professional armies; rather, it had prohibited a standing army "within the kingdom in time of peace," and even then, "consent of Parliament" would make it permissible. It would be some time before William and Mary's England would be at peace. William did indeed help lead an international confederacy against Louis XIV. The fighting would last from roughly the time of William's invasion until the 1697 Treaty of Ryswick.

The existence of an English army of professional soldiers was not controversial as long as England was at war, even if politicians and civilians alike complained about the enormous burden and the army's inconsistent results.[35] But in 1697 peace was approaching. The English and the French—along with the Dutch and the Spanish—all signed the peace treaty. William, though, wanted to keep a part of his army intact. England's army had grown to seventy-six thousand soldiers during the fighting. Another forty thousand men were in the navy.[36] With most of those men set to return to their homes, William wanted to maintain an army of professional, full-time soldiers, including his own Dutch Guards.

John Trenchard and Walter Moyle responded to this request with their pamphlet *An Argument, shewing that Standing Army, is inconsistent with a Free Government, and absolutely destructive to the constitution of the English Monarchy.* "When I consider what a dismal Scene of Blood and Desolation hath appeared upon the Theatre of *Europe* during the Growth and Progress of the *French* Power," the pamphlet began, "I cannot sufficiently applaud and admire our thrice happy Situation." England, the authors wrote, had been able to escape from the problems that had befallen the nations of the continent, where "we see most Nations in *Europe* over-run with Oppression and Slavery." This was the fate that awaited England, the authors warned, should England follow the lead of France and the rest of the European powers and grant William his wish for a professional peacetime army.[37]

The standing army controversy had begun. There would be several other essays from Trenchard, along with essays by friends of his supporting the anti-standing-army position. There were responses from supporters of the policy as well (including one from Daniel Defoe). In this process, the vision of an armed citizenry expanded beyond anything that earlier writings had portrayed and became something very close to the vision that would lead the authors of the US Bill of Rights to declare well-regulated militias necessary to the security of a free state.

Andrew Fletcher of Saltoun reentered English history during the standing army controversy. William's invasion had already made it possible for Fletcher to return to Great Britain. Though his participation in the Monmouth Rebellion had earned him a conviction for treason in absentia, in 1690 this conviction was lifted.[38] But if Fletcher was glad to be back in Britain, things there did not always turn out as Fletcher wished. During the first years of the eighteenth century, Fletcher fought hard against the union between Scotland and England, but the pro-union forces won out. Many of his other political endeavors also failed. He even took part in the Darien scheme, an attempt to establish a colony in Central America in which many Scots invested and whose failure weakened the entire Scottish economy. But his treatise on militias and standing armies, *A Discourse of Government with Relation to Militias,* was a masterpiece of political writing and one of the best defenses of citizen-soldiers.

Fletcher started with the foundations that Machiavelli had first established, arguing the superiority of citizen-soldiers and the uselessness of mercenaries. This is not to say that Fletcher attributed this theory to Machiavelli. Although many British authors owed an intellectual debt to Machiavelli, some were more explicit about it than others. Fletcher did not mention Machiavelli in his *Discourse of Government,* though he would mention him in other writings. Not everyone was eager to fly Machiavelli's flag, given how closely it was associated with a darker legacy of backstabbing and cruelty. Even those writers who did acknowledge Machiavelli's influence tended to play it down.[39] But Machiavelli's basic foundation was there: citizens made better soldiers; therefore rulers were best off if they armed their citizens.

As shown in chapter 2, Machiavelli had argued against mercenaries. Instead, any wise ruler would insist that his citizens be armed, "for when they are armed, those arms become yours."[40] But in Fletcher's writings the benefits of a citizens' militia went far beyond what Machiavelli had written. The warnings Machiavelli gave about mercenaries, meanwhile, reemerged in a somewhat different form: a warning that any professional army would be a threat to the society's freedom. For Fletcher, as for Trenchard and others, the dangers of a standing army became much greater than anything Machiavelli had warned about the shortcomings of mercenaries. The basis of Machiavelli's theory had been that citizens made better soldiers, and his goal was to make as strong an army as possible. Militia advocates of seventeenth-century Britain, Fletcher among them, agreed with this principle. They also believed that part-time soldiers made better citizens. Societies as a whole could only flourish when citizens ensured their own security.

In calling for citizen-soldiers rather than professional soldiers, Fletcher and his fellow travelers were using the foundation that Machiavelli had laid down but not for exactly the same purposes. Machiavelli's main concern was to build a strong fighting force. The seventeenth- and eighteenth-century British writers who praised the militia wanted to build a strong and free society. The problem was, for a writer who starts with the belief that a standing army is incompatible with a free society, the question of how to have a nation that is both strong and free becomes difficult. What good is it to employ men to defend a nation if that nation then becomes dependent on its defenders? Or, as Fletcher put it, "What security can the nations have that these standing forces shall not at some time or other be made use of to suppress the liberties of the people?"[41] Fletcher's answer—along with those of Moyle and Trenchard and generations of writers to come—was to rely on a citizens' militia. An army made up of citizens would not march on its fellow citizens; a citizenry trained to arms would be able to defend itself if attacked. To prove their argument, they had to prove several supporting points: that standing armies were incompatible with free societies, that requiring citizens to participate in the militia was compatible with a free society, that citizens would participate in those militias when called upon, and that militias were capable of defending a society, including against other nations' professional armies.

In *A Discourse of Government with Relation to Militias,* Andrew Fletcher of Saltoun did all that and then some. In the flourishing literary genre that was the early modern pro-militia pamphlet, some authors found more readers; other authors were reprinted more frequently. But none captured the argument quite as well as Fletcher, and none imbued their writing with more passion. To understand his views on militias and citizen-soldiers, on mercenaries and standing armies, is to understand the views on these topics that would remain dominant among intellectuals for the following century in England and in British North America. To understand Fletcher's views is also to understand how opposition to standing armies and support for citizens' militias could continue over decades and decades, even as the empirical results failed to measure up to the writers' promises. In reality, the militias that existed in the eighteenth century were not the equal to professional armies on the battlefield. Citizens continually balked at the prospect of increasing their participation in their local militias. Yet writer after writer continued to bestow a near-mythic status on the potential that citizens' militias had to offer.

Fletcher began his *Discourse* with a history of European and British military forces. For Fletcher, there had been a good system at work in the Europe that emerged after the decline of the Roman Empire. After "the Goths, Vandals, and other warlike nations" had destroyed the Roman Empire in the west, they set up new nations. The generals became kings, but those kings had only limited power. "There was no longer any standing army kept on foot" in those nations, but "when the defence of the country required an army, the king summoned the barons to his standard, who came attended with their vassals."[42] In Fletcher's account, this system would last for over a thousand years, from Rome's fall until around the year 1500. If it had been up to Fletcher, things would never have changed, because this system represented a balance of power between the different parts of society: "This constitution of government put the sword into the hands of the subject, because the vassals depended more immediately on the barons than on the king, which effectually secured the freedom of those governments. For the barons could not make use of their power to destroy those limited monarchies, without destroying their own grandeur; nor could the king invade their privileges, having no other forces than the vassals of his own demesnes to rely upon for his support in such an attempt." This description of medieval society requires a bit of explanation for those unfamiliar with the relationships between barons, vassals, and kings. Fletcher was pointing to medieval society's relatively decentralized military forces, its hierarchy, and its mutual bonds of obligation. The king's army was made up mostly of smaller armies each under the control of a local noble—a "baron," in this terminology, though that baron might go by the title of earl, count, or other equivalents in other languages. Those barons commanded forces made up of their vassals, who enjoyed partial ownership of their baron's land in return for certain obligations the vassal had toward the baron—including military obligations. So for the king to raise his army, he called on the barons, and those barons, in turn, called up their vassals. The king's power therefore depended on the power of those who ranked beneath him; but as those who ranked beneath them had direct control over these smaller military forces, kings had to choose wisely when deciding what orders to issue. Barons, meanwhile, had to choose wisely which orders to disobey, at the risk of "destroying their own grandeur," as well as that of their king. The result, in any case, was an arrangement that kept kings from becoming overly powerful. Or, as Fletcher put it, "There was a balance that kept those governments steady, and an effectual provision against the encroachments of the crown."[43]

Around 1500, though, things began to change. "The sword fell out of the hands of the barons," and "those vast armies of mercenaries which this change has fixed upon Europe" began bringing Europe "to her affliction and ruin."[44] Fletcher, then, was telling the story of the military revolution—the rise, in continental Europe, of large standing armies and equally large administrative states.[45] What was a story of military and administrative change, for military historians, was for Fletcher the story of free peoples losing their freedom—and a story of kings becoming too powerful.

There were two forces at work in this story, according to Fletcher. One was the kings' desire for greater power. The other was a desire on the part of the barons, and on the part of citizens more generally, for greater luxury and refinement in their lives. This change began in Italy, where the people "began to come off from their frugal and military way of living, and addicted themselves to the pursuit of refined and expensive pleasures." From there, "this infection spread itself by degrees into the neighbouring nations."[46] People became less focused on their obligations to their society and more focused on their pleasures. This trend hit the barons hardest, and those barons soon fell into debt; those debts, in turn, forced the barons "to turn the military service their vassals owed them into money."[47] These vassals were now tenants, and the men who made up the barons' armies were no longer soldiers. Thus it was that "the sword fell out of the hands of the barons."

The barons' loss was the kings' gain. With their military training and background—and little else in the way of what would today be considered "transferrable skills"—nobles were still eager to take part in the army. But without their own armed men to command, their only place in any sort of military force was as officers in the king's army. So the barons, once the defenders of the nation from the encroachments of the Crown, "were now the readiest of all others to load the people with heavy taxes, which were employed to increase the prince's military power, by guards, armies, and citadels, beyond bounds or remedy."[48] These armies' existence could seem justified; kings and nations needed some military force to protect them, and the one that had previously existed no longer did. But when paid soldiers became the norm, they brought with them taxes and tyranny. Or, as Fletcher put it, "Princes were afterwards allowed to raise armies of volunteers and mercenaries. And great sums were given by diets and parliaments for their maintenance, to be levied upon the people grown rich by trade, and dispirited for want of military exercise." And while these were at first only temporary forces, "princes soon found pretences to make them perpetual."[49]

This process had occurred throughout Europe and on the British Isles but had not happened everywhere equally. It was furthest along in France. Other continental nations, according to Fletcher, were in fear of "falling into the subjection to which they saw the kingdom of France already reduced"[50] by means of its standing army. England had thus far been lucky. Though England's barons had lost their armies, its kings "had no pretence to keep up standing forces, either to defend conquests abroad or to garrison a frontier towards France, since the sea was now become the only frontier between those two countries."[51] So "no mercenary troops are yet established," even though "the power of the barons be ceased."[52]

England, along with Fletcher's native Scotland, was sick but curable. France, not so much. In Fletcher's account, France was beyond dead; France was the disease itself. After all, it was the French model that inspired James II to build up England's army, and it was the threat France still posed that inspired William III to propose maintaining a standing army. "But we are told," Fletcher wrote, "that only standing mercenary forces can defend Britain from the perpetual standing armies of France."[53] In order to disprove this claim, Fletcher had to prove that France's standing armies were not the threat that they appeared to be. Fletcher went beyond that, showing that while France's armies did not pose a real danger to England, emulating France's armies was indeed dangerous.

Like militia-advocating authors since Machiavelli, Fletcher believed that a good militia was a superior fighting force to a professional army. He too scoffed at the thought that "mercenaries would fight more bravely for the defence of other men's fortunes, than the possessors would do for themselves or their own; or that a little money should excite their ignoble minds to a higher pitch of honors than that with which the barons are inspired, when they fight for the preservation of their fortunes, wives and children, religion and liberty."[54] It was a lesson that might sound like a bit of stretch, given Fletcher's own experiences fighting with Monmouth. But Fletcher was not blind to the problems that the militias of his age faced. For one thing, the militias of Fletcher's age were a sort of replacement force that had evolved so that they were no longer independent of the king. Or, as he put it, "After the barons had lost the military service of their vassals, militias of some kind or other were established in most parts of Europe. But the prince having everywhere the power of naming and preferring the officers of these militias, they could be no balance in government as the former were."[55] In these new militias, too many men avoided their duty. As a result, even in England and Scotland "there is but a small number of the men able to bear arms exercised." To make matters worse, for Fletcher, a man born into Scotland's nobility and who always remained conscious of matters of birth and status, "Men of quality and estate are allowed to send any wretched servant in their place . . . by which means the militias being composed only of servants, these nations seem altogether unfit to defend themselves."[56]

Even then, the militias were not as bad as they appeared. Rather, "ambitious princes" were engaged in a campaign to sabotage the militias and destroy their reputations. These princes, "who aimed at absolute power, thinking they could never use it effectually to that end, unless it were wielded by mercenaries, and men that had no other interest in the commonwealth than their pay, have still endeavoured by all means to discredit militias, and render them burdensome to the people, by never suffering them to be upon any right, or so much as tolerable foot, and all to persuade the necessity of standing forces."[57] In other words, yes, the militia was in bad shape—but it was not in as bad a shape as its critics claimed.

The decline of England's militia posed a problem for Fletcher. It implied the necessity of replacing it with a standing force or risk invasion by a foreign power. Here, Fletcher assured his readers that even in its current state, the militia was still prepared to defend England from France. "For Britain cannot be in any hazard from France; at least till that kingdom, so much exhausted by war and persecution, shall have a breathing space to recover."[58] But this did not mean that the militia should be allowed to remain in its current state. The first step was to make sure that all eligible men fulfilled their obligations. These men, Fletcher wrote, "should blush to think of excusing themselves from serving their country, at least for some years, in a military capacity, if they consider that every Roman was obliged to spend fifteen years of his life in their armies."[59] But beyond that, Fletcher proposed a radical project to regenerate the militia. He proposed establishing four training camps—three in England, one in Scotland—"into which all the young men of the respective countries should enter" once they turned twenty-two. Those who could afford to maintain themselves would stay for two years; the rest would remain for one year, "at the expense of the public." There they would be trained, including in "the use of all sorts of arms."[60]

The proposal was breathtaking in its aims, not least because of how unpopular among the population it would be. The English on the whole were wary of their militia duty, which they found onerous. Yet here was Andrew Fletcher of Saltoun proposing not only to increase that militia duty but to do so beyond what any European society was attempting.

Yet Fletcher was in some ways not unique in this proposal. Vast plans to regenerate the militia—plans that would often entail significant changes to the entire society—would reappear periodically, from the late seventeenth century into the first decades of the nineteenth. US politicians would float similar (if less radical) proposals in the aftermath of the American Revolution, as had other writers in Great Britain and even in France.[61] These proposals all shared similar traits. One was that they never made it into practice. More substantively, they tended to share a counterintuitive belief that people who disliked the relatively minor obligations involved in militia training as it existed would come to appreciate a far larger obligation. In this view, people who were complaining that there was already too much militia duty were really complaining that there was too little militia duty. Counterintuitive, yes, but it would prove to be one of the most brilliant arguments that ever came about to justify militias. Whatever shortcomings any particular militia might have came not from the shortcomings of the militia system itself but from a society that had insufficiently embraced its obligations. The answer to a militia's shortcomings was always the same: more militia.

To understand why Fletcher believed such a project could succeed is to enter the mind-set of the purest early modern militia advocates. For these men—and they were invariably men—the problem with a standing army was not only that soldiers were no longer citizens; it was also that citizens were no longer soldiers. And because they were no longer soldiers, they had become soft and undisciplined. Once they were properly trained—once they had learned to appreciate their discipline—they would come to embrace it. Citizens forced to sacrifice several Sundays a year to militia training and found it a waste of time would come to appreciate the training and discipline that came from devoting a year or two of their lives to the militia. The hypothesis was not only counterintuitive; it was also untestable, short of actually adopting the proposal in full. Until that time, it was always possible for militia advocates to reply to any criticism of the militia by calling for more militia.

Fletcher, like Machiavelli, believed that citizens made the best soldiers. And Machiavelli, too, saw the advantage of a citizenry that was used to the discipline and hardships that military training and battle experience brought. But there had been a change of emphasis. Fletcher was no longer primarily concerned with creating the strongest army possible, nor did he want to recreate a conquering army that would bring soldiers away from their homes for extended times. Fletcher's focus was on the domestic arena, and the main goal of his proposals, including his training camps, was not to make a better army. It was to make a better society.

As noted above, Fletcher believed that the taste for luxuries had not only taken the sword from the barons' hands; it had also begun to make the men soft and undisciplined. In an ideal society, men had little need for luxury, embraced their military obligations, and lived in freedom. But in a society with a standing army, men embraced luxury, lost their freedom, and were saddled with heavy taxes in order to support that army. In other words, exactly the situation that Fletcher saw across the channel, "where the king has power to do what he pleases, and the people no security for anything they possess."[62] Everything that Fletcher feared for Great Britain had already happened in France—the professional army, the absolutist state. Fletcher would come back to this theme in 1698, when he wrote that "we are told there is not a slave in France; that when a slave sets his foot upon French ground, he becomes immediately free: and I say, that there is not a freeman in France, because the king takes away any part of any man's property at his pleasure; and that, let him do what he will to any man, there is no remedy."[63]

It was because of France's army that William III had proposed maintaining a standing army in England as well. Yet this brought back the central question that republican militia advocates posed during the seventeenth and eighteenth centuries: How can a nation defend itself without being threatened by its defenders? For Fletcher, there was no doubt that this standing army would become permanent and that it would, in turn, suppress the people of England and Scotland. There was no point in England defending itself against France by fielding a standing army, as that army's presence would turn England French.

Fletcher would come back to this theme in the closing words of the *Discourse*. There he warned of the fate that might await Great Britain should it follow France's path. It was a dire warning indeed, of a fate that would befall all of England's people, yet for some reason, would hit England's women hardest:

> Shall we see the once happy commonalty of England become base and abject, by being continually exposed to the brutal insolence of the soldiers; the women debauched by their lust; ugly and nasty through poverty, and the want of things necessary to preserve their natural beauty. Then shall we see that great city, the pride and glory, not only of our island, but of the world, subjected to the excessive impositions Paris now lies under, and reduced to a peddling trade, serving only to foment the luxury of a court. Then will Britain know what obligations she has to those who are for mercenary armies.[64]

It was a fitting closing note for the pamphlet—a call for England (and Scotland as well) to do all that it could to maintain its liberties, to resist the temptation of luxuries, and to avoid being French. The closing note showed how, for Fletcher, the issue of a standing army not only brought up issues of national pride—a complicated issue for a Scotsman in the world of English politics—it brought up questions of manliness and femininity as well. To be a man was to bear arms; to cease to bear arms was to cease to be a true man. It was a theme that was present in some other passages in the texts as well, including Fletcher's insistence that, during the military training young men were to experience, "No woman should be suffered to come within the camp, and the crimes of abusing their own bodies any manner of way, punished with death."[65]

A Discourse of Government with Relation to Militias stood out in a few ways from the rest of the pamphlets attacking the proposed standing army. Fletcher's was the most radical training plan; he had the best sense of the economic implications of a standing army. He also stood out among the writers on militias in the extent of his military experience.[66] But he was nevertheless part of a movement, and the details of each proposal, of each pamphlet attacking the proposed standing army, were less important than the traits that tied them together.

For Fletcher, the golden age of the citizen-soldier came in the aftermath of the fall of the Roman Empire rather than in the Roman Republic. Still, Fletcher was a fan of the Roman Republic, which he used as a model for his training plans, and he wrote, "The militia of ancient Rome, the best that ever was in any government, made her mistress of the world."[67] He also pointed to the contrast between Rome's militia and Carthage, which "used mercenary forces, was brought to the brink of ruin by them in a time of peace, beaten in three wars, and at last subdued by the Romans."[68] To this he added the cases of ancient Sparta, where the people "continued eight hundred years free, and in great honour, because they had a good militia," and added that "the Swisses at this day are the freest, happiest, and the people of all Europe who can best defend themselves, because they have the best militia."[69]

Texts from other militia advocates also sang Rome's praises. Trenchard and Moyle drew the sharpest lessons from Julius Caesar and the Marian reforms that had made his rise possible. Early in the republic, they wrote, "we find amongst the *Romans* the best and bravest of their Generals came from the Plough, contentedly returning when the Work was over." But when "luxury" increased, "the strict Rule and Discipline of Freedom soon abated." At that point, "Necessity constrained them to erect a constant stipendiary Souldiery abroad in Foreign Parts," and this long-term paid service made it possible for "*Cesar* totally to overthrow that famous Commonwealth; for the Prolongation of his Commission in *Gaul* gave him an opportunity to debauch his Army."[70] Moyle, in a later work on Rome's history, would refer to "the seven consulships of Marius, the early and multiplied honours of Pompey, and the long continuation of Caesar's command in Gaul" as "the direct and immediate causes of the ruin of the commonwealth."[71]

The role that the history of Rome played here was important for a few reasons. Rome remained a model of republicanism, and even in an England that could no longer embrace a fully republican model of governance, the example of Rome remained one to emulate. As Levillain points out, Rome also became a more comfortable place to discuss than England itself. "One of the striking aspects of the standing army debates of 1697–9," he notes, "is the relative dearth of references to Cromwell, as if the memory of Caesar more or less eclipsed that of the Lord Protector."[72]

In the works of Fletcher, Trenchard, Moyle, and their colleagues, the key points of militia advocacy were coming into focus. The beliefs that citizens make better soldiers and that soldiers make better citizens; that standing armies and freedom were incompatible; that these truths had been proven throughout history, in example after example; and that the Roman Republic made the best example. All of these were present in the writings of the standing army controversy. The ideas that George Washington, writing in 1783, considered to be "conceded on all hands," the lessons from history with which his readers were "too well acquainted with . . . to require information or example," dated back to this time.[73]

Although they did not phrase it in exactly this way, these seventeenth-century British authors would have agreed that a well-regulated militia was necessary to the security of a free state. And they would have agreed that the right to bear arms should not be infringed, provided that only a certain part of the population would enjoy that right.

For scholars who study the relationship between the right to bear arms, as found in the 1689 Bill of Rights, and the language of the Second Amendment, much of this debate has been over the difference between England's limitations to "subjects which are Protestants . . . suitable to their condition" against the Second Amendment's more inclusive language, which refers only to "the people." As the following chapters will make clear, American practices were less inclusive than the language of the Second Amendment indicated. The writers of the standing army controversy found no problem with the prospect of limiting weapons access to men of property. John Toland is also worth mentioning here. In his *The Militia Reform'd,* he wrote that "my First Proposition shall be, that *England* consisting of Freeman and I understand Men of Property, or Persons that are able to live of themselves; and those who cannot subsist in this Independence I call Servants."[74] Here, too, he looked to the Romans, "who understood the Art of War beyond all the World." During the republic, they "did not make Soldiery a Refuge to Poverty and Idleness; nor none but Men of Fortune and Property, whose private Interest lay firmly engag'd them to the Publick Good, had the honor of serving in their Armies."[75] Toland came back to this theme with his claim that "all those who aspir'd at Tyranny or any unlimited Power above the Laws, as *Marius* for example, did constantly make Levies of the poorer sort, putting Arms into the hands of those that had no stake to lose, and who for that Reason would be sure not to design the Good of the Commonwealth, but only his Profit that employ'd them."[76] It was a theme present in other writers as well, one that had been present in Harrington's writings earlier that century: the goal was not to arm all of the citizens but, rather, to arm only citizens of means. Fletcher himself was no egalitarian. In a later text, he would propose a form of slavery for Scotland's poorest peasants.[77] As noted in chapter 2, when Machiavelli called for the prince to arm his subjects, he also wrote that "because all subjects cannot be armed, if those whom you arm are benefited, one can act with more security toward the others." [78] It would prove to be one of Machiavelli's more prophetic thoughts on arming citizens.

Andrew Fletcher of Saltoun would live until 1716. He continued to be active in politics, in the same fully committed way he had been throughout his life: dedicated, energetic, and unpredictable. In 1705, he challenged a fellow member of Scotland's Parliament to a duel, which was only halted at the last moment.[79] In typical Fletcher fashion, the member of Parliament in question was not a political opponent but a former supporter of his. Fletcher's signature issue during the early eighteenth century would be the nature of the union between England and Scotland. Here again, events fell short of his goals—he had wanted a union with England that gave Scotland more autonomy. He voted against Scotland's 1707 Acts of Union but was in the minority. His last recorded words would be in sympathy for his native Scotland: "Have mercy on my poor country that is so barbarously oppressed."[80]

There would be one curious footnote to Fletcher's life. Another Scottish nobleman, George Keith, the tenth (and final) Earl Marischal, served for some time as governor in the Swiss city of Neuchâtel, near the French border. Like Fletcher, Marischal lived a life of adventure, battle, and exile—though, unlike Fletcher, the earl died in exile, and his title died with him. During his time in Switzerland the earl had a chance to speak with the author Jean-Jacques Rousseau. As the story goes, Marischal's tales of Andrew Fletcher inspired Rousseau to the point that Rousseau hoped to write Fletcher's biography. To that end, the earl had many of Fletcher's papers transferred to Rousseau. But Rousseau never wrote that biography, and the papers never resurfaced. Nor has the story ever been confirmed; it is precisely the kind of story that is all but impossible to confirm.

Papers or no, more than a few traces of Fletcher's thinking would show up in some of Rousseau's later writings. In 1772, Rousseau wrote a piece called *Consideration on the Government of Poland,* where he called standing armies "the plague and depopulators of Europe," good only for conquering neighbors or to "bind and enslave citizens," and called on Poland to instead form a militia, as in his native Switzerland, "where every inhabitant is a soldier, but only when necessary."[81] Rousseau's theories would go on to be quite influential among French readers, including those who, in the 1790s, would lead France's revolution. At that time, Rousseau's writings on the revolution would be less influential than some of his other writings—including his work *On the Social Contract,* a more widely read and discussed philosophical tract. There, Rousseau made the cryptic statement that men must be "forced to be free."[82] In its odd mixture of obligation and promise, it recollects the idea that Fletcher and his allies had during the standing army controversy: that whatever shortcomings a militia might have, and whatever misgivings a population might have over their obligations to that militia, those problems were best solved by increasing the commitment to the militia—in Fletcher's case, through the year or two that all men would spend training. The solution to the militia's problems was always the same: more militia. Once society is reconstituted and the people have been properly trained, they will appreciate the training that they had at first resisted. At that point, they would have been forced to be free.

As for England, the standing army controversy died down at the turn of the century. Politically, it was settled with a compromise solution: William III would be allowed to retain a peacetime army, but one much smaller than he had hoped. The king had wanted a total of around thirty thousand soldiers, including the Dutch Guards who had been with him since before 1688. He would get seven thousand soldiers and had to disband his Dutch Guards, a bitter pill for him to swallow.[83] But England would have a peacetime standing army, and, in that sense, it was a defeat for Fletcher and his allies. That army's subsequent history would even prove those critics correct: once England came to rely on its standing army, that army continued to grow and grow. Over the course of the eighteenth century, England would come to have a very effective standing army. The close of the seventeenth century marked the final defeat, in Great Britain, of any hope that England would ever again rely on the militia alone, or that together, the militia and the navy would suffice. The 1689 Bill of Rights had not outlawed standing armies; it had only insisted on Parliament's consent. Year after year, Parliament would give that consent—along with the necessary funding. It did so in a curious manner, via its Mutiny Acts, which authorized the army and included its funding, along with codifying laws regarding the discipline and punishment for soldiers.[84] As difficult as it had been for William to keep a portion of his army in 1697, it became easier for the Crown as the years went by. The army grew, and the people of Great Britain grew less wary of its potential for oppression at home.[85]

There is also some evidence that, for all of the support that Fletcher and Trenchard received in Parliament, their views were less popular with the public at large. True, no pamphleteers had volunteered to defend the proposal—the only defenses that came were ones that the king paid for.[86] But in the world of public entertainment, things were less clear cut. As Hannah Smith shows in a history of theater and drama at the time, supporters of a standing army were far more popular among theatergoers than were their opponents. Pro-army playwrights showed soldiers who were "the quintessence of political virtue and manliness."[87] Meanwhile, Fletcher and Trenchard would become less relevant in Great Britain. Their ideas would filter into the Commonwealth man tradition in eighteenth-century England, even though that movement failed to attract many people in Britain.[88] England's militia did have something of a revival during the eighteenth century, but it never became the kind of institution Fletcher had wanted. Meanwhile, the militia in Fletcher's native Scotland would enjoy no such revival. During the eighteenth century, the British government did what it could to disarm the people of Scotland and disband the militias there.[89]

They did leave quite a legacy, though. In the writings of the men of the standing army controversy—including Fletcher, but not only Fletcher—the ideas that would later lead the US Congress to declare a well-regulated militia necessary to the security of a free state were in place. The key beliefs behind that amendment can still be found in the writings of Trenchard, Fletcher, Moyle, and their friends. Those writers repeated over and over the ideas that citizens made better soldiers because they fought harder and that soldiers made better citizens because of their discipline. And they told their readers time and again that a society with a standing army of professional soldiers could never be free. For true freedom, citizens needed to participate in the militia; therefore citizens had to be militiamen, and to be a citizen meant bearing arms for one's nation. To prove these points, these writers invoked their own version of history. In their praise of Sparta, of Switzerland, and especially of the Roman Republic, they tried to show how a society could be free by requiring citizens to be soldiers. With their criticisms of the Roman Empire, and especially of absolutist France, they tried to show the dangers of relying on professional soldiers. These ideas that would later be central to American views on militias and armies, on governments and citizenship, could be found in these writings of the 1690s.

Still, it would take some time before these lessons became important for the British colonies in North America. For most of the eighteenth century, practical matters regarding the militia took priority over philosophical ones in the colonies. It was an irony of the path that would eventually lead to the Second Amendment: the theories praising militias and criticizing standing armies flourished first in England, and they flourished at a time when England's own standing army was emerging. In colonial North America, it was the militia itself that flourished, not because of any ideologies behind it but because the colonists who settled North America had no access to professional armies. Instead, they were forced to provide for their own military needs. In that sense, those militias were just what Andrew Fletcher would have recommended. What Fletcher would not have imagined, though, was the importance that chattel slavery would come to have in the American colonies and, therefore, in the colonial militias.

SEVEN

The Stono Rebels Head for Florida

1739

It was late in the morning of 9 September 1739. William Bull, the lieutenant governor of South Carolina, was traveling through the colony with several companions when by chance they came upon a group of African men who were heading south. By the time Bull encountered them, they were probably around fifty or so strong. And while Bull did not yet know it, they had already killed several white South Carolinians.

The African men had first gathered sometime after the last sunset near a bridge over the Stono River, around fifteen miles inland from the colonial capital of Charles Town. Before beginning their rebellion, they had been living as slaves on nearby plantations. The first people they killed were two men who were running a store that sold guns and gunpowder. They took what they needed from that store and left the two men's heads on the front steps. They then started their journey south, passing through several plantations, killing a number of white slave-owning families, and encouraging other enslaved people they encountered to join them.

Bull might not have known the specifics, but upon seeing the men gathered it would have been easy enough for him to figure out the basic outlines of the situation. There was nothing unusual about what Bull and his companions were doing—several white men traveling through the colony on horseback. But a gathering of African men in South Carolina was not only unusual; it was illegal. The colony's 1721 Act for the Better Settling and Regulating the Militia had established patrols to monitor the enslaved population, search their homes for weapons, and "prevent any caballings amongst negroes."[1] Bull would have immediately suspected that he was seeing a slave revolt. The fear of such a revolt had existed long before enslaved labor came to dominate the colonies of the American South, and that fear would continue to exist for as long as slavery itself, if not longer. As historian Winthrop Jordan has noted, whites' fear that the people they had enslaved would rise up against them "was ever present in the West Indies, the plantation colonies on the continent, and even, with less good reason, in some areas in the North."[2]

This fear, according to Jordan, was based on both rational fears of the repercussions of such a brutal institution and "a response to more complicated anxieties," including "the spectre [of] an appalling world turned upside down, a crazy nonsense world of black over white, an anti-community which was the direct negation of the community as white men knew it."[3] These concerns had led some of the colonies, including South Carolina, to prohibit enslaved people from "caballing" together in large numbers, so any such gathering was by definition a sort of rebellion. Bull, though, realized that what was going on was, from his perspective, far more than just an unlawful assembly, and he "deserned the approaching Danger time enough to avoid it." The rebels, for their part, do not seem to have realized that Bull was anything other than a typical white Carolinian.[4] He and his fellow travelers fled quickly, managing to escape, even as one of the few remaining accounts claimed that Bull was "pursued" and only escaped with "much difficulty." According to that anonymous account, once away Bull "raised the Countrey," as the rebels continued their movement south. Or, as Bull would put it, his escape allowed him to "give notice to the Militia."[5]

By the end of that month when Bull took the time to write out his own account of the uprising, he would have known all of the details. He shared relatively few of them in his description, though, writing simply that "a great number of Negroes Arose in Rebellion, broke open a Store where they got Arms, killed twenty one White Persons, and were marching the next morning in a Daring manner out of the Province, killing all they met, and burning Several Houses as they passed along the Road."[6]

The anonymous account, titled simply "An Account of the Negroe Insurrection in South Carolina," gave more details. That account was in all likelihood the work of James Oglethorpe, founder of the Georgia colony and an observer, at least from a distance, of the goings on in South Carolina. The surprisingly central role that Oglethorpe plays in the account—"The Lieutenant Governour sent an account of this to General Oglethorpe, who met the advices on his return from the Indian Nation"—seems to lend credence to this theory. So too does Oglethorpe's background, which included more experience writing than Bull's (and even a prior anonymous publication).[7]

"An Account of the Negroe Insurrection in South Carolina" identified the rebels' leader as "one who was called Jemmy." It detailed the places that

Jemmy and his men had reached, starting with the arms store, naming the several plantations through which the rebels had passed, and noting that the rebels had spared the life of a tavern owner who was "good and kind to his slaves." At another slave owner's home, one of the enslaved people there had protected the owner. That account also noted that by the late afternoon the rebels were convinced that they were "victorious over the whole province." They began to drink, dance, sing, and beat drums.[8]

It was at this point, less than a day after the rebellion had begun, that Bull and the militia caught up to Jemmy and his men. South Carolina's militia opened fire on the rebels and soon put an end to the rebellion. Or, in Bull's own words, "The Militia who on the Occasion behaved with so much expedition and bravery as by four a Clock the same day to come up with them and killed and took so many as put a stop to any further mischief at that time."[9]

That was the end of the rebellion, over less than twenty-four hours after it had begun. "In the whole action," the author of the "Account" wrote, "about 40 Negroes and 20 whites were killed."[10] A significant number of the men who had participated were still on the run, and it would take some time to capture the last of them; the active resistance, though, and the violence toward the slave owners, was over.[11] Some of the men who had participated returned to the plantations where they had previously been enslaved, claiming that they had been forced to participate. Enslaved people who had defended their enslavers during the uprising were rewarded. As for those rebels who died during the fighting, "Planters . . . Cutt off their heads and set them up at every Mile Post they came to."[12]

It was the largest rebellion of enslaved people in the history of colonial North America. And yet one is struck less by the scope and impact of the revolt than by how quickly the militia put it down and how few traces it left.

Historians hoping to reconstruct the event are forced to make do with relatively little concrete evidence. Information is especially scarce on the men who rose up at Stono. Bull described them simply as "Negroes" or "Our Negroes." The anonymous account gave a few more details. Along with referring to the leader as "one who was called Jemmy," the account referred to the rebels who began the revolt as "Some Angola Negroes . . . to the number of Twenty."[13] These men were, in other words, men who had been born in Africa, sold into slavery there, and then brought over on slave ships, rather than multigenerational African Americans or men who had come to the American mainland from Barbados or other islands in the West Indies. As John Thornton has pointed out, this African background was significant—even if the men were more likely Congolese than Angolan. The African origins helped explain several aspects of the revolt. It made their desire to flee south to Spanish Florida even more plausible, given the large number of Congolese who could speak Portuguese and, more importantly, were already familiar with—or even believers in—Catholicism. Congolese men would likely have military training, hence their ability to capture the weapons and their familiarity with firearms. Hence, too, their dancing and drumming later that day, which, as Thornton notes, fit in with African warrior traditions.[14]

Thornton's interpretation helps make more sense of the specifics of the Stono rebels' actions. Still, for understanding who these men were as individuals, there is not much to go on. There were no court cases later whose transcripts could help shed light on the situation or on the day's events. The closest thing that exists to any direct testimony from any of the participants came from a 1930 interview with a man named George Cato who described himself as the great-grandson of "de Stono slave commander"—whom he called "Cato," not "Jemmy." The account is strikingly similar to the written accounts, showing the continuing importance of the story in his family lore. "He die but he die for doin' de right, as he see it," George Cato noted—and he also claimed that "from dat day to dis, no Cato has tasted whiskey"—a reference to how the rum and the dancing made it easier for the planters to catch up to the rebels.[15]

South Carolina's newspapers did not discuss the revolt at the time. As Smith notes, those papers were silent because "whites feared that news of the revolt would only incite other rebellions."[16] Bacon issued a declaration of principles in 1676; Jemmy did not. The Stono Rebellion had nothing that would remotely approach the "confession" that Nat Turner left after leading an 1831 revolt in Virginia.[17] Stono lacked the sort of prerevolt statements that the abolitionist John Brown had given before attempting to lead a revolt in 1859. Nor did Stono lead to the quantity of ex post facto analyses and descriptions that Bacon's Rebellion had.[18]

There is more information available about the men who put down the revolt but not much more. The men involved were not ones to put pen to paper in order to share their deepest convictions, as Machiavelli and Fletcher had; nor did they have the importance of a Julius Caesar or an Oliver Cromwell, such that their contemporaries were inspired to write about them. William Bull was the lieutenant governor at the time; he was also from one of South Carolina's most prominent families. His father had been one of the men who founded Charleston—then Charles Town—in 1670. Bull grew up, then, in the center of South Carolina's powerful circles, and by the standards of early South Carolina, his was a well-documented life. He was granted land for a significant estate around fifty miles southwest of Charles Town. This location put him halfway to the eventual site of Savannah, Georgia, a town that he helped start. (One of Savannah's main streets still bears his name.) Still, at the start of the eighteenth century, South Carolina's elite were the biggest fish in a small pond. The start of the South Carolina colony was touch and go for some time, as the founders struggled to set up a society that for decades amounted to little more than a distant and poor outpost of Britain's sprawling empire. At several points it looked like the colony could be wiped off the map, particularly during the Yamasee War of 1715–17, in which Bull had served as captain. It was one of several wars against neighboring tribes during the colony's early decades, at a time when South Carolina's biggest threats came from those tribes and not from their own labor force. Bull also fought in the Tuscarora War earlier that decade. He was, in short, a prominent but otherwise fairly typical member of South Carolina's emerging ruling class.

Ironically, the one person involved in this story about whom the most information *might* be available, was Oglethorpe, the "anonymous" author. It was Oglethorpe's other activities that left a record, not his involvement—however marginal it may have been—in the Stono Rebellion. Again, the rebellion itself left few traces. And while part of this lack of evidence stems from white fears that news of the rebellion would spark another rebellion, that is not the only reason. By some measures, the Stono Rebellion was not that important.

That verdict is not one all historians share. For Peter Wood, the rebellion hastened a "concerted counterattack" from the slave owners, as the earlier frontier society gave way to a plantation society. For others, including historians Michael Mullin and Eugene Sirman, the event lacked that importance.[19] The deaths of twenty-five whites and fifty or so Africans mattered relatively little in the grand scheme of the colony's history. A pair of epidemics around the same time had killed far more South Carolinians, white and black alike. Even Bull's account makes the uprising seem merely a part of a larger conflict, that of England against Spain, played out in the New World as a battle between South Carolina and Florida. Those arguing for Stono's unimportance would seem to be bolstered by the relative lack of information available about it. Again, Bacon's Rebellion had produced far more documentation and far more inquiries from London. But then, Bacon's men had torn apart the colony and burned Jamestown to the ground during an uprising that had lasted for several months.

For understanding the history of colonial American militias, though, Stono merits as much attention as Bacon's Rebellion. The two events showed different sides of the colonial militia. Bacon's Rebellion showed, in its earliest forms, the emergence of what would be a long-term American pattern: citizen militias could be unstable. By arming its citizens and relying on those citizens to enforce the laws, Virginia had no way to enforce unpopular laws. Laws that divided the citizenry would divide the militia as well. Berkeley had little ability to impose his will on Bacon and his men. Bacon's Rebellion also showed how white colonists could tolerate a significant amount of violence when that violence came from other whites. Many of the settlers who did not support Bacon were still unwilling to heed Berkeley's call to fight against Bacon.[20] Yet Britain's North American colonies would continue to rely on militias, despite the instability that would occasionally result. There would continue to be uprisings among white colonists angry at government policies, and colonial governments would be similarly hamstrung in their responses—a pattern that would continue into the early years of the republic.[21]

Stono showed the other side of colonial militias. It showed how colonial militias could do what the law intended them to—quell insurrections rather than start them. There was no hesitation on the part of Carolinians to rush out and suppress Jemmy and his followers, the way Virginians had hesitated to suppress Bacon's Rebellion. For better or for worse, the South Carolina militia responded to the Stono Rebellion by doing everything a militia was supposed to do: springing into action, engaging the rebels, defeating them, punishing them, and restoring order to the colony.

That a colonial militia would be more effective in suppressing a revolt of enslaved people than in suppressing an internecine fight between different colonists is not surprising. A slave revolt did not draw on the militia's personnel the way an uprising like Bacon's Rebellion would. The insurgents would not have the organizational structure that the militia did—even if the Stono rebels themselves probably had military backgrounds. But there is no point here in overlooking the obvious: this was a black and white issue. Militias were unstable institutions when it came to disputes between different factions of white colonists. They were far more stable, and far more effective, when dealing with neighboring indigenous tribes. And they were most effective when policing enslaved people. Militia politics, like so much of colonial America, were racial politics. In much of British North America, citizens' militias' most important role was to police the enslaved population. In colonial America, militias' main role was to maintain white colonists' domination over nonwhites. This was true in the northern colonies, and it was truer still in the slave colonies of the South.[22]

Understanding Stono and its aftermath, then, has an importance that goes beyond what happened on that one day in 1739. The more unique men in the story—Jemmy/Cato and Oglethorpe—pointed out paths that Britain's North American colonies did not follow. William Bull was exemplary not for his uniqueness but because of how typical he was: settler, planter, slave owner, citizen-soldier.

The differences between the 1676 Bacon's Rebellion and the 1739 Stono Rebellion, then, were stark—as were the differences between the role that the militia and the militiamen played in each event. The main source of those differences lay in how Britain's North American colonies had changed during the intervening decades. In other words, the militia was not more efficient at Stono because of anything Fletcher or Trenchard wrote during the 1690s. South Carolina did not rely on a militia because of the rights that England had declared in 1689, and the different role that the militia played was not a result—or was at most a tangential result—of the upheavals England experienced during that period. The transformations were inextricably intertwined with developments in the broader Atlantic World that allowed Britain to become an imperial power in the first place, allowed its North American colonies to trade their agricultural products across the ocean, and allowed those same colonies to purchase human beings from Africa.[23]

By 1739, Britain's North American colonies had grown considerably from what they had been during Bacon's Rebellion. The Carolina colony, which had barely existed in 1676, had, by 1739, grown and then split into the two colonies of North and South Carolina, to be followed, in the 1730s, by Oglethorpe and Georgia. Up and down the Atlantic coast, European settlers had pushed further and further into Native Americans' lands. The combined population of the existing colonies that would eventually unite in the American Revolution, in 1680, had been perhaps 150,000; by 1740 it would be roughly six times that many. The population of Virginia itself had roughly quadrupled, from 45,000 to 180,000.[24]

For Virginia, this was more than just quantitative growth; it was also a qualitative change in the colony's makeup. In the Virginia of Berkeley and Bacon, for a white settler to become rich, he had to rely on the labor of other white settlers—men who had arrived more recently and who were hoping to, in turn, have their own farms and their own indentured labor. This had meant a continuing supply of poorer whites, men who had no guarantee for their future prosperity but who were required to participate in the militia, creating the population that Berkeley had called "a People where six parts of seaven at least are Poore Endebted Discontented and Armed."[25]

Bacon's Rebellion had shown the instability inherent to that system. When Bacon began his rebellion, the men loyal to him brought not only their grievances but also their weapons and their training. Berkeley, meanwhile, could not count on the loyalty of his own militia, as many of those men sympathized with Bacon—or at least were sympathetic enough to not risk life and limb trying to suppress the rebellion. Yet, when one looks at the century separating Bacon's Rebellion from the American Revolution, it is not the continued instability of Virginia that stands out but rather its relative stability. Colonial Virginia did not have another similar revolt, despite the instability that Bacon had helped expose.[26] The most likely reason for this lies in the ways in which Virginia changed during the remainder of its colonial period. In 1670, Virginia had about three thousand Africans and African Americans living in slavery, in a population of thirty-five thousand people. That number would triple over the next decade, during which the white population would also increase but only slightly. By 1740, Virginia had sixty thousand enslaved Africans. By 1750, Virginia would have a total population of around 230,000, of whom 100,000 were living in slavery.

By 1739, Berkeley and Bacon's Virginia was gone. Chattel slavery had replaced indentured servitude. As planters instead began relying on African people imported into the colony, not only would the people working the land no longer have the opportunity to earn their freedom but their children would be born into a life of slavery. In the process, Virginia changed. Scholars distinguish between "societies with slavery" and "slave societies." Many societies have had slavery, but not all of these were slave societies; a slave society is one where slavery is the society's central organizing principle, determining that society's values and institutions.[27] Since at least 1619, Virginia had been a society with slavery. It took some time, though, for Virginians to think through what slavery meant, and for decades slavery's legal status there was unclear, as was its relation to racial divisions.[28] At the time of Bacon's Rebellion, Virginia was still a society with slavery. But Virginia was an evolving society, and that evolution was heading toward the slave society that colonial Virginia would soon become. In doing so, white Virginians reshaped their colony, which became more like what Carolina's founders, Bull's father included, had always intended for their colony to be.

Carolina's founders had come over from Barbados, not the British Isles. This alone set the Carolina colony apart from the other colonies of British North America. Carolina's first generation of leaders were not attempting to re-create England on the other side of the Atlantic; rather, they wanted to replicate the society they had helped shape in Barbados. By 1650 Barbados was the richest of England's New World colonies; by the late seventeenth century, the island's elite were "the wealthiest men, by far, in British America," and the sugar they shipped back to the British Isles was worth more than all of the crops and products from the mainland combined.[29] In the process, the leaders of Barbadian society helped shape a world that was quite different from the England they had left. By the time they began exporting that society to the American mainland, Barbados was dominated by large sugar plantations owned by wealthy white planters and reliant on the labor of enslaved Africans.

Carolina's elite, then, wanted it to be a slave society from its very beginnings—although it took some time for the plantation economy that had made white plantation owners rich in Barbados to take root in Carolina. Mostly, it took time for the people who settled the region to figure out which crops would best grow there. The first generations of Carolinian settlement were based more on raising livestock. During this period, most of the enslaved people in the region were responsible for pasturing the animals, which gave them a higher level of autonomy than other enslaved peoples had in the Americas. They were America's original "cowboys"—a term used for enslaved black people in the Carolinas before it was ever used for white Americans in the West.[30] During the first quarter of the eighteenth century, landowners began planting rice and selling it for export. Rice's profitability allowed Carolina's elites to begin re-creating the plantation society of Barbados. This shift meant that the autonomy of previous work gave way to the monotony of plantation labor—among men who, unlike future generations of enslaved Americans, were used to a different way of life.[31] It also meant that slave owners were now eager to purchase more African people to work in the rice plantations. Many of those men, as Thornton shows, had military experience and the memory of a preslavery life.

There were already reasons, then, why in the late 1730s South Carolina was ripe for an uprising by enslaved people there. Within that period 1739 was particularly ripe. The colony was still recovering from a 1738 smallpox epidemic, enduring a yellow fever epidemic, and facing food shortages that year.[32]

For Bull, though—and for the anonymous chronicler who may well have been Oglethorpe—the key contributing factor was the hostilities between England and Spain. Those hostilities played out in North America as a rivalry between British Carolina and Spanish Florida. Both men began their accounts by pointing to a recent proclamation from Spanish Florida promising freedom to, in Bull's words, "all Negroes who should Desert hither from the British Colonie." Word of this promise had already reached enslaved people in South Carolina. There was something of a tradition during this era of people seeking their freedom in Florida—though most acted independently or in small groups, hoping to flee quietly.[33] In 1739 hostilities between Britain and Spain were ramping up, putting British South Carolina and Spanish Florida into an even more hostile opposition than normal—a situation of which the people who rebelled may or may not have been aware.[34] For Bull, though, the issue of Spain's role in inspiring Jemmy and his followers to rise up pointed to a danger that remained after he and his fellow planters had put down the rebellion: "If such an attempt was made in a time of Peace and Tranquility," Bull asked, "what might be expected if an Enemy should appear upon our Frontier with a design to invade us?" In asking this question, Bull was pointing to one of the fundamental truths about living in a frontier society with enslaved labor: those enslaved people, especially in large numbers, posed a security risk to the people enslaving them.[35]

The allegiance of the enslaved African people to the white population of South Carolina had previously been more ambiguous than might be expected. During the Yamasee War, Carolina raised an army of a thousand men, of whom four hundred were black.[36] As South Carolina became the plantation society its founders had always intended, though, blacks stopped being a major part of any military forces.[37] The "Account of the Negroe Insurrection" noted that a Mr. Rose "was saved by a Negroe who, having hid him, went out and pacified the others" and that a number of the men who participated had been "forced & were not concerned in the Murders & Burnings." White South Carolinians rewarded the enslaved people who helped whites during the uprising.

None of that changed whites' overall approach to living with a large enslaved population. The white population knew that if they were going to live in a society with that many enslaved people, they needed a way to maintain their control. What they needed to decide was how best to accomplish that task—and if it should be done by hiring full-time professionals or if it should be done by the citizens themselves.

Here, too, Carolina's Barbadian legacy played a key role. Barbados's enslaved majority had posed real questions for the whites as to how to maintain their control over the island. Other West Indian islands had relied on private slave catchers to catch individuals who had emancipated themselves and on overseers to prevent enslaved people from organizing uprisings or keeping weapons. Barbadians, however, took a different approach. In 1661, Barbados established a militia system to monitor the enslaved population. This move, as historian Sally Hadden points out, "shifted the job of slave control firmly onto the shoulders of all whites."[38] Rather than rely on bounty hunters, overseers, or some other sort of professional force, the 1661 Act for the Better Ordering and Governing of Negroes placed the responsibility for policing the enslaved population on the white citizens themselves, who would be both militia members and slave patrollers, two functions that were often indistinguishable from one another.

Barbadians were, like the Virginia colonists of the same period, acting in ways consistent with the English tradition of citizen-soldiers and militias. As in Virginia, the Barbadians were far more committed to the militia in practical terms than were their countrymen in England. And, as in Virginia, the Barbadians' choice to rely on a militia lay more in the practical and economic necessities of the colonial setting than to an ideological or philosophical commitment to an armed citizenry. In such a context, traditional justifications for citizen-soldiers were a way to make a virtue of necessity. Even more than the Virginians, though, the Barbadians knew that their situation could not be a simple exportation of their traditions into a new setting. Life in Barbados was different, and it was different because of slavery. The 1661 act claimed that their code was "not contradictory to the Laws of England." Still, the English traditions alone would not suffice for the Barbadians' purposes, "there being in all the body of that Law no track to guide us where to walk nor any rule set us how to govern such Slaves."[39]

The Barbadian planters, then, had to develop their own system that would allow them to maintain their control over a population of which a majority were enslaved. Early modern militias had always combined internal policing with external military duties. More often than not, militias were more effective at policing than they were on the battlefield. This policing, moreover, had always been intended as a way of maintaining some form of control, of maintaining order—which, in England and continental Europe, had always involved class domination. Hence the insistence from Harrington, and from the writers of the standing army controversy, that landowners participate in their local militias rather than servants.[40] Those class divisions, though, would never play as much of a role in American politics as they had in the Old World. Nor would those divisions play the role in American militias that they had in England. Because colonial militias, in Barbados as in Massachusetts, in Virginia as in Carolina, were always about race.

Up and down the Atlantic Coast of North America, militias became, to use a scholarly formulation, military organizations aimed at establishing and maintaining racial domination. In the first waves of settlement, those militias had been what the Virginia militia had been during Bacon's Rebellion: an armed organization of white men who fought against the indigenous population. The nature of those confrontations could vary, as the disagreements between Berkeley and Bacon showed, but all of the colonial militias played a role in claiming land that had been previously inhabited by Native Americans and in defending the colonies against attacks by Native Americans. All of those militias also combined an obligation on the part of white males to participate in the militia with restrictions on nonwhites' ability to participate.

These regulations were specific to each colony. That is, there was no "American" law governing or regulating the colonial militias, only acts, laws, and regulations specific to each colony—to Delaware or New Jersey, to Virginia or Rhode Island. Colonies would borrow ideas, habits, and practices from their neighbors. The colonies would also reissue their regulations fairly often, including those governing the militia. Sometimes the new regulations would have no changes, sometimes slight changes, and sometimes the colonial governments would give their regulations a major overhaul. As a result, between all of Britain's North American colonies, by the end of the colonial era the colonial legislatures had issued scores of militia codes. Some had their own quirks and features, especially regarding who was eligible and who was exempt. Pennsylvania stood alone in resisting using a militia—not because it preferred paid soldiers or policemen but because its Quaker leaders did all they could to avoid instituting any sort of military organization there. Everywhere else, though, the militias' broad outlines shared several key features, repeated over and over from year to year and from colony to colony.

First, these regulations usually included criteria dividing the men in the population. Some men were required to participate in the militia, others were exempt, and a third group were either prohibited from taking part or could only take part in a limited capacity. To put this in more concrete terms: the regulations would state that all men "16 to 60," or "above seventeen years and under sixty," or "21 to 60," etc., would be members of the militia. There were often qualifiers to this, such as "all able-bodied men," or "all free male persons." These men would make up the personnel of the militia. This made these men subject to a series of requirements. They had to make themselves known to their local militia leader, and that leader, in turn, had to keep and maintain a list of eligible men in his region. Those men would be required to equip themselves with certain weapons, often a "musket" or a "fuzee," along with the accompanying ammunition. They would be required to attend a certain number of training sessions per year—"musters"—often including one that would be a combined training exercise with other neighboring militia units. The regulations would also include details on the militia's hierarchy, method of choosing electors, methods of discipline permitted, and penalties for various infractions.[41]

Certain men who were eligible for participation were nevertheless exempt from the requirement to attend the musters. These typically included government officials and teachers, though regions would have other classes of men exempt as well—usually based on occupations. South Carolina's 1721 Act for the Better Settling and Regulating the Militia mentioned at the start of this chapter, for instance, included in its list of exemptions "all members of the Council, all members of the Assembly, and clerks of the same, all judges and their clerks," and a number of other government officials, as well as "ministers of the gospel," "coroners," and "attornies," along with a number of others.[42] New Jersey issued regulations the following year, with exemptions that also included members of the government and clerics, along with "Physitians, School-Masters, [and] Millers."[43] Virginia's list of exemptions in 1723 included, along with those in the colonial government, "any minister in the Church of England, or the president, masters, professors, or students, of the College of William and Mary," as well as "persons emploied in or about any iron, copper, or lead work, or any other mine." They also exempted any "overseer . . . having four or more slaves under his care."[44]

Then there were the regulations that prohibited certain groups of people from participating in the militia or limited the extent to which they could participate. These restrictions were almost always racially based; they were intended to make sure that the militia was an organization of white men. In 1656, for instance, Massachusetts declared that "no negroes or Indians, although servants to the English, shall be armed or permitted to traine."[45] Virginia's 1738 militia act prohibited "free mulattoes, negroes and Indians" from participating as armed members of the militia, though they could serve as "drummers or trumpeters" or "other servile labor."[46] New York declared in its 1702 militia regulations that nothing in it "shall be Construed or taken to allow or give Liberty unto any Negro, or to any Indian Slave or Servant to be Listed or to do any Duty in the Militia of this Province."[47] Maryland also declared in 1718 that "all Negroes and Slaves whatsoever shall be exempted the duty of training or other military service."[48] Maryland also prohibited any "Negro or other slave within this Province" from carrying weapons.[49] Such regulations were common; colonial laws often prohibited blacks from owning weapons or made such ownership subject to the approval of the enslavers. In South Carolina at the time of the Stono Rebellion, slave quarters and other "negro houses" were subject to searches for "guns, pistols, swords, cutlasses, and other offensive weapons" by whites, who would then be able to take the weapons for their own use, unless the enslaved person could produce a "ticket or license in writing from his master."[50]

There were also restrictions on selling weapons to Indians, although these were more complicated. A colony's ability to sell weapons to specific tribes but not others was a major factor in the colonists' diplomacy, and this task was complicated by the independent nature of each colony. At several points in the seventeenth century, Virginia announced strict fines for any colonists who sold weapons to Native Americans, even declaring in 1657 that any colonist doing so forfeited his whole estate—a far harsher penalty than those for other offenses that, when viewed from a modern perspective, might seem comparable. Two years later, however, the same Virginia legislature announced that "it is manifest that the neighboring plantations both of English and fforainers do plentifully furnish the Indians" with weapons, and allowed colonists to "freely trade" weapons with their indigenous neighbors.[51]

Again, the colonists' commitment to the militia system was based on practical and economic considerations, not on ideological ones. The colonial militia codes reflected that: they were practical documents. They did not tend to begin with statements on the evils of standing armies or list the problems that a mercenary force could cause. The regulations at times began with a statement emphasizing the importance of an armed citizenry or something along those lines. South Carolina, for instance, began its 1703 militia act by declaring that "the defense and safety of any people, under God, consists in their knowledge of military discipline."[52] The militia regulations also tended not to expound at length on the importance of military training for a virtuous society; if anything, they would begin with a statement bemoaning the current state of the colony's militia. Virginia's 1738 militia regulations, for instance, began by noting that "the laws heretofore made, have proved very ineffectual" at keeping the colony's militia in proper order.[53] The 1755 regulations also began with the complaint that previous measures "hath proved very ineffectual," adding that as a result "the colony is deprived of its proper defence in time of danger."[54] More common was a general statement outlining the necessity for a militia. Or, as Massachusetts's 1693 Act for Regulating the Militia declared, "WHEREAS for the Honour and Service of Their Majesties, and for the Security of this Their Province against any Violence or Invasion whatever: It is necessary that due care be taken that the Inhabitants thereof be Armed, Trained, and in a suitable posture and readiness for the ends aforesaid" and required of its inhabitants that "all Male Persons from *Sixteen* years of Age to *Sixty,* (other than such as are herein after excepted) shall bear Arms, and duely attend all Musters and Military Exercises of the respective Troops and Companies where they are listed or belong."[55]

Virginia's 1748 Act for Making Provisions Against Invasions and Insurrections would make a similar statement, declaring, "Whereas the frontiers of this dominion, being of great extent, are exposed to invasions of foreign enemies at sea and incursions of Indians at land, and great dangers may likewise happen by the insurrections of negroes, and others, for all which the militia settled by law is the most ready defence: And forasmuch as the militia of those counties, where any the dangers aforesaid shall arise, must necessarily be first employed, and may by the divine assistance, be able to suppress and repel such insurrections and invasions."[56]

Like Massachusetts's earlier act, Virginia's declaration made a similar statement of the militia's role: to ensure the colonists' safety by requiring many of them to participate in the militia. Yet Virginia's statement also showed the difference between the two colonies, particularly by the middle of the eighteenth century: as slavery grew, the militias in slavery-dominated regions took on a different role—closer to the one played in seventeenth-century Barbados than the one played in seventeenth-century Virginia. They were slave patrols.

Again, Barbados set much of the template here. During the seventeenth century, Barbados relied on citizens to police the enslaved population—which, in relying on citizens to serve as part-time police, was broadly consistent with English traditions. Barbados also pioneered population-control measures that had been unknown in the Old World but would become staples of New World slave societies. Barbadian whites set strict limits on enslaved people's movements. Those traveling off of their plantations had to carry passes. Whites who found enslaved people traveling were required to inspect their passes; should they come across any who were not carrying passes, those who had "not apprehend[ed] them or endeavour[ed] to do so, and having apprehended them and shall not punish them by a moderate whipping" were subject to fines. Whites were also responsible for inspecting enslaved people's quarters and making sure that there were no weapons there.[57]

Carolina's laws and slavery codes grew out of Barbados's laws and codes, even as it took a few generations for the mainland colony to develop the kind of plantation economy of Barbados. Carolina's first slave code, the 1690 Act for the Better Ordering of Slaves, copied the basics of Barbados's codes, including requiring any enslaved person traveling off of his or her master's plantation to carry a ticket authorizing his or her travel and requiring whites to inspect those tickets. That code also required slave owners to "cause all their slaves houses to be diligently and effectually searched, once every month, for clubs, guns, swords, and mischievous weapons."[58] The goal was not to create an "armed society" but rather a divided society, where one half was armed, and the other half was not.

By 1712, as North and South Carolina were emerging as separate colonies, South Carolina's new slave code declared that "the plantations and estates of this Province cannot be well and sufficiently managed and brought into use, without the labor of and service of negroes and other slaves." That updated code established two distinct law codes for white and black South Carolinians, as it deemed nonwhites as too "barbarous" to be governed by the same laws as whites.[59] The basics of the Barbados system remained in place, though, with enslaved people's movements restricted, with tickets required for travel off of plantations, and with whites expected to inspect those tickets. And as in Barbados, for the enforcement of that code, South Carolina relied on its citizens' militia.

Colonial South Carolina did experiment with paid slave patrols early in the eighteenth century. These patrolmen's duties were limited to patrolling the enslaved population, and members of the patrols were exempt from the militia service required of other Carolinians. Even this exemption shows the overlap between the two institutions, though. In any large-scale disturbance, the militia would be required to act alongside the patrols. In any case, the distinction would not last for long. In 1721 Carolina returned to relying on its militia to police its enslaved population.[60] The white population of colonial South Carolina, as in Barbados, was responsible for its own protection and safety, whether from the indigenous population on its frontier or from the people whom it had enslaved. Hence the two different wordings for the suppression of the Stono Rebellion, in Bull's account and in the anonymous account: Bull wrote that he had "decserned the approaching Danger time enough to avoid it and to give notice to the Militia," while the other account wrote that Bull "escaped & raised the Countrey," but both authors were writing the same thing.[61]

Commentators on colonial militias often found that they were less than fully effective and that their preparedness measures could at times be lacking.[62] As shown earlier, even the militia codes themselves would describe the militias in less than flattering ways.[63] At Stono, the militia was effective. Part of this success came by chance, as a result of Bull and his men having stumbled upon the rebellion even before hearing of it. A more delayed response might have led to a more successful revolt. In all likelihood, it would not have been that much more successful. There seems to have been little hesitation from the militia to spring into action and to catch and capture the rebels. Bull wrote that before the day was over, "Fort[y] four of the Rebels have been killed & executed, some few yet remain concealed in the Woods and expecting the same fate seem desperate."[64] South Carolina's militia had ended the revolt. The anonymous account again gave more details, but its overall message was the same:

> The Planters with great briskness pursued them and when they came up, dismounting, charged them on foot. The Negroes were soon routed though they behaved boldly, several being killed on the Spot, many ran back to their Plantations thinking they had not been missed, but they were there taken and Shot, Such as were taken in the field also, were, after being examined, shot on the Spot; and this is to be said to the honour of the Carolina Planters, that notwithstanding the Provocation they had received from so many Murders, they did not torture one Negroe, but only put them to an easy death.[65]

Over the next several weeks, South Carolina's militia set out to find the remaining missing rebels. They also began measures meant to prevent further uprisings, during a time when white South Carolinians were willing to put aside other differences.[66] To prevent enslaved Africans from rising up again, the South Carolinians took several measures. As mentioned above, they had left the heads of several rebels on mileposts as warnings. In 1740 the South Carolina colonial government issued An Act for the Better Ordering and Governing Negroes and Other Slaves in This Province. That act had two clear goals. The first was to prevent another Stono from happening. The second was to make sure that South Carolina continued to be a slave society and not lessen its reliance on enslaved labor.[67]

There were, to be sure, no regrets about how the militia had put down the rebellion. "Whereas, several Negroes did lately rise in rebellion, and did commit many barbarous murders at Stono," the act read, "all and every act, manner, and thing" done to suppress the rebellion, "is and are hereby declared lawful, to all intents and purposes whatsoever, as fully and amply as if such rebellious negroes had undergone a formal trial and condemnation."[68] The act added some minor measures that were meant to soften the treatment enslaved people received, as a possible way of preventing a future uprising. "Cruelty is not only highly unbecoming those who profess themselves Christians, but is odious in the eyes of all men who have any sense of virtue of humanity," the act read, subsequently listing the fines for anyone who would "willfully murder" their own enslaved laborers and lesser fines for those who would "willfully cut out the tongue, put out the eye, castrate, or cruelly scald, burn, or deprive any slave of any limb or member." Maximum working hours per day were limited to fourteen or fifteen (depending on the time of year). The act also tried to crack down on the problems posed by Florida and its policy of welcoming any fugitives who escaped South Carolina. Such a resolution, though, would have to wait quite some time.[69] South Carolina also instituted a duty on importing enslaved Africans for the next ten years.[70]

For all of its changes, the slave code South Carolina issued in Stono's aftermath stuck to the main principles of the codes that had preceded it and the codes that Carolina's founders had brought with them from Barbados. Nonwhites, especially Africans, were "by the honorable William Bull, Esquire, Lieutenant Governor and Commander-in-chief, by and with the advice and consent of his Majesty's honorable Council, and the Commons House of Assembly of this Province . . . hereby declared to be, and remain forever hereafter, absolute slaves, and shall follow the condition of the mother."[71] The ticket system remained in place, and whites were still required to inspect enslaved people's tickets. There was a renewed emphasis on prohibiting owners from allowing their enslaved workers some of the little remaining autonomy they had, especially gatherings on Sundays.[72] There were also more limits on enslaved people's movements. And the enforcement of this slave code still remained in the hands of white South Carolinians—both as citizens and as members of the militia, which is to say as citizen-soldiers.

South Carolina's militia regulations and its slave codes were two sides of the same coin. The slave codes prohibited enslaved people from gathering; the militia codes required the militias to break up any such gatherings. The slave codes prohibited enslaved people from owning weapons; the militia codes required the militias to search for any weapons.

Life never went according to code, of course. Throughout the colonial era, men who were required to attend musters found ways to avoid them, and men who did attend found ways to turn them from military trainings into social gatherings. Some enslaved people owned their own firearms—a practice that the slave codes noted, even in the aftermath of Stono. The 1740 act allowed enslaved people to possess weapons while "in the presence of some white person" or with a ticket from their master, as long as it was not on Sunday. Some masters allowed their enslaved workers to hunt, both for themselves and for their masters, though if they were unaccompanied, they could only hunt on their master's property.[73] Guns were an important daily tool in colonial South Carolina, and it would have been difficult to completely eliminate enslaved people's access to them. Still, the goals of the slave codes were still clear: the creation and maintenance of a divided society, where one part was armed and trained and the other part was unarmed and isolated.

Hence the difference between Bacon's Rebellion, where much of the fighting involved whites fighting against each other, and the Stono Rebellion, where free whites fought enslaved black people. The Virginia of 1676 was still evolving, the social divisions still not completely clear. Berkeley had identified it as a question of class, an uprising of "the lowest of the people."[74] Historians have been less willing to accept Berkeley's description of the fight as a battle along class lines, but it was still a fight that involved white soldiers on both sides. Stono would be much clearer, not only in ways that would shift racial balance but where the racial divisions would help soothe over any class divisions that might have existed. As historian Alan Taylor points out, in South Carolina, "the common planters felt bound more tightly to the rule of the great planters who, in turn, recognized their own dependence upon the common militia. As in the Chesapeake, the common and the great planters of Carolina established a white racial solidarity that, in politics, trumped their considerable differences in wealth and power."[75] Revolts more like Bacon's Rebellion would continue during the colonial era and even into the early years of the republic. But they would not come in slave regions.

The Stono Rebellion took place at a time of transition in South Carolina, from a frontier economy to a plantation economy. Neighboring Georgia was just getting started. The men who rose up were, like many of their fellow South Carolinians, new arrivals to the colony, with memories of their former lives. All of these factors made a rebellion more likely in 1739 than it would be in the decades that followed. But the transitional nature of South Carolina in 1739 is worth underlining, in part because it provides a view of the other paths the people of the region could have taken. Virginia and South Carolina, though their origins were different, were already evolving in similar directions. The people who owned Virginia's tobacco plantations had already stopped employing so many indentured servants and instead forced enslaved Africans and African Americans to do the work. South Carolina's slave society was shifting from a frontier economy to a plantation system, growing rice. Both were heading toward a plantation economy based on enslaved labor. Between them lay North Carolina, where slavery was also widespread, especially along the coast, but where large plantations were less common.

To the immediate south lay Georgia, which would soon become another colony where plantation slavery was the key to the economy—and, therefore, to the lives of most of its inhabitants. In 1739 Georgia was not there yet, though. When Oglethorpe founded Georgia, he had a very different vision in mind. Like Berkeley, Oglethorpe was born into English nobility and spent his adult life in both England and North America. Like Berkeley he was a bit of a Renaissance man, with a career that included experience as a member of Parliament, military service, and political advocacy, along with his time in North America. It was his political advocacy in England that led him to found Georgia. Oglethorpe had been disturbed by the large number of Englishmen in prison, especially those who had been locked up for debts. His proposal was to give those debtors a chance to make it as farmers and as landowners in the New World. Oglethorpe had envisioned a Georgia where Englishmen worked on the land and provided for themselves and where the laws of the colony would ensure that they led upstanding and moral lives. It would have no large-scale plantations and no rum either. Most notably, Oglethorpe envisioned a colony free of slavery—and, for that matter, free of Africans.[76] Georgia would not long remain true to Oglethorpe's vision, though, and white Georgians would bristle under the rule of Georgia's early laws.

Further south still lay Florida, and while it might be a stretch to view this Spanish colony as an "alternative model" to English colonies, there were communities in northern Florida whose inhabitants were descended largely from people who had successfully fled from slavery during previous years.[77] Florida was one of several places in the New World with "maroon" communities made up largely of fugitives and their descendants. There were other such maroon communities in Jamaica and in the marshlands along the Virginia/Carolina border known as the Great Dismal Swamp.[78]

One by one, alternative models would fall by the wayside. The Europeans who settled in Georgia did not embrace Oglethorpe's vision the way he had hoped; soon they were fighting against the colony's laws and calling for "liberty and property without restrictions"—that is, for the liberty to own slaves. In 1751, the men who had originally created Georgia as a destination for English debtors gave up and relinquished their control over the region. The new leaders embraced slavery with a vengeance and imported as many enslaved Africans as they could. By the time of the Revolution Georgia, too, was a slave society. Even Oglethorpe's vision of small farms had given way to large-scale plantations. Georgia's slave codes and its militia codes would soon mimic South Carolina's in all major points.

Florida's maroon colonies would last for several generations, as Florida itself would go back and forth between Spanish rule, British rule, independence, and eventually statehood. As those alternative models fell by the wayside, the one model left standing was the kind of economy, and the kind of society, against which Jemmy and his followers had rebelled: a society of plantation slavery, where political power was in the hands of wealthy plantation owners, where chattel slavery was the lot for most of the population, and where the lines between the free and the enslaved were based on people's race. If there had ever been an opportunity for that region to take a different route, that opportunity had been missed—put down less by the South Carolina militia on that day than by all that the men who made up the militia, across the colony, had done in the preceding years. As Wood puts it, 1739 "was slightly too late, or far too soon, for realistic thoughts of freedom among black Americans."[79] Slavery won out.

The victory of slavery over other competing social models brought with it a specific form of militia society: the civilian policing of the enslaved populations. A significant portion of the militias in British North America would focus their attention on the African American population. These militias would play a larger role in the day-to-day life of the southern colonies than would the militias of the northern colonies, especially off of the frontier. This was part of the overall nature of the history of militias in the eighteenth-century Atlantic World and, therefore, of the road to the Second Amendment. The ideology of the citizen-soldier was a British product, but as an institution there the militia was fading away.[80] In British North America the militia was thriving as an institution among men who had little interest in the lofty ideals of civic virtue. During the first part of the eighteenth century, there were two roads to the Second Amendment: one that passed through the laws of England and the writings of the republican theorists and another that lay in the growth of the militias in Britain's North American colonies. These two roads would reconverge before the century was over. Before that could happen, the colonies would have to join together and fight for their independence. In that struggle the militia would again have to act as an army rather than a domestic police force.

EIGHT

The Minutemen Turn Back the Redcoats at Concord Bridge

1775

Years after the "midnight ride" that made him famous, Paul Revere wrote out his recollections of that night in April 1775, when he and several other men rode west from Boston to warn the people of Lexington and Concord about the impending invasion by British troops. His version was quite a bit different from the version Longfellow would later put into his poem—"Listen, my children, and you shall hear / Of the midnight ride of Paul Revere." To start with, Revere himself was a silversmith, not a wordsmith. He was much more interested in recounting the event than he was in dramatizing it. Still, his version did reveal not only the drama of that night but the tensions that already existed between the people of Massachusetts and the British soldiers stationed there. "On Tuesday evening, the 18th," Revere wrote, "a number of Soldiers were marching towards the bottom of the Common. About 10 o'Clock, Dr. Warren Sent in great haste for me, and beged that I would imediately Set off for Lexington, where Messrs. Hancock & Adams were, and acquaint them of the Movement, and that it was thought they were the objets." And set off he did—though first, as he was away from his own home, "went to git me a horse." Having gotten one, he set off to warn the people along the route that led to Lexington and then Concord. He would make it to Lexington before being stopped by soldiers; his fellow riders would make it further. As he rode, Revere noted, "I alarmed almost every House, till I got to Lexington." The warning he gave to his fellow New Englanders was simple: "The regulars are coming out."[1]

The "regulars" were indeed coming out. That is, professional British soldiers—not militiamen, not citizen-soldiers, but men from England's standing army—were on their way to both Lexington and Concord. Their goal was to capture the military supplies stored there (and not, as Revere believed, to arrest local opposition leaders Samuel Adams and John Hancock).[2] These professional soldiers were loyal to and acting on behalf of the government in London but stationed in New England. The people of New England faced a choice: agree to their demands or stand up to them with only their militia and stare down professional soldiers.

By this point, the impending arrival of such a confrontation was not much of a surprise. Relations between the British government in London and the British colonists in North America had been deteriorating for the past decade. Both sides had hardened their positions during the first half of the 1770s. The Boston area had been at the center of a series of confrontations between the two sides. King George III and Parliament had stationed more British soldiers in or near Boston. New Englanders who were leading the local opposition to the British government also stepped up their game. Towns in Massachusetts supplemented their existing militias with elite groups of "minutemen." The old training schedules of monthly musters gave way to two training sessions per week.[3]

It was at once the dream and the nightmare of those British writers who, for generations, had been warning about the evils of standing armies. They had been claiming for decades that a ruler could use a professional standing army to stamp out the flames of freedom—hence the nightmare. But it was also a dream come true because those writers had also been telling their readers that because citizens made better soldiers, militiamen, motivated by the need to protect their homes and families, would outfight professional soldiers motivated only by money. The battles of Lexington and Concord represented a chance to test these theories, a chance to test the ability of committed part-time soldiers to stand up to a professional army. In 1775, England was an imperial power with a very effective standing army and an even better navy. England's newfound military strength had allowed it to defeat France during the Seven Years' War, which had ended twelve years earlier.[4] Now imperial power England was looking to maintain its hold on some recently recalcitrant colonies on the other side of the Atlantic. Men like Revere were not making that easy.

After he left Lexington but before he reached Concord, "Six officers, on Horse back" stopped Revere and ordered him to dismount. "One of them, who appeared to have the command, examined me, where I came from, & what my Name Was? I told him. it was Revere, he asked if it was Paul? I told him yes." Revere warned the officers that because the English were slow in getting started, "There would be five hundred Americans there in a short time," as he had already "alarmed the Country all the way up." At that point another British officer arrived, "Clapped his pistol to my head, called me by name, & told me he was going to ask me some questions, & if I did not give him true answers, he would blow my brains out."[5]

No one did blow Revere's brains out that day. He was able to return to Boston soon enough. But his actions helped prepare the two towns for the regulars' arrival, especially since one of the men riding alongside Revere had eluded the regulars and made it all the way to Concord. Both Lexington and Concord had enough time to let the militias there prepare for the regulars' arrival. And the militias were ready. The previous months of increased training and the creation of the minutemen had been for just this kind of confrontation.[6]

The "regulars" were under the command of Lieutenant General Thomas Gage, who at the time was both the governor of Massachusetts and the commander in chief of the British forces stationed in America.[7] Gage had given instructions to one of the army's colonels that the colonial government had "received intelligence, that a quantity of Ammunition, Provision, Artillery, Tents and small arms, have been collected at Concord, for the Avowed Purpose of raising and supporting a Rebellion against His Majesty." Gage therefore ordered the soldiers to "March . . . with the utmost expedition and Secrecy to Concord, where you will seize and destroy all artillery, Ammunition, Provisions, Tents, Small Arms, and all Military Stores whatever."[8] It was Gage's attempt on behalf of the British government to take control over the developments in Massachusetts and to put an end to all of the rebellious stirrings there.

Gage himself was from England, but by 1775 he was no stranger to North America. Like Berkeley the century before, Gage was a member of England's aristocracy—though Gage was from even higher aristocracy. It was a sign of the increasing importance of England's North American colonies that the men sent there were now from Great Britain's elites. Thomas Gage had grown up the second son of a family who had been on the same estate since the fifteenth century. He had chosen a military career, which brought him to North America in 1755 to fight in the French and Indian War—the colonial theater of Europe's Seven Years' War. Gage had an uneven record in that war, and he would have an uneven record in his subsequent military assignments as well.

In a 1994 study of Revere's ride, historian David Fischer describes Gage as "a tragic figure." While sympathetic to Gage, even Fischer acknowledges the key dynamic in Gage's career trajectory: he kept failing up. After each of his defeats on the battlefield, Gage was promoted. After the French and Indian War he remained in North America as the highest military commander of British troops in North America. As the Boston area bristled more and more under British rule, the existing colonial governor of Massachusetts, Thomas Hutchinson, made himself the object of the ire of Revere, Hancock, Adams, and their fellow Boston patriots. At that point Gage, popular in many of the colonies, came in to replace Hutchinson in 1774.[9]

It was in this context that Gage became responsible for putting an end to the rebellious stirrings that had been going on in the area. He saw the dilemma he faced, having written at one point that the "strictest orders have been given, to treat the inhabitants with leneity, moderation, and justice." But he also wrote that "lenient measures, and the cautious and legal exertion of the coercive powers of government, have served only to render them more daring and licentious."[10] Perhaps no man could have handled the job, but if any man could have, it was not Gage. He also miscalculated in his approach to colonial Massachusetts, though here he was hardly alone. Like many others in the British government, Gage thought that the resistance was mostly the matter of a small number of militants, something that could be nipped in the bud with a sufficient display of force. "A large force will terrify," he wrote to England, "and engage many to join you."[11] Gage was going to try to do just that—hence his plan and his orders, in April 1775, for the regulars under his command to march inland and seize the colonists' military supplies.

By all accounts, Gage's plan was not a good one. In his classic 1976 account of Concord, historian Robert Gross describes Gage's plans as "entirely predictable" and "what every well-informed colonist had been anticipating for weeks." Beyond that, it was "plagued by miscalculations, leaks, and delays that helped ensure its failure."[12] Included in those miscalculations was Gage's own assessment of the New England citizens' prowess as soldiers, which he arrived at during his time in the French and Indian War. In June of 1775 Gage would complain that "in all their Wars against France," the men of New England "never Shewed so much Conduct Attention and Perseverance as they do now."[13] Like most professional soldiers—and like George Washington, for that matter—Gage did not expect a citizens' militia to pose much of a threat to his professional army.

Nothing in the first phase of fighting would have changed Gage's opinion on the matter. The British troops arrived in Lexington at around sunrise of April 19. There, they fought against men from the local militias—though it was not much of a fight. As one of the militiamen would testify later, after "being drawn up sometime before sunrise, on the green or common, and I being in the front rank," he saw a large number of British regulars approaching. As the soldiers galloped toward the center of Lexington, the officers yelled, "Throw down your arms, ye villains, ye rebels." At that point, according to this witness, the officers ordered their men to "fire, by God, fire."[14] The British soldiers began shooting, and the colonists—including the witness himself—fell. The colonists never recovered, and the fighting was over soon. A British officer would give a different version of the start, claiming that the colonists "fired one or two shots" before the British fired, but from there, the two accounts are similar: once the first shots were fired, the officer claimed, "our Men without any orders rushed in upon them, fired and put 'em to flight; several of them were killed, we cou'd not tell how many, because they were got behind Walls and into the Woods; We had a Man of the 10th light Infantry wounded, nobody else hurt."[15] Gage's regulars were able to impose their will on Lexington in less than an hour.[16] The officers gathered their men back to Lexington's town square and proceeded along the road toward Concord. Regulars 1, militiamen 0.

Down the road in Concord the alarm bell had been ringing all night, and the militiamen had been gathering in the town center. "The roads," Gross writes, "began to fill with men advancing on Concord from all directions."[17] They chose positions at higher ground, knowing that the regulars would be arriving on the main road. When those regulars arrived, then, they would be standing in the middle of the town, wearing their bright red uniforms. Representatives of a powerful military machine, these redcoats would soon find themselves outflanked and outnumbered by a group of men who had "resolved to . . . defend their homes, or die in the attempt."[18] One of the colonists who fought that day—Solomon Smith, from nearby Acton—described being alarmed "about day-break" and then heading east toward Concord "when the sun was something more than an hour high." He would be joined on the road by other colonists, including the militia's officers. They would head to the center of Concord, particularly to the Concord Bridge. Then, with the regulars still on their way, they "proceeded to the high ground, north of the bridge. There was a considerable number of men from Concord and other towns assembled there," he added, and "others were fast joining them." From there, they saw the British arriving in the town. "The sun was rising," one colonist later noted, "and shined on their arms, and they made a noble appearance in their red coats and glistening arms."[19] Later the colonists would also see smoke start to rise up, though they did not yet know from what. Most of the men waited for the officers to give them the order to march down toward the bridge and engage with the regulars.[20]

This was the immediate lead-up to the Battle of Concord Bridge and the fighting that would only end six years later with the Battle of Yorktown and the British surrender. But how had things gotten to that point? Answering that means asking not only why the relations between Britain and her colonies had soured but why the thirteen colonies were willing to unite. It also means asking, since when did the British government have such a large professional army at its disposal?

As shown in chapter 6, England embarked on a paradoxical path following the Glorious Revolution. The 1689 Bill of Rights had declared that "the raising or keeping a standing army within the kingdom in time of peace, unless it be with consent of Parliament, is against law." That article grew out of James II's attempt to build a true standing army in Britain, modeled after Louis XIV's royal army. The English overthrew James II, and the weight of that standing army was one of the reasons for their actions. But after 1689, year after year, Parliament renewed its Mutiny Acts and thereby gave its consent, and England had at its disposal a professional army. In the immediate aftermath of 1689, maintaining that army seemed a necessity during the ensuing war with France. The 1697 Peace of Ryswick had led to a confrontation. Writers like Andrew Fletcher and John Trenchard fought to eliminate Britain's standing army; King William III fought to maintain that army. The result was a compromise where the king maintained a standing army that was smaller than he had hoped.[21]

That army did not stay small. As historian John Brewer has shown, from 1688 to 1714 the British state went through a "radical transformation" in which it acquired "all of the main features of a powerful fiscal-military state: high taxes, a growing and well-organized civil administration, a standing army, and the determination to act as a major European power."[22] This expansion began as a reaction to Louis XIV's continued belligerence, which, within England, made Fletcher's argument less tenable. From the Glorious Revolution to the end of the American Revolution, England and France would be at war with each other more often than not—and preparing for the next war the rest of the time.[23] Fletcher had argued that there was no point in building up a standing army to defend Britain against France because by doing so, the British would, in essence, turn themselves French. But during the eighteenth century, this argument found fewer and fewer adherents within Britain itself. Fletcher's calls for a rejuvenation of the militia also fell on deaf ears for the first half of the century. No one was interested in the sort of commitment to the militia Fletcher and his fellow travelers had called for, and few Britons believed that a militia made up of part-time soldiers could replace an army of professional soldiers. England would finally reform its militia in 1757—though its goal then was to re-create it as a domestic police force to complement the armed forces, especially the navy, rather than as an alternative to the standing army.[24] For the first time in centuries, England was successfully asserting itself militarily outside the British Isles and becoming, once again, a major player in European power politics. That success seemed to pave over some of the hesitancy with which earlier Britons had viewed the threat of a strong army.

So England built up its armed forces—army and navy alike. During the wars following 1689, Parliament had approved a navy of forty thousand and an army of seventy-six thousand. That would go down after 1697—the compromise solution of the standing army controversy—but would grow again five years later when fighting resumed. By the time of the American Revolution, those numbers had grown to 82,000 in the navy and 108,000 in the army.[25] The numbers were smaller during peacetime, but the English still kept a significant number of men under arms when not at war. Behind all of this growth was the equivalent growth in Britain's administrative state, which provided the infrastructure and logistics that made this growth possible. Beyond that, in turn, were the taxes British citizens—at least those in Great Britain itself—had to pay.[26]

And yet England would emerge not only as a military power with a centralized state, a large standing army, and a powerful navy; it would also maintain its self-understanding as a nation proud of its liberties. Whether this reputation was deserved within Britain itself remains debatable. For Brewer, the English insistence on civilian control over military power prevented the sorts of privateering and other abuses that had plagued nations with earlier military revolutions.[27] This fear of a standing army also helped explain England's insistence on a strong navy throughout this period (and beyond), as Britons had less fear that a navy would impose its will on the nation militarily the way that Cromwell's New Model Army had.[28] Yet Brewer acknowledges that within England "the military was an important means of maintaining public order and one to which the civil authorities, for all their soul searching, had frequent recourse. Indeed by the last quarter of the eighteenth century, rioters in England were more likely than those in France to be confronted by armed soldiers."[29] England was a nation with a standing army, and England's government used that army to impose its will on the nation, even if it did so less blatantly than had been the case during Cromwell's rule. Critics of the standing army had lost; England rejected their vision in favor of a British Empire that allowed London to again be a major player in international politics.[30]

Still, the critiques of the standing army would have their legacy. The tradition of English thought that went back through Fletcher and Trenchard, and even to Machiavelli's vision of the Roman Republic, would develop a legacy in British North America, particularly during the buildup to the Revolution. That legacy would allow the colonists to formulate their opposition to English rule in ways that were familiar to them—and would be familiar to people in England as well. In other words, as the colonial militias prepared to oppose a standing army, England provided the colonists both the intellectual legacy of opposition to a standing army and the standing army itself that British North American colonists would oppose.[31]

When colonists read about the dangers of standing armies and the virtues of militias, it tended to be via Trenchard. Fletcher died in 1716. His works remained somewhat popular, though not especially so, over the course of the century. Trenchard would live on until 1723 and continued to be productive. During the last three years of Trenchard's life he teamed up with the Scottish writer Thomas Gordon and wrote a series of essays knowns as *Cato's Letters,* named after the Roman politician Cato the Younger. In Plutarch's telling, Cato accused Caesar of trying to "ruin the commonwealth." Later, unwilling to tolerate Caesar's eventual victory, Cato committed suicide.[32] In other words, Trenchard continued to view the Roman Republic as a model to emulate and Julius Caesar as the man who had killed that republic. *Cato's Letters* covered more issues than Trenchard's earlier writings, ranging from topics of the day to general principles of the role of virtue in society. Trenchard did return to the question of standing armies in two of those letters, where he reminded his readers that "all parts of Europe which are enslaved, have been enslaved by armies; and it is absolutely impossible, that any nation that keeps them amongst themselves can long preserve their liberties."[33]

As criticism of the standing army became less popular in Britain during the eighteenth century, *Cato's Letters* went on to be quite popular in Britain's North American colonies. They helped keep alive the intellectual tradition that would eventually lead to the Second Amendment—the fear of a standing army, the belief in citizen-soldiers, and the idea that not only did citizens make better soldiers but part-time soldiers made better citizens. Most crucially, *Cato's Letters* helped keep those ideas familiar to British colonists in North America.[34]

Trenchard and Gordon's influence grew in the buildup to the Revolution. The developments of the 1770s, with Britain seeking to impose its policies on the colonies via its standing army, made the traditional critiques of standing armies relevant and useful for the colonists.[35] Those theories' influence early in the century, though, should not be exaggerated. Until midcentury, militias were usually all that the colonists had. As chapters 5 and 7 have shown, militias were a key part of Britain's North American colonies—but for practical reasons, not for ideological ones. There was rarely any money for professional soldiers. Virginia did at times employ professional soldiers to patrol its western frontier, but those were relatively small units of dubious military ability.[36]

Bacon's Rebellion showed some of the dynamics that came into play when citizens were required to participate in the militia. Citizens would prove to be capable of military actions but not always willing to follow orders. Governor Berkeley had discovered that in the 1670s, when Nathaniel Bacon was able to command the loyalty of a significant portion of Virginia's citizens. Other colonial governments would make similar discoveries. In the decade leading up to the Revolution, the North Carolina government was unable to contain the "Regulators," a group of colonists who, like the men who had flocked to Bacon, were from the western part of the colony and felt that the coastal government was not acting in their interests.[37] New York and New Hampshire both had trouble dealing with Ethan Allen and his Green Mountain Boys, to the point where they eventually gave up and allowed Allen to help establish Vermont as a state in the 1790s.[38]

The case of Allen and the Green Mountain Boys showed that sometimes these uprisings could be successful—a trained and armed citizenry could succeed in imposing its will on the government that had trained them. Of course, the American Revolution provided a similar lesson. In 1775, Massachusetts's colonial governor was facing a crisis that in many ways paralleled the one that Berkeley faced. Compared to their seventeenth-century counterparts, the New England colonists were not "poore," and they were not disproportionately indebted. They were most certainly discontented and armed, though, and by April 1775 they were trained and organized as well.

That the militias' unruliness was proving useful in 1775 does not mean that the colonists had maintained the militias out of some sort of clairvoyance, some future knowledge that they would need the militias in order to stand up to their colonial overlords at an unknown later date. No one in the colonies could have foreseen the arrival of the Revolution even a decade before it happened.

The militias had also shown that in other situations, they were useful and effective—even brutally effective. That had been one of the lessons of the Stono Rebellion. Southern states' attachment to their militias had always been tied to the need to police the enslaved population. This aspect of the militias came out in events like Stono, but it was the relative lack of such events that showed the effectiveness of the militias in the southern colonies.

New England's militia tradition was less tied to policing the enslaved population than were the southern militias, but colonial New England was no utopia of racial harmony. It was still a society with slavery, even if, unlike South Carolina or Virginia, it never became a slave society.[39] It also had a history of dealings with the local indigenous tribes that was more or less similar to the history of the other colonies up and down the Atlantic Coast. As Anne Little notes, for the men of colonial New England—English and non-English alike—war was not only a way of establishing mastery over one's enemy but also a way for men to prove their manhood. The result was the development of a "particular puritan warrior tradition" that linked military duty with leading a household and, eventually, with a conception of manhood that incorporated a recognition of British liberties as well.[40]

Massachusetts militia regulations went back to the seventeenth century and were, for the most part, typical for a British colony in North America. When the British government reorganized New England in 1692, Massachusetts's charter gave the governor command over the militia.[41] A 1699 Act Regulating the Militia declared that "Whereas for the Honour and Service of Their Majesties, and for the Security of Their Province against any Violence of Invasion Whatsoever, it is necessary that due care be taken that the Inhabitants thereof be Armed, Trained and in a suitable posture and readiness for the ends aforesaid: and that every Person may know his duty and be obliged to perform the same."[42] The earliest regulations even called for pikemen,[43] although the colonists soon realized that New World warfare required different tactics and by the early eighteenth century stopped providing soldiers in the militia with "a good sword or cutlash," as "it is found by experience that baionets are of more use, as well for offence as defence."[44]

Massachusetts was also typical in requiring citizens to participate while carving out exceptions for certain groups—members of the government and clerics were usually exempt and, just as Virginia had exempted the students and professors of William and Mary, so Massachusetts exempted the students and professors of Harvard.[45] Participation was also required of men who had the physical ability to do so; therefore "Lame persons or otherwise disabled in Body" were exempted.[46] And then there were the restrictions—classes of people who were not only exempted from the requirement but forbidden from participating. The New England militias were not slave patrols, like the southern militias, but they still made sure that the militias were limited to white colonists.

New England had not always been that way. A 1652 militia regulation declared that "all Scotchmen, Negroes and Indians inhabiting with or servants to the English . . . are hereby enjoyned to attend trainings as well as the English."[47] But four years later new regulations (cited in the previous chapter) prohibited "negroes or Indians, although servants to the English" from being armed or training.[48] That would be the rule going forward, as subsequent regulations would keep "*Indians* and *Negroes,*" including "free negro's and molatto's," out of the militia.[49] The Massachusetts militia had been a typical colonial militia—down to the complaints about it, both from those required to participate and from the officers who commanded it. The regulations themselves make clear that the participation was not always up to the level the colonists hoped for. In 1666 the militia regulations already stated that the existing orders were "not so attended as is to desired."[50] A 1679 regulation added that the training days were being derailed by people who brought "considerable quantities of wine, strong liquors, cider, and other inebriating drinckes" to the training.[51]

During wars, Massachusetts would organize provincial forces, which usually had a less representative cross-section of the white population and instead were mostly the poorer and more marginalized white citizens, either by impressment early in the colony's history or through recruiting volunteers later on when impressed soldiers turned out to be bad soldiers.[52] As Taylor points out, the colonial militias relied on poorer whites, which gave those poor whites some political leverage. "To avoid alienating the militiamen, British colonial elites gradually accepted a white racial solidarity based upon subordinating 'blacks' and 'reds.' Once race, instead of class, became the primary marker of privilege, colonial elites had to concede greater social respect and political rights to common white men."[53] This dynamic was not unique to New England. As one Virginia planter told a British officer during the Revolution, "Every one who bore arms, esteemed himself on an equal footing with his neighbor. . . . No doubt, each of these men conceives himself, in every respect, my equal."[54]

The colonial militia, then, could play an important role even while its military preparation was lacking, and even when the musters were more of a party than training session. Still, there were times when a militia did need to be what it was supposed to be—an effective military force. In those situations, the musters would regain their sense of gravity, and the military training would again become paramount. Such was the case in the lead-up to Lexington and Concord. Hence the announcement from the first Provincial Congress of Massachusetts that "while the British ministry are suffered with so high a hand to tyrannize over America, no part of it, we presume, can be negligent in guarding against the ravages threatened by the standing army now in Boston. . . . The improvement of the militia in general in the art military has been therefore thought necessary, and strongly recommended by this congress." In that situation, they added, "each of the minute men" should be sufficiently armed, and towns should begin paying them a "reasonable consideration."[55]

Thus were born the minutemen, who then began their paid training. The Provincial Congress's suggestion was "three times a week, and oftener, as opportunity may offer,"[56] though the frequency varied from town to town. It was not a change in who participated—the new regulations included the same exemptions and restrictions, including "Negroes, Indians and Mullatoes."[57] But those who did participate would be training more often, and with a different goal in mind, than previous New England militias. They were at once traditional and new: new because the level of training and readiness far exceeded what had existed for most of the colonies' history, traditional because they still grew out of the practice in the colonies, by that point over one hundred years old, of requiring citizens to participate in the militia. Solomon Smith would later report that "we turned out to drill and exercise, twice a week. . . . I think the company was raised by voluntary enlistment. The town paid us eight pence for every half day."[58] The training was also done with a different adversary in mind: instead of preparing to fight against local indigenous populations, this militia was preparing to go up against the professional soldiers from Britain's army—soldiers who had been mostly absent during the first century of England's colonial settlement of North America but had come during the French and Indian War and had been a presence there ever since.

The French and Indian War not only brought Gage to the New World. It also brought British troops to North America in numbers never seen before. The earlier large-scale actions against France or Spain also brought British professional soldiers to North America, but those had been both smaller, more episodic, and not the tens of thousands of regulars arriving in the 1750s and 1760s.[59] These new levels of engagement became possible thanks to the growth of England's standing army throughout the eighteenth century. England now had the possibility to send troops across the ocean by the tens of thousands and, seeing an opportunity to take out their French rivals, the leaders of England's government chose to do just that. So when Gage arrived, he was one of many British officers, along with tens of thousands of professional soldiers fighting in Britain's army. There, the British fought alongside colonists, who brought with them their own training and traditions from the colonial militia system.[60]

It was in this fighting that Gage met a young Virginian named George Washington. The two struck up a friendship that would last for some years after the war. It was here, too, that Washington would get his first real military experience. He wrote to his brother after one of his battles, "I fortunately escaped without a wound, tho' the right Wing where I stood was exposed to & received all the Enemy's fire and was the part where the man was killed & the rest wounded. I can with truth assure you, I heard Bulletts whistle and believe me there was something charming in the sound."[61]

With English professional soldiers fighting alongside colonists, it was also a chance for both sides to get a sense of each other's potential as a fighting force. And here, more often than not, the professional soldiers found the colonists wanting. In many places, it was hard to gather enough soldiers. Virginians were often uninterested in the fighting. Like their neighbors to the south, they were more concerned about policing the enslaved population than they were about fighting the French.[62] This meant they were wary of weakening the militia itself or diverting the militiamen from their standard duties. Those colonists who fought would have been members of the militia, but they did not fight as militia units. They fought rather as "provincial" troops. Benjamin Franklin described the distinction in a letter to a friend, noting that "those men posted on the frontier are not militia, but what we call our provincial troops, being regularly enlisted to serve a term, and in the pay of the province," while the rest of the militiamen continued to "follow their respective callings at home." Franklin described these men as something close to British regulars.[63] Not everyone would have agreed with that statement. The colonists had less training. Many were attracted simply by the promise of pay and clothing. In the case of Virginia's provincial troops, those who were sent to fight came from the lowest levels of white Virginian society and often deserted.[64] These men were "needy," according to Washington, and even "loose, idle persons quite destitute of house and home."[65] The same was true of Massachusetts's provincial troops, which had a long tradition of relying on the poorer colonists.[66]

So the provincial troops were not identical to the militia units, though they drew from the same overall pool of manpower. Such statements could often be made of the British soldiers as well—and often would be, particularly by Bostonians who didn't appreciate their presence in New England. But the British regulars had been trained before arriving in the New World, and that training far exceeded what the average colonial militiaman received. Those American soldiers did not always appreciate the disdain they received from British soldiers.[67] As for Washington himself, the war provided an opportunity to familiarize himself with the tactics and practices of the professional soldiers. He would copy those practices with his own Virginia regiment during the French and Indian War, just as he would later try to adopt those same practices when he was commanding the Continental army.[68]

The French and Indian War started poorly for the British regulars in North America. In 1755 General Braddock, a sixty-year-old British career military man with only European experience, led an expedition to capture Fort Duquesne, at the site of present-day Pittsburgh. Braddock lost decisively at the Battle of Monongahela and was killed in the fighting, along with five hundred other soldiers from the British side, while the French only lost a few dozen. Gage, one of the highest-ranking officers below Braddock, had helped organize the retreat—allowing Washington, who was also there, to survive as well.[69]

England would eventually dominate the fighting in North America and in Europe as well. The 1763 Treaty of Paris cemented England's place at the top of Europe's power heap. France had to renounce its North American territories. It would be the dawning of a new vision of the British Empire in the New World: one where the colonies would be better integrated into the empire, where there would be a standing army of ten thousand professional soldiers stationed in the colonies, and where the colonists themselves would pay a larger portion of the costs involved in maintaining those troops.[70] It was a vision that the British were never able to impose on the colonists themselves. And while the first disagreements between London and the colonists began over taxes, the issues would eventually turn to the soldiers stationed in the New World.

Ironically for the British, their victory in the French and Indian War would be the start of their undoing. Managing that much of an empire was beyond what London was capable of in the eighteenth century—and beyond what the English were willing to foot the bill for as well. What would ensue—and historians have covered this at length—was a series of proposed taxes on Britain's North American colonies, ensuing opposition from the colonists, then British measures meant to put an end to that opposition.[71] Starting with the 1764 Sugar Act, followed by the 1765 Stamp Act and its subsequent repeal the following year and then the 1767 Townshend Acts, the British tried to find new sources of revenue for their increasingly expensive colonies.[72] The colonists not only opposed the taxes; they also linked that opposition to arguments about the liberties that they, as British citizens, enjoyed. This dynamic made it impossible for the two sides to come to an agreement about British rule in the colonies. Parliament's Declaratory Act of 1766 stated that its North American colonies "have been, are, and of right ought to be, subordinate unto, and dependent upon the imperial crown and parliament of Great Britain." The government in London therefore had, in its own view, "full power and authority to make laws and statutes of sufficient force and validity to bind the colonies and people of America, subjects of the crown of Great Britain, in all cases whatsoever."[73] The colonists claimed for themselves a right to disagree, whether or not London agreed. It was, in the colonists' view, an attack on their identity as British citizens.[74]

If the laws on taxation offended one aspect of colonists' conception of themselves as British citizens, the laws concerning the colonies' new standing army offended another. This discontent was slower in manifesting, however. Colonists in most places did not immediately chafe at the standing army's newfound presence in North America.[75] The exception was the area around Boston. There colonists were particularly vocal in their opposition to the new British policies toward the colonies—both the taxation policies and the soldiers' increasing presence. Bostonians' opposition would lead the colonial government to station more soldiers in the area; those soldiers would in turn incite more opposition from the colonists.[76]

Five years before Lexington and Concord, the mutual animosity between the Bostonians and the British soldiers led to the 1770 Boston Massacre—a confrontation between British soldiers and the Bostonians that grew out of the daily tensions between the two groups. The soldiers had been stationed in the area for some time, but the Bostonians did not much like the soldiers, and many of the soldiers—trained to fight other soldiers, not to police civilians—were not always fond of the citizens. On 5 March 1770, the mutual animosity and name-calling gave way to a more heated confrontation. According to Captain Thomas Preston of the British army, the Bostonians—"the mob," as he called them—started calling out the soldiers with cries of "Come on you rascals, you bloody backs, you lobster scoundrels, fire if you dare, G-d damn you, fire and be damned, we know you dare not." A witness named Theodore Bliss saw "about 100 people in the Street." As tensions grew, Bliss "saw the People throw Snow Balls at the Soldiers and saw a Stick about 3 feet long strike a Soldier upon the right." Then, Bliss added, that soldier "sallied and then fired. A little time a second. Then the others fast after one another." Preston, too, mentioned that Bostonians began throwing snowballs and that the soldiers fired at them in retaliation. Whether or not Preston ordered them to do so was a matter of dispute at the time, though he denied having done so. Once the soldiers began shooting, according to Preston, "the mob then ran away, except three unhappy men who instantly expired."[77] The soldiers would kill five of those Bostonians (three died on the spot; two others died soon afterward from their wounds). Hence the title of "massacre," though as historical massacres go, this was on the mild side.

It was obvious to both sides that the confrontation grew out of the tensions between the Bostonians and the soldiers. In testimony afterward, Preston told the court that it was "a matter of too great notoriety to need any proofs that the arrival of his Majesty's troops in Boston was extremely obnoxious to its inhabitants." Preston's sympathies were with the soldiers; Bostonians, he complained, "have ever used all means in their power to weaken the regiments," while "constantly provoking and abusing the soldiery." In this context—wherein, according to Preston, "The insolence as well as utter hatred of the inhabitants to the troops increased daily," some sort of confrontation was all but inevitable.

The Boston Massacre, then, had grown not only out of opposition to British tax policies; it also grew out of opposition to British military policies. Bostonians did not like having the professional soldiers stationed in their town. It was at this point still a largely local phenomenon: in 1770, Virginians were not as likely to see their interests so closely tied in with those of Massachusetts.[78] But from 1770 to 1775 that would change. Bostonians continued to make their displeasure known, but they were joined more and more by colonists from New York, from Philadelphia, from Virginia. Case in point: the 1773 Boston Tea Party, in which Revere also participated, became a rallying point for colonists up and down the Atlantic Seaboard in ways in which the Boston Massacre had not.[79]

This was the context in which, as noted above, colonists themselves began upping their military training. Meanwhile, twelve colonies sent delegates to Philadelphia, where the first Continental Congress began meeting. In Virginia, still the most populous and influential colony, the royal governor was finding himself in as much trouble as his Massachusetts counterpart. Lord Dunmore, who had been in charge of Virginia since 1770, dissolved the House of Burgesses in 1774, only to find that its members continued to meet. Leading Virginians, including George Washington, along with his friend, neighbor, and long-time burgess George Mason, began organizing a militia that would be independent of the royal government. Dunmore was becoming as unpopular in Virginia as Gage—and Hutchinson before him—were in Massachusetts.[80]

But it was in Massachusetts that the fighting began.

The Battle of Concord itself was a short affair, as battles sometimes are, and a chaotic affair, as battles usually are. The fighting in Concord itself took only a few minutes. The general outlines were clear enough: the British arrived in the center of town, where the colonists charged them and forced them to retreat. Some of the other details would never be clear, and the debate over who shot first began almost as soon as the fighting did. The debate on that issue would be quite intense for quite some time. Josiah Adams, when he wrote about the battle sixty years later, particularly focused on establishing "that Americans were *killed*, at Concord, before they fired."[81] And while the salience of that argument has died since, the answer is no more certain.

By the time the colonists rushed the British soldiers, the British had already spent some time in Concord. The soldiers had even mingled some with the townspeople. Accounts after the fact would often mention the British officers who had eaten at a nearby tavern and insisted on paying for their food. Some other accounts pointed to soldiers who had gone beyond their intended goal and found ways to steal from people's homes in Concord. Though the people of Concord had had plenty of time to prepare for the fight and had done what they could to hide the various stores of ammunition and gunpowder there as well, the British still found some of them, as they had information from a spy who helped them. So while many of the stores remained hidden, the soldiers did find some supplies. Some of these the soldiers threw into the water. Others they lit on fire—the source of the smoke that the colonists saw rising up from the town and that some imagined came from the burning of houses.[82]

The key moment, though, was the fighting on Concord Bridge. Smith recalled an officer saying to the men, "'I haven't a man that is afraid to go,' and gave the word, 'march.'"[83] After the shooting began, one of the Massachusetts officers would yell out, "Fire, for God's sake fire!"[84] Whoever fired the first shot, soon both sides were shooting at each other. Several Americans were shot right away. Two of the British soldiers were also shot on that bridge. As one of Smith's fellow minutemen noted, "Two of the enemy were killed;—one with a hatchet, after being wounded and helpless. This was a matter of horror to us all. I saw him sitting up and wounded, as we had passed on the bridge."[85] It would lead to a second major question about the events of that day—whether or not that British soldier had been scalped.[86]

At that point the British began to take stock of their situation. Outnumbered and outpositioned, they chose to retreat. Many ran. Some of the colonists took up a position behind a nearby stone wall. There would be no second attack by the British that day, though the colonists too were at a bit of a loss as to what to do next. Smith noted that the soldiers who had been roaming through the town destroying military stores then "passed us without molestation." Smith would blame this on "our want of order and our confused state," as the colonists could easily have taken those regulars prisoner.[87]

At the end of the battle, the losses on the Americans' side were low. Two Americans, including one officer, died during the first round of shooting. The British casualties were also low, up to that point—"3 Men killed; 1 Sergt. and several Men wounded," according to a British officer who was there—but their troubles were just beginning. As they retreated along the same route they had taken to Lexington, they found themselves facing a countryside that had risen up against them. "After getting as good conveniences for the wounded as we cou'd, and having done the business we were sent upon, We set out upon our return," the officer wrote. But

> before the whole had quitted the Town we were fired on from Houses and behind Trees, and before we had gone a mile we were fired on from all sides, but mostly from the Rear, where People had hid themselves in houses till we had passed, and then fired; the Country was an amazing strong one, full of Hills, Woods, stone Walls, & c., which the Rebels did not fail to take advantage of, for they were all lined with People who kept an incessant fire upon us, as we did too upon them, but not with the same advantage, for they were so concealed there was hardly any seeing them: in this way we marched between 9 and 10 miles, their numbers increasing from all parts, while ours was reducing by deaths, wounds, and fatigue; and we were totally surrounded with such an incessant fire as it is impossible to conceive; our ammunition was likewise near expended.

The regulars' troubles calmed when reinforcements met up with them on the way back to Boston. They reached Boston that evening. "Thus ended this Expedition, which from beginning to end was as ill plan'd and ill executed as it was possible to be," the officer wrote.[88]

The battle was over. The war had begun.

From that point on, the British and the colonists would be at war with each other through the 1781 Battle of Yorktown and the subsequent peace treaty established US independence. The shooting was a point of no return. The following January, Thomas Paine wrote—not without hyperbole—that "no man was a warmer wisher for reconciliation than myself, before the fatal nineteenth of April 1775."[89] And though this may not have been immediately clear to the various colonists up and down the Atlantic Coast in April and May 1775, it would be clear by the time Paine wrote.

As battles went, Concord and Lexington were a big deal, but not because of the towns themselves, and not because of the British casualties—they were bad, but this was not the Battle of Cannae. The British government's military capacity was essentially the same after the battle as it had been before. The military supplies at Lexington and Concord had never been all that important to begin with—"a few trifling Stores," according to the British soldier quoted above.[90] Like many events, the importance of Lexington and Concord lay in the meanings people made of them. And those meanings had everything to do with the contrast between the citizen-soldiers of Massachusetts, on one side, and the professional soldiers on the other. The fighting began when American militiamen stood up to England's professional soldiers, just as their advocates had always said they would.

Militias, for that one shining moment, were everything that their advocates had claimed they would be. As shown in chapter 6, Andrew Fletcher had scoffed at the idea that "mercenaries would fight more bravely for the defence of other men's fortunes, than the possessors would do for themselves or their own."[91] And on this day, Fletcher was right. The colonial militia, which had persisted and evolved in North America out of practical necessity, was, on that day, what its ideological cheerleaders in Great Britain had claimed it could be. In that moment, in that event, the two roads heading toward the Second Amendment reconverged.

As shown in the previous chapters, starting in the middle of the seventeenth century, the history of militias in the British Atlantic had been evolving along two separate trajectories. In Britain, the theorists of the standing army controversy had created a philosophy and worldview that stressed the importance of militias and the dangers of standing armies. In that worldview, only a society where the citizens were soldiers, and where soldiers were citizens, could truly be free. Any standing army would enslave the population it was meant to defend. Those writers also believed that a citizens' militia was a better fighting force than a professional army and that men fighting for their homes and their families would defeat professionals fighting only for pay. Yet in Great Britain, those ideologies could not stop the decline of the militia there, nor could they stop the growth of England's standing army—which became the most powerful army in the Atlantic World. In Britain's North American colonies, meanwhile, the militia itself was a vital institution in which many men participated. Their reasons for doing so, however, were practical rather than ideological: the colonies were too poor, and too sparsely populated, to have a professional army. Even if the participation was never what it should have been, even if it caused its own problems, and even if its main accomplishments lay not in defeating foreign armies but in enforcing racial domination, the militia was a key part of colonial life. On one side of the Atlantic the militia thrived as an ideal even as the institution itself was dying. On the other side, the militia thrived as an institution but with few of the noble virtues its advocates claimed for it. The road to the Second Amendment had split, as it were.

In the 1770s those two roads began to reconverge. The colonists stepped up their training; they prepared themselves to put that militia into the field against a professional army. The colonists did not need to create a militia from scratch because the militia had always been there, and most of the men who participated could use whatever skills and training they already had. The colonists did not need to create their criticisms of the British soldiers from scratch, either; they had an entire tradition and legacy to draw on to justify their actions, to explain—to others, and to themselves—what they were doing and why they were doing it. That legacy was why the first Provincial Congress of Massachusetts not only complained of the soldiers' presence and the excess of taxation but also specified the threat of "the ravages threatened by the standing army."[92] That legacy was also why, when the first Continental Congress met in 1774, it called out the British government for "keeping a Standing army in these colonies, in times of peace"[93]—evoking the 1689 Bill of Rights, even though England itself had had a standing army ever since.

In the aftermath of Lexington and Concord, Americans would highlight the injustice of the British using professional soldiers, both before and during the fighting. The *Massachusetts Spy* wrote in its next issue about British regulars who, at Lexington, "unmolested and unprovoked wantonly, and in a most inhuman manner fired upon and killed a number of our countrymen, then robbed them of their provisions, ransacked, plundered and burnt their houses!" As for the colonists, the *Spy* reported, "We have pleasure to say, that notwithstanding the highest provocations given by the enemy, not one influence of cruelty, that we have heard of, was committed by our Militia; but, listening to the merciful dictates of the Christian religion, they breathed higher sentiments of humanity."[94] It would be a story that found a receptive audience: the evils of the professional soldiers, bent on destruction, against the goodness of an American people, forced to take up arms when needed but ready to return to their homes once the fighting was over. These same themes would reappear during the following years—eventually being written into the Constitution's Second Amendment. But there would be other steps before then.

The following summer, when Thomas Jefferson compiled the list of grievances that made up the bulk of the Declaration of Independence, he included the British having "kept among us, in times of peace, standing armies." It was a claim that Fletcher or Trenchard, or even Harrington, could have foreseen. Jefferson also attacked the British for "transporting large armies of foreign mercenaries" to North America—a criticism that even Machiavelli might have made. All of those forces served to "render the military independent of, and superior to, the civil power"—a topic about which British politics had been concerned since Parliament began debating jurisdiction over the militia in 1642.

One month before the Declaration of Independence, Jefferson's native Virginia issued its own Declaration of Rights—written, for the most part, by George Mason. Its thirteenth article declared "That a well regulated militia, composed of the body of the people, trained to arms, is the proper, natural, and safe defense of a free state; that standing armies, in time of peace, should be avoided as dangerous to liberty; and that, in all cases, the military should be under strict subordination to, and be governed by, the civil power."[95] This, too, was something that Fletcher or Trenchard could have written, and that stood as a direct intellectual heir to the writings of the standing army debate. Mason presented the militia not just as an institution with which he, as a colonist, had long been familiar but as the alternative to a standing army and a necessary one for a people who wished to remain free.[96]

Virginia was not alone in issuing some sort of bill or declaration of rights that year, and it was not alone in including some sort of statement that criticized standing armies and placed its trust instead in the militia and in an armed citizenry. Pennsylvania's Declaration of Rights that year included a similar article stating "That the people have a right to bear arms, for the defence of themselves and the state; and as standing armies in the time of peace are dangerous to liberty, they ought not to be kept up; And that the military should be kept under strict subordination to, and governed by, the civil power."[97] Also in 1776, North Carolina and Maryland included statements calling for an armed and organized citizenry rather than a "dangerous" standing army as a way of ensuring civil authority over the military. Even Vermont issued a similar statement in 1777, though it would not become a state until 1791.[98] These declarations were part a larger link in people's minds between the American cause and the traditional critique of standing armies—a link that would prove quite enduring. As James Martin and Mark Lender point out, there was a "mythology about the War for Independence" that emerged at Lexington and Concord, managed to survive through the war itself, and became key to the stories Americans told about the Revolution ever since. In this mythology, the American Revolution was a war fought by citizen-soldiers "reluctantly forced into war," where they had to face off against professional soldiers. The story, they note, has "just enough plausibility" to make it believable. But only "up to a limited point," because "the Lexington and Concord paradigm came apart quite early in the conflict."[99] In the summer of 1775, Congress created the Continental army and began filling it with men willing to enlist as full-time soldiers.[100]

For most of the Americans who participated in the Battles of Lexington and Concord, it would be the defining event of their lives. In the following years, enthusiasm for the war would decline in the towns, especially after the focus of the fighting shifted south. When the Continental army began demanding the towns meet a certain quota of soldiers, Concord struggled to meet its minimum. The men who fought, as in earlier wars, tended to be "landless younger sons" and "the permanent poor." Once the army began allowing them, Concord also sent African American men into the army.[101] Concord never fell short but did only what was required of it.

For Paul Revere, too, his nighttime ride was his moment in the spotlight, so to speak. He remained active during the war, becoming an officer in the Massachusetts militia. He saw little action, though, and what action he did see went poorly. He participated in a 1779 failed invasion of British Canada and resigned his post in the militia afterward. Thomas Gage had followed up his loss at Concord with a pyrrhic victory at Bunker Hill. After that he was relieved of his position and returned to England, where he lived out the rest of his life on his family's estate.[102] Samuel Adams and John Hancock would both remain active in politics—including representing Massachusetts in the Continental Congress. Both would go on to be signers of the Declaration of Independence—Hancock famously at the top, but both Samuel and John Adams were among the signers from Massachusetts. According to one account, Hancock may have expected the prestige to earn him the leadership in the Continental Congress and the command of the new Continental army. That position went, of course, to George Washington.[103] When Washington became the head of that army, he brought many of the beliefs he had held during the French and Indian War—including a preference for a well-trained professional army over a citizens' militia.

NINE

Hamilton, Madison, and Jay Publish *The Federalist* 1787–1788

On 15 March 1783, George Washington addressed a group of army officers in Newburgh, New York. It was a transitional moment in the Revolution. It had been over a year since the British surrender at Yorktown, but the two sides had not yet agreed on a peace treaty, and there was still sporadic fighting between the British and the Americans. The United States was no longer actively at war with England, but it was not quite at peace, either. The British still occupied New York City. The new US government was also behind in paying its soldiers—a frequent occurrence in European history and also a frequent cause of unrest, given that the complainants were armed, trained, and organized. Many American soldiers were beginning to doubt that the new government would make good on the pensions they had been promised. These fears were not limited to the rank and file either. In December 1782, the officers at Newburgh had written to the Congress, "We have borne all that men can bear—our property is expended—our private resources are at an end . . . the uneasiness of soldiers, for want of pay, is great and dangerous; any further experiments on their patience may have fatal effects."[1]

There was speculation at the time—and since—that some of those officers planned a military coup d'état in the young republic. Historians have debated how far the planning got and how serious the threat was. Some historians have speculated that the conspiracy was not intended to spur a successful coup but rather a failed coup that would in turn bolster calls for a stronger central government.[2] It was, in short, the sort of quasi event that in retrospect provides fertile ground for creative interpretations. But the officers were indeed angry—that much was clear—and so too were the soldiers. In early March, Washington wrote to Alexander Hamilton about the possibility of a conflict between the army veterans and Congress. "The predicament in which I stand as Citizen & Soldier," he wrote, "is as critical and delicate as can well be conceived—It has been the Subject of many contemplative hours." He sympathized with the "Sufferings of a complaining Army," and bemoaned "the inability of Congress & tardiness of the States" in paying the soldiers but hoped for a resolution—and that the "just claims of the Army" would win over Congress and the various state legislatures.[3] The following week, Washington was more pessimistic and worried that the officers were on the "precipice" of "plunging themselves into a gulph of Civil horror from which there might be no receding."[4] It was this impending crisis—or at least, the possibility thereof—that led Washington to address the officers on 15 March.

In his address, Washington warned the men about the dangers of "sowing the seeds of discord & seperation between the Civil & Military powers." He even warned that they might "overturn the liberties of our Country . . . open the flood Gates of Civil discord, & deluge our rising Empire in Blood."[5] His most memorable action during that speech, though, came during an offhand moment, saved for posterity in a description of Washington's address to the officers by one of the men there, which included this passage:

> One circumstance in reading this letter must not be omitted. His Excellency, after reading the first paragraph, made a short pause, took out his spectacles, and begged the indulgence of his audience while he put them on, observing at the same time, that he had grown gray in their service, and now found himself growing blind. There was something so natural, so unaffected, in this appeal, as rendered it superior to the most studied oratory; it forced its way to the heart, and you might see sensibility moisten every eye.[6]

Any threat those officers might have posed to the republic ended there. The officers involved were so moved—some wept—that any possibility of continuing to threaten Congress was gone. The "Newburgh Conspiracy" would not join the Battle of Concord or the Constitutional Convention in the list of key events in the founding of the republic, nor would it join Benedict Arnold's betrayal or Shays's Rebellion (about which more below) among the key threats of the era. Its greatest appeal for historians remains the anecdote itself, the humanizing touch of a historical icon and his relationship with those who had served under him. Even the historian who did the most to bring the Newburgh Conspiracy back into academic discussions claimed that it was important primarily "for what did not happen."[7] But it also remains worth noting for what it revealed. Most obviously, it revealed the extraordinary influence and charisma that Washington himself had at the time. During the earlier phases of the war, not everyone had been sure he was the best man for the job. As the war continued and the Americans gained the upper hand, those doubts had diminished. In the aftermath of Yorktown, Washington commanded the respect of both the nation and the army, in a way no one else could. But the problems that surfaced at Newburgh also revealed a more fundamental issue at work, as Washington himself recognized: "discord . . . between the civil & military powers"[8] a threat to any nation, was especially dangerous to a nation just starting out.

Hamilton shared Washington's concerns and, on these issues, shared his priorities as well. In his letters to Washington, Hamilton communicated his hope that Congress would pay the soldiers and his overall impatience with the situation. He attributed the difficulties in paying the soldiers largely to the problems of Congress. Hamilton was among those who thought that the United States' form of government at the time was not sufficient to the task of running the nation. But Hamilton also pointed out that "Republican jealousy has in it a principle of hostility to an army whatever be their merits," leading the government to not take seriously the demands of the men who had fought in the war. Still, he cautioned that "to seek redress by its arms would end in its ruin." All of this frustrated Hamilton to no end. "I often feel a mortification," he wrote, "which it would be impolitic to express, that sets my passions at variance with my reason."[9]

Hamilton had served in the militia early in the American Revolution and had some success doing so. George Washington then hired Hamilton as an aide de camp, allowing Hamilton to spend much of the war working for Washington, gaining the general's trust, writing letters on his behalf, and representing Washington in important missions. Even then, Hamilton was not satisfied; he wanted to command troops in the field instead of handling Washington's correspondence. Eventually Washington relented. Hamilton emerged from the Revolutionary War not only as one of Washington's most trusted associates but as one of the heroes of the Battle of Yorktown.[10] He also emerged from the war convinced that Congress was unable to sufficiently govern the United States. During the war he had dealt with the frustration of working with a Congress that would not—or could not—supply the army as Washington wished.[11]

Hamilton was quite different from the men who surrounded him. For one, while almost all had been born into wealth, and many were from families who held people as slaves, Hamilton had been born into poverty. Yet his background did not make him egalitarian and certainly not a defender of the rights of the people. Of all the leading revolutionaries, Hamilton was probably the least tempted by ideals of the republican tradition. He feared anarchy and wanted a strong government.[12] He would later write that for a republic to thrive it needed a strong executive power, pointing out that anyone "the least conversant in Roman history" knew the benefits of the dictatorship.[13] It was a reasonable point to make but one that few of his colleagues at the time would have been interested in making. So Hamilton was not a fan of the Articles of Confederation, which, with their large degree of state autonomy, kept the central state weak. Hamilton's views would put him among the nationalists during the 1780s—though "nationalist" meant something different then than it does now. Hamilton was one of those who sought a strong national government rather than keeping so much government power at the state level. "Every day proves more and more the insufficiency of the Confederation," he wrote in January 1783.[14] For Hamilton, then, the crisis averted at Newburgh was one more example of the need for a strong national government—one that would have been able to avoid such a situation by paying the soldiers in the first place.

Thomas Jefferson would later write of a somewhat similar event that occurred in Philadelphia a few months after the events in Newburgh that "there was indeed some disatisfaction in the army at not being paid off before they were disbanded, and a very trifling mutiny of 200 souldiers in Philadelphia."[15] A trifling mutiny indeed. Jefferson's comments did foreshadow what would be a recurring theme over the following decades; Jefferson was more willing to tolerate certain kinds of unrest and upheaval than were Hamilton or Washington.

The relationship between civil and military power—an issue that any society has to deal with, at least implicitly—had been a central issue in British politics off and on since 1642, when Parliament and King Charles I battled over control of England's militia. It would come back to center stage in the debates over a standing army in the 1690s. As colonial America evolved, such debates tended to be less central, especially with such a small government and an almost exclusive reliance on the militia. For most of the history of Britain's North American colonies, the militias flourished for practical reasons rather than ideological ones. And for most of the colonies' existence, there were relatively few professional soldiers there. The aftermath of the French and Indian War changed matters, bringing the now militarily powerful British government to station a permanent force in North America. That force's presence helped spur the American Revolution, which, in turn, Americans liked to portray as a battle between the citizens of the United States and the professional soldiers fighting on behalf of King George. But the War for Independence had led the Americans to form their own wartime professional army. As the fighting was winding down, and with the army in the process of decommissioning, the problem of the relationship between the military and civil authorities was again surfacing—this time, for reasons both practical and ideological.

The Newburgh Conspiracy was less than a decade after the Battle of Concord Bridge, but it might well have been in a different world, given all that the United States had been through during the time in between and all of the battles that its army had fought. The "militia-only" phase of the war was brief. The United States fought the war itself with the Continental army, far more than with the militias. The Continental Congress authorized the establishment of the Continental army in June 1775. Washington was pleased.[16] Not everyone else was. The following year, Samuel Adams warned that "a standing Army, however necessary it may be at some times, is always dangerous to the Liberties of the People. Soldiers are apt to consider themselves as a Body distinct from the rest of the Citizens. . . . Men who have been long subject to military Laws and inured to military Customs and Habits, may lose the Spirit and Feeling of Citizens." A militia, on the other hand, "is composed of free Citizens. There is therefore no Danger of their making use of their Power to the destruction of their own Rights, or suffering others to invade them."[17] American leaders were concerned about the dangers of "new modeling" of the Continental army, out of fear that it, too, would produce another man to continue the tradition of Caesar and Cromwell.[18]

Volunteers for the war were hard to come by after the initial surge—hence Thomas Paine's complaint in 1776 about the "summer soldier and the sunshine patriot" who would "shrink from the service of their country."[19] But it was Washington's viewpoint that won out in 1775 and would remain in place for the duration of the war—especially as militia contributions diminished and military service became primarily an affair of poorer Americans. Wealthier Americans largely stopped fighting after 1775. In the northern states, an increasing number of African Americans also joined the Continental army—a step southern leaders refused to take.[20]

English debates about the militia had always distinguished between professional wartime armies and standing peacetime armies. The 1689 Bill of Rights had set limits on "keeping a standing army within the kingdom in time of peace," and William III did not face opposition for wanting to have an army during wartime. It was his desire to keep that army after the Treaty of Ryswick that sparked the standing army controversy. So the Continental army, as a wartime army, was not out of line with the ideals of 1688, even if some of the most strident republicans opposed the idea.

From 1778 on, the standing army par excellence was fighting alongside the Continental army.[21] It was not the least of the Revolution's ironies that France's army—the army that descended from the one that Richelieu and then Louis XIV had built up, the army that had represented everything Fletcher feared and opposed—fought alongside the Americans in their war against England's own professional mercenary army. "What a miraculous change in the political world!" wrote Massachusetts politician (and future vice president) Elbridge Gerry. "The ministry of England advocates for despotism. . . . The government of France an advocate for liberty. . . . The king of England considered by every whig in the nation as a tyrant, and the king of France applauded by every whig in America as the protector of the rights of man. . . . Britain at war with America, France in alliance with her! These, my friend, are astonishing changes."[22]

The Continental Congress was in no position to decline the help—not that anyone wished to. As the war dragged on, Americans' idealism turned to pragmatism, if not fatigue. "By the spring of 1777," Martin and Lender note, "rebel leaders fully comprehended that troop quotas resting upon abstract notions of public virtue would go largely unfilled." In 1779, one general complained that citizens expected other Americans to display "Spartan virtue" while themselves "wallowing in all the luxury of Rome in her declining state."[23]

The war, then, was fought mostly by professional soldiers. On the English side was a combination of Britain's own professional soldiers and the "Hessians"—the roughly thirty thousand German soldiers the British government had hired to fight for them, and a smattering of activity from armed loyalists.[24] On the American side, too, the fighting came from professional armies—both American and French—though the militia continued to contribute. The militia fought well at times.[25] Its actions at the Battle of Saratoga helped turn not just that battle but the war itself. Its actions in the Battle of Camden (South Carolina), on the other hand, were disastrous; the militia fled from the battlefield and left the continentals to face the British on their own. There were many other examples of militias' worthy, and less worthy, contributions to the war effort, and historians have debated ever since how much the militias contributed to the Americans' victory; indeed, that debate did not need to wait for the historians; it began during the war itself. Washington criticized the militia from the start. In 1776, he wrote to Hancock, "The Militia instead of calling forth their utmost efforts to a brave & manly opposition in order to repair our Losses, are dismayed, Intractable, and Impatient to return. Great numbers of them have gone off; in some Instances, almost by whole Regiments—by half Ones & by Companies at a time," an example that risked infecting the rest of the army.[26] Washington's ideal army remained what it had been since the French and Indian War: a professionalized force, along the lines of the very army he was fighting against.[27] Hence his claim in that same letter that "no dependence could be put in a Militia or other Troops than those enlisted and embodied for a longer period than our regulations heretofore have prescribed" and his open advocacy the following year for conscription.[28]

If the militia was less than effective on the battlefield, that does not mean that it played no part in the Revolution. As shown in earlier chapters, the militia had always been at least as much of a domestic police force as it was a form of an external army facing a foreign nation. That continued to be true during the Revolution itself. Ever since John Shy's 1963 "A New Look at Colonial Militia," historians have focused on how the militia's main accomplishments during the Revolution took place away from the battlefield.[29] In the slave states, the militias continued to police the African American population. That task often took precedence over the Revolution itself, as traditional fears of slave revolts were now linked to a British policy of offering freedom to enslaved people who fought on the British side.[30] The militias also acted as a sort of politicized police force, ensuring that towns remained on the patriot side and fighting against loyalists.[31]

During the American Revolution, the militia was a multifaceted entity. In the shadow of Lexington and Concord, it remained the embodiment of the citizen-soldier ideal. The army's leaders viewed it as an unreliable aid (and times even a hindrance) to the war effort. Away from the battlefield, the militias remained what they had long been—an often effective if unpredictable and unstable domestic police force and, in the southern states, a way of policing the enslaved population. The years of fighting had shown most American politicians that they could not rely on it to win a protracted war. Die-hard defenders of the militias, though, could continue to see things in the light of the militias' few victories. The militias' strongest defenders could still take the position that men like Andrew Fletcher had taken and blame any shortcomings of the militia on society's lack of commitment to the cause of the citizen-soldier.[32] Americans of the day continued to see in the militia what they wanted to see.

Once the fighting began to wind down after the Battle of Yorktown, there was never a question that most—if not all—of the army would be decommissioning. The events at Newburgh had shown that that process might not go smoothly. Nor was it clear what would come next for the nation's military.

These questions formed the background to Washington's *Sentiments on a Peace Establishment,* discussed in this book's introduction. For Washington, unlike for some of his contemporaries, even during peacetime there should still be some permanent establishment. "Altho' a *large* standing Army in time of Peace hath ever been considered dangerous to the liberties of a Country," he wrote, "yet a few Troops, under certain circumstances, are not only safe, but indispensably necessary. Fortunately for us our relative situation requires but few." The bulk of *Sentiments* is, in fact, a detailed plan for a peacetime standing army for the United States, albeit one of only "a few troops." Washington hoped to be able to rely on trained long-term soldiers who had committed to a term of at least three years. Such a professionalized group would enable the United States to avoid delays in crucial moments, such as the time "which it would take to form an excellent body of Infantry from a well regulated Militia."[33]

As for that militia, Washington hoped to see it become more than it had been. Part of that was to propose a two-tiered system, relying more on "able-bodied young men" from eighteen to twenty-five who would be "the Van and flower of the American Forces," easing the reliance on those who, due to "bodily defects, natural awkwardness or disinclination, can never acquire the habits of Soldiers."[34] Washington's vision was something less than what the militia's most avid defenders had called for. There would be no multiyear training as Fletcher had proposed the century before. Washington's plan was based on the longer American militia tradition: a militia established on the limited means of the young nation. If anything, it hearkened back to the tradition of trained bands of Elizabethan England discussed in chapter 4. It was also based on the necessity, as he saw it, of acknowledging that other political leaders were wary of standing armies.

Washington was not fully on board with the long tradition of writers who, going back to the standing army controversy and beyond, believed that citizens made better soldiers. And yet even Washington—a man who was both the single most influential man in the United States at the time and was at best wary of the militia—had to spend time praising the militia. Having sought more than anyone to create a US Army on the model of the British army in which he had served at midcentury, and against whom he had fought in the Revolution, Washington would be unlikely to sing the militia's praises. Yet there he was, describing it as

> the basis of our system, that every Citizen who enjoys the protection of a free Government, owes not only a proportion of his property, but even of his personal services to the defence of it, and consequently that the Citizens of America (with a few legal and official exceptions) from 18 to 50 Years of Age should be borne on the Militia Rolls, provided with uniform Arms, and so far accustomed to the use of them, that the Total strength of the Country might be called forth at a Short Notice on any very interesting Emergency.[35]

As Washington had been critical of the militia during the war, his praise of it in the war's aftermath can look like cynical pandering or pro forma republicanism.[36] That he included it showed both how unfeasible it was for the United States to have a large standing army at that time and the relative consensus that the nation did need at least some form of active militia participation from a significant portion of the citizenry. Yet it was still not enough. His praise for the militia and the small size of the standing army he proposed could not convince the Congress that was running the United States at the time. The government followed none of Washington's recommendations. Congress initiated no permanent army during the 1780s. Nor did Congress take any measures to reform the militia itself—neither those that Washington had proposed nor those proposed by Henry Knox a few years later.[37] Alexander Hamilton led a committee of delegates who put together a different proposal, also calling for a small permanent standing army. Hamilton tried to argue around the limits that the Articles of Confederation presented in order to argue for a force that was both professionalized and national rather than relying on citizens from the different states.[38]

There were a variety of reasons neither Washington nor Hamilton could pass any such reforms. First, nothing in the Articles of Confederation authorized such a reform or, indeed, any kind of national reform of the thirteen different state militias, despite Hamilton's logical gymnastics. Beyond that, even after all that had happened during the Revolution itself, after the Continental army, along with troops from France's royal army, had won the war, the fear of standing armies was still strong. Washington knew as much, or else he would not have included the criticisms of large standing armies in his own call for a small standing army.

While the Revolutionary War had not borne out militia advocates' view that militias would outfight professional soldiers, other aspects of their criticism had turned out to be accurate. The army did grow to be a separate body, increasingly alienated from the rest of American society. Soldiers felt unappreciated by the society for whom they were fighting. They would at times loot surrounding areas, increasing any resentments toward them and in turn furthering the alienation they felt.[39] These tensions between an army and the citizenry as a whole were typical, but the tradition of republican thought that criticized not only permanent armies but also the professional soldiers themselves amplified that.

As the war wound down, the success of the Continental army did not lead men who had long advocated militias to overly rethink their views. The militia had won some battles; the professional army caused some problems in society (and had made taxes higher to boot). But the Americans did their best to move ahead. In 1784, the United States did develop a small force to patrol the western frontier. It consisted of fewer than a thousand men "for securing and protecting the northwestern frontiers of the United States . . . and for garrisoning the posts soon to be evacuated by the troops of his Brittanic majesty."[40] Those soldiers would be supplemented by nearby militia troops. Theoretically, it was the nation's first step toward a standing army; in practice, it had little impact on people's lives. If it was a potential tool of despotism, it was not a very good one. Those politicians who had wanted a stronger national government in the early 1780s continued to want a stronger national government as the decade wore on.[41]

As the United States transitioned from a collection of insurgent colonies to a new republic, the militia remained one of its key institutions. A belief in citizen-soldiers, a tradition of militia service, and a fear of standing armies were integral parts of the American identity going into the war; the shortcomings of the militia during that war had not dislodged them. As a result, the politicians who praised militias and criticized standing armies in the 1780s sounded a lot like the politicians who praised militias and criticized standing armies in the 1770s—and they did not sound that different from the men who had made those arguments back in the 1690s. In 1784, Gerry addressed the Massachusetts legislature and gave a speech that sounded many of the same themes that Americans had sounded in the lead-up to the war. "If we have no standing army," he said, "the militia, which has ever been the dernier resort of liberty, may become respectable and adequate to our defence . . . but if a regular army is once admitted, will not the militia gradually dwindle into contempt? And where then are we to look for the defence of our rights and liberties?"[42]

Beyond that, there were the tasks the militia had long accomplished and Americans could expect them to keep accomplishing. First among these was the policing of the enslaved population in the southern states. Second was the role that militias had always played along the frontier in interactions with Native American tribes. Third was the role that the militias had played during the Revolution, supporting the war effort, harassing loyalists, and keeping recalcitrant citizens in line. As in most other discussions of the militia, their advocates compared them to armies, but they had always been more effective as a police force, and they would continue to be one going forward. Which leads to their final role—and their most ambiguous one: that of suppressing domestic insurrections. The militias' difficulties in suppressing an insurrection in Massachusetts would prove the final spark to push American politicians to abandon the Articles of Confederation and create a new system with a stronger central government. The Articles of Confederation made it difficult for the national government to do much of anything; this would be a particular problem for dealing with military matters. At the start of the era of the United States living according to the Articles of Confederation, the Newburgh Conspiracy had shown that—it grew out of the inability of the nation to pay its veterans. Just a few years later, Shays's Rebellion, as that uprising came to be known, tipped the balance—convincing enough people in the United States that the articles did not provide a strong enough national government.

Some notes, then, on the Articles of Confederation themselves—and the extent to which they did, and did not, provide the United States with a workable government. The Continental Congress wrote the Articles of Confederation during the war and, at the time the Congress approved them, they provided a good model of republican government. The Articles reflected the ideals behind the 1776 Declaration of Independence, but in the 1780s, with the government running a real nation, the political leaders were finding that a "firm league of friendship" was not enough.[43] As the problems at Newburgh and at the "very trifling mutiny" showed, they would have to tackle the problem of governing the new nation at the same time as they handled demobilization. More than 200,000 men had served in the Continental army over the course of the war. Keeping these men—or, for those who died in the war, the beneficiaries of their pensions—paid had always been a challenge for the national government, as had keeping them supplied and fed. The Articles of Confederation made it difficult for the central government to bring in revenue and, as a result, also made it difficult for the government to pay soldiers and veterans.[44]

The articles reflected republican principles, including the traditional criticisms of standing armies. There would be limits on what forces could be "kept up by any State in time of peace," to be "such number only, as in the judgement of the United States in Congress assembled, shall be deemed requisite to garrison the forts necessary for the defense of such State." The articles also stated that "every State shall always keep up a well-regulated and disciplined militia, sufficiently armed and accoutered, and shall provide and constantly have ready for use, in public stores . . . a proper quantity of arms, ammunition and camp equipage."[45]

These militias were state militias, not national ones. The articles gave control over these militias to the state governments, not the national government. Each state's militia was in many ways a remnant of the colonial militias from before the war. The requirement that states "keep up" these militias lacked any national enforcement mechanism. It was unclear, too, what the militia could be used for—or, at least, what the national government could use the militias for, as their regulations were contained not in the national laws but in the state constitutions, and the leadership lay with the governors. The articles did pledge each state to the "common defense" against "attacks made upon them," including from "some nation of Indians." In the case of domestic unrest, though, the national government's authority was less clear. Nor did the articles provide for any sort of enforcement mechanism across state lines.[46] This loose government structure stood in the way of any sort of reform along the lines that Washington, Hamilton, and Knox had proposed. As it would turn out, it also hamstrung the national government when it came to dealing with uprisings from within—including one that came just a few years after Washington had talked down the men at Newburgh.

In late August 1786, a veteran of the Revolutionary War named Daniel Shays led several hundred men into Northampton, Massachusetts. These men were "armed with guns, swords, and other deadly weapons," according to the governor, "with drums beating and fifes playing, in contempt and open defiance of the authority of this Government."[47] Like the men at Newburgh, they were men concerned about their financial well-being—though in this case, not about salary or pensions owed them, but about the debts and taxes they needed to pay. Unlike the men at Newburgh, Shays and his men had passed from planning to action and, in doing so, put the state government of Massachusetts into a very difficult situation.

During the war, Shays had been a successful soldier. He had fought in some of the most important battles that took place in the northern states—Lexington and Bunker Hill in 1775, then Saratoga in 1777, before being wounded in 1780 and returning to his farm. He had fought well enough to rise up to the rank of captain. At one point, the Marquis de Lafayette gave Shays a ceremonial sword as a way of recognizing Shays's accomplishments. Needing money, though, Shays sold it.[48] In the war's aftermath, Shays's financial complaints continued. Many of his neighbors in western Massachusetts shared those same financial problems, viewing themselves as the victims of the financial speculations of the wealthier Massachusetts men near Boston. Western Massachusetts became a hotbed of dissent against the state government, especially since Massachusetts itself was more aggressive in using taxation to pay off war debts than were some of the other states.[49]

As the men in the region pushed for a confrontation with the state authorities, Shays's military experience made him an obvious leader for the movement. By all accounts, Shays saw himself as more of a voice of the people than their leader; as a recent article points out, Shays "conceived of his role as a spokesperson for the collective opinions of the residents of Western Massachusetts." He wrote little, and when he did, he used the first-person plural, "we," portraying himself as a speaker for his community, not their commander. His critics chose to see in him a leader of an angry anarchic mob—or perhaps a would-be Caesar, ready to march on Boston itself—even if the chances of Shays taking power in Massachusetts were quite small indeed.[50]

Shays, then, was a very different man than Nathaniel Bacon had been, just as the Massachusetts of the 1780s was a far cry from the Virginia of the 1670s.

Still, much of Shays's Rebellion fit into the same American pattern as Bacon's Rebellion had over a century before. (It was a battle between the elites along the seaboard and citizens farther west. It was not based in hostility toward Native Americans as Bacon's Rebellion had been. By the 1780s, the areas most affected by Shays's Rebellion were far from the frontier.) Once again, armed white men rose up against their colonial—now state—government, the government was largely powerless to respond, and the surrounding community was either sympathetic to the insurgents or, at least, unwilling to take action against it.[51]

Three days after Shays and his men marched on Northampton, Massachusetts's governor issued a proclamation. "Insurgents have frequently embodied, and with a military force, repeatedly interrupted the Judicial Courts . . . the Government is held by them at open defiance; and that the laws are, in those Counties, laid prostrate." To handle the situation, the governor "ordered a part of the Militia to assemble in arms" to protect the courts, which Shays and his men had closed down.[52] But the Massachusetts government found itself facing the situation Governor Berkeley had faced: they were governing a population that was, if not exactly "poor"—the actual economic hardships faced by Shays and his followers remains a matter of some dispute—their economic situation was not what they were hoping for. Many were indebted. And of course they were armed. They were also trained. Many of them were even veterans of the Continental army.[53]

Shays's Rebellion showed the same tensions inherent in relying on the mi litia. The Massachusetts militia had been involved in Shays's Rebellion since before it was even clear that there was a rebellion—though, again, determining its exact role is not easy, given the way that the militia and the citizenry blended into each other. The men who followed Shays—like the men who followed Bacon—were members of the militia and brought with them their training and their weapons. In the case of Shays's Rebellion, they made a point of organizing themselves into regiments and going to great lengths to distinguish themselves from just being "the mob" that they were accused of being.[54] They were local men with an allegiance to their region, and their sense of region did not necessarily coincide with state boundaries. But state boundaries were what determined command over the militia. The Massachusetts governor could only command the Massachusetts militia, and when he ordered them to Springfield to suppress the insurrection, many men in the militia—again, as in Bacon's Rebellion—refused to fight against their fellow citizens.[55] Beyond that, nothing in the Articles of Confederation authorized anyone to send militiamen from one state to another to deal with domestic issues, nor did the national government have much of an army at its command that could act independently of state governments. The governor of Massachusetts had lost control of much of his state, and there wasn't much that either the state government or the national government could do about it. Washington wrote to Knox about the insurgency, warning that "if government shrinks, or is unable to enforce its laws; fresh manœuvres will be displayed by the insurgents—anarchy & confusion must prevail—and every thing will be turned topsy turvey in that State."[56] Another Virginia politician wrote to his own governor, complaining that

> here is felt the imbecility, the futility, the nothingness of the federal powers; the U.S. have no troops, nor dare they call into action, what is called the only safe guard of a free government, the Militia of the State, it being composed of the very objects of the force; neither can reliance be placed upon that of neighboring states: N. Hampshire has already shewn her kindred to revolters; Connecticut is not free from the infection; and, the Legislative Acts of Rhode Island, have discovered that an opposition to baseness, can be expected from no order of people there.[57]

Congress was eventually able to send troops to Massachusetts from neighboring states, though in order to do so it had to pretend that the problems stemmed not from domestic unrest but from an attack by Native Americans.[58] Wealthy businessmen from eastern Massachusetts were also able to pay men—mercenaries!—to help put down the uprising. In early 1787, those troops were able to put the movement down. The Massachusetts government regained control over the state; Shays himself went into exile in Vermont, which was going through its own series of uprisings.[59] Shays's Rebellion was over; its impact was just beginning.

Shays's Rebellion helped prove exactly what nationalists like Hamilton had been saying for years: the United States needed a stronger government. It was not by chance that the politics and practices of the American militia were at the center of the crisis. Like the Newburgh Conspiracy, Shays's Rebellion posed the question of the relationship between civil authority and military power. The threat of a standing army thwarting the will of the legislature was gone, at least for the time being—the United States had barely any permanent army at the time, not even one that could put an end to the rebellion. Instead, the nation seemed to be drifting toward anarchy, with the state militias unable to put an end to an insurrection that threatened the ability of either the Massachusetts government or Congress to get anything accomplished.

Shays's Rebellion had not been the only domestic unrest in the United States since Yorktown. Already in March 1782, a group of Pennsylvania militiamen had killed almost one hundred unarmed Lenape Indians, many of them children.[60] This event, which came to be known as the Gnadenhutten Massacre, had led to some outrage by political leaders but not to punishment for the perpetrators. There had even been some newspaper accounts that sympathized with the militiamen.[61] That event fit into its own tradition of American violence against Native Americans. When the Paxton Boys killed twenty Native Americans in 1763, even though those Native Americans were under the protection of the colonial government, Benjamin Franklin had called them a "disgrace of their country and colour" and "Christian white savages."[62] But they too would face no punishments—and often had the support of their communities, especially closer to the frontier. This kind of violence, between whites on the frontier and Native Americans, never led to the kind of reassessment that Shays's Rebellion had. When Shays led his men into Northampton, it was enough to push the balance to the side of those who, like Washington and Hamilton, wanted a stronger central government, and convinced a critical mass of political leaders that the Articles of Confederation did not provide the United States a sufficient form of government.

In May 1787, delegates from the colonies met again in Philadelphia. Soon—though this had not been the original goal of the meeting—those delegates began discussing how to replace the Articles of Confederation with an entirely new Constitution. This was no easy task. The men represented thirteen states used to making their own decisions and living by their own laws. In less than four months, though, the delegates emerged with the new Constitution—based largely on a plan written by one of the Virginia delegates, James Madison.[63] Madison was a Virginian like Washington and Jefferson—and a wealthy landowner and enslaver like them as well. He had been involved in revolutionary politics since 1775. The Revolution itself had not been a good fit for Madison's skills, though; he was a sickly man, smart and bookish, uncomfortable with public speaking. Madison was not an inspiring military leader, nor had he mastered oratory. Still, Madison was present when Virginia wrote its Declaration of Rights in 1776. He later served in the Continental Congress, where he found the lack of central power frustrating. When his term in the

Continental Congress was up in 1783, he returned to his estate in Virginia. As historian Jack Rakove writes, Madison's time back on his estate recalled Machiavelli's own return to his lands in 1512. Both men retreated reluctantly from public life to their own private lives, both men sought comfort and companionship in the writings of the ancient world, and both men asked how they could apply the lessons of the ancients to their own world.[64]

Madison would go on to be the fourth president of the United States, so to call him only a "man of ideas" would be inaccurate. Yet it was his ideas, and his ability to convince others that he was correct, that allowed Madison to rise to prominence in 1787. A recent biography of him begins by pointing out that there was "nothing flamboyant" about Madison, and that he seemed "incapable of fiery oratory."[65] But at the Constitutional Convention he established himself as the man of moment. He had spent years studying the history of politics and thought he knew what would give the United States the best possible constitution. As Rakove notes, Madison was "soft-spoken and unprepossessing" with "an aptitude for committee work." Still, "much of the history of the Convention can be written as the story of his efforts to persuade his colleagues that his diagnosis was accurate." He did not win all of the battles—including, most notably, his desire for both houses of the legislature to be based on proportional representation—but "when he was done briefing an issue, it was hard for anyone to avoid perceiving the problem in the terms he had used."[66]

Madison wanted the central government to be stronger. But only by so much. Madison was no Richelieu, and neither Washington nor his successors would be a Louis XIV—or even a William III. The president would not be a king and certainly would be no absolutist. The Constitution still shared powers between the national government and the state governments, and within the national government, the Constitution divided power between the government's different branches.

The United States would also remain a society where the state militias would be the main military institution. Those militias, meanwhile, would be largely—though not completely—as they had been before. For both practical and ideological reasons, the US Constitution did not include any attempt to establish a professional army, nor did it set up a two-tiered militia system. Politically, those had proved impossible. Instead, the Constitution maintained the state militias but established Congress's right to maintain a minimum level of standards binding for each state. It also allowed Congress to coordinate between these militias at a national level and gave the president the potential to play a primary role in directing militias that would have been impossible under the Articles of Confederation.

Under the Constitution, the president, as the head of the executive branch, would be commander in chief of the army and navy. He would also be the commander in chief of "the Militia of the several States, *when called into the actual Service of the United States.*"[67] This power would be controversial—it took away some of the state governments' authority over the militias, though not all of it. But the Constitution gave more power over the militia to Congress than it did to the president. It also gave the Congress the same ability to control funding for the army that the British Parliament had enjoyed since 1689. According to Article I, Section 12, "Congress shall have Power . . . To raise and support Armies, but no Appropriation of Money to that Use shall be for a longer Term than two Years."

The most controversial aspects of the Constitution's changes to the military revolved around Article I, Sections 15 and 16. These together make up the Constitution's "militia clause" (or "militia clauses"). Congress would now have the power "to provide for calling forth the Militia to execute the Laws of the Union, suppress Insurrections and repel Invasions; [and] To provide for organizing, arming, and disciplining, the Militia, and for governing such Part of them as may be employed in the Service of the United States, reserving to the States respectively, the Appointment of the Officers, and the Authority of training the Militia according to the discipline prescribed by Congress."[68]

These laws were an attempt to reconcile republican principles and the need for stability. In 1787 the United States stepped back from the extremes of the Articles of Confederation, but the new Constitution was still designed, in good British oppositional tradition, to ensure that military leaders would be under civil authority. For their critics, though, this article was a thinly veiled attempt to abolish the state militias; any national control over the militia would seem to be the equivalent of a peacetime standing army. This would be the debate between the two sides, from the ratification debates through the publication of *The Federalist* and the Constitution's eventual ratification. But before going into those, it is worth asking: What exactly did the militia clause do? And what was it intended to accomplish?

Again, the Constitution was written in the shadow of Shays's Rebellion. Massachusetts's inability to put down the rebellion promptly and the central government's inability to help had showed the weakness of the central government and the need to reinforce its power. The new Constitution put the national government in a better position to respond to such events in the future. By allowing Congress to call forth the militia, it offered the possibility that a state like Massachusetts could call on the help of neighboring states, should its own militia refuse to be a party to the suppression of the insurrection. This would indeed represent an improvement over the existing situation, and the events of the Whiskey Rebellion during the early 1790s, discussed in this book's epilogue, would bear this out. Yet in 1787 it was also one of the possibilities that most frightened the Constitution's opponents (about which more below). But from today's perspective, what is striking is not how much of a change this was but how little. There was still no significant professional or permanent force under the command of any of the governments, especially not the national government. The window for any possible permanent standing army along the minimal lines that Washington had called for in 1783 was closed.

As for how the Constitution could prevent a recurrence of Shays's Rebellion from happening in the first place, the answer was: it would not. For all of the insistence that Shays's Rebellion had spurred political leaders to embrace a stronger government, the factors that had allowed that rebellion to spiral out of the Massachusetts government's control remained in place. Nothing in the new Constitution protected Americans from their debts. And nothing prevented Americans from being armed. If anything—though the Constitution was not as explicit on this as many state constitutions were—those who counted as full citizens were required to arm themselves and to participate in their militia. But then many men who lived in the United States did not count as full citizens.

For all of the importance of Shays's Rebellion in spurring the Constitutional Convention, it was not a repeat of that kind of rebellion that most scared the men who wrote the Constitution. The men in the Constitutional Convention knew what the militias were, and they expected the militia to remain something along the lines of what it had always been. It was an event like the Stono Rebellion that scared the founders more—a fear that was stronger in the slave states but was by no means limited to them.[69] The Revolution had seen more unrest and resistance from enslaved people than had existed during the colonial era. Back in 1775, Virginia's royal governor Dunmore issued a proclamation promising that "all *indentured servants, Negroes,* or others (appertaining to rebels) *free,* that are able and willing to bear arms, they *joining his Majesty's troops.*" Jefferson would refer back to this proclamation in the Declaration of Independence, noting that the British government had "excited domestic insurrections amongst us."[70] Politicians would debate just how much they should tolerate domestic unrest when it came from white Americans. Thomas Jefferson, it should be noted, was somewhat of a dissenting voice on the response to Shays's Rebellion. Writing to Madison in January 1787 Jefferson included the Latin phrase "Malo periculosam, libertatem quam quietam servitutem" (I would rather have a disturbed liberty than a quiet slavery).[71] He would follow that up at the end of the year by noting, again to Madison, that "the late rebellion in Massachusetts has given more alarm than I think it should have done."[72] At the time, though, Jefferson was in Paris and unable to influence the events there much, beyond furnishing Madison with much of his reading material as he prepared his planned Constitution. But they were all unwilling to tolerate the idea of an enslaved people rising up. The Constitution did what it could to make sure that they would not have to.

The Constitution, by giving the national government the ability to call forth the militia, also ensured that, should there be another uprising by enslaved people, the federal government would be able to respond rather than leaving that responsibility only to state or local governments. This led northerners to worry that they would be forced to travel to the south to suppress slave uprisings there. There was even some fear that Quakers—pacifists and in large part abolitionists—would be forced to do so. None of this appears explicitly in the text of the Constitution, but then, that was par for the course when it came to the way the Constitution dealt with slavery, enshrining it into law while avoiding mentioning it by name. This pattern appears most infamously in Article I, Section 2, which referred obliquely to enslaved African Americans by distinguishing between the "whole number of free persons" and "three-fifths of all other persons." It was a phrase that everyone understood. As David Waldstreicher argues, the need to maintain slavery was the Constitution's great unwritten focus—its "curious silence." The authors studiously avoided mentioning slavery in the document, and thus "slavery would be protected by several interlocking provisions, but not mentioned explicitly."[73]

The southern states were dedicated to maintaining slavery. The northern states might not have wanted to maintain slavery, but they were not dedicated to abolition and, in any case, feared slave uprisings and did what they could to avoid them. And their approach to slavery helped shape their approach to the militia as well. The Constitution, by maintaining state militias, ensured that slave states would be able to keep their own militias in place, as a way of policing their enslaved populations. The men in the Constitutional Convention knew what the militias were. They knew that in the slave colonies of the South, those militias had served as slave patrols and would continue to do so as state militias in the new republic.

The Constitutional Convention's delegates finished writing the Constitution in September 1787. The immediate responses were mixed. Jefferson wrote to Madison that December, noting that while there was much he liked about the Constitution, there was also much he did not. The first shortcoming he listed was "the omission of a bill of rights" which would include protections for freedom of religion and the press, trials by jury, and "protection against standing armies," among other matters.[74] This would be one of the most common criticisms of the Constitution but not the only one. Within weeks, papers began printing the first major letters critical of the Constitution. These "Anti-Federalist" letters would soon appear in various newspapers from various authors, using pseudonyms like "Centinel" and "Federal Farmer" and, more tellingly, "Brutus," named after the Roman who had helped assassinate Julius Caesar, and "Cato," after Cato's letters and, beyond that, the Roman citizen who had killed himself rather than live under Caesar's dictatorship. These writers would lead a loosely (if at all) organized opposition to the new Constitution, based largely on the resistance to the Constitution's shift of power away from the state governments. There was a wide range of anti-federalist sentiment, though. Some wished to retain the Articles of Confederation and wanted the new Constitution rejected in its entirety; others only hoped to add a Bill of Rights to it.[75] The Constitution's militia clause was also the focus of much criticism from the Anti-Federalists.

It was at this point that James Madison and Alexander Hamilton teamed up with John Jay and, together, stated their case for ratifying the Constitution. For Madison and Hamilton, it was an extraordinary collaboration in what was to be only a short-term alliance. As a recent biography of Hamilton puts it, "People tended either to embrace Hamilton or to abhor him; Madison stands out for having alternated between the usual extremes."[76] By the early 1790s, when the rivalry between Hamilton and Jefferson began to define the nation's political landscape, Madison was on the side of Jefferson, his friend and fellow Virginian.[77] In the late 1780s, though, Hamilton and Madison both agreed on the need for a stronger central government. Together they produced the strongest statement of the principles and beliefs behind the new Constitution. Joining them—though only writing five of the essays—was Jay, a New Yorker like Hamilton who would go on to be the first Supreme Court chief justice. In 1787 Jay's most important experience was as the US secretary of foreign affairs, and that was the main subject of his essays.

They published the letters one by one, and at a very fast clip. The first *Federalist* appeared in newspapers in late October 1787 and announced the intention to "offer arguments to prove the utility of the UNION . . . by examining the advantages of that Union" and "the certain evils and the probable dangers, to which every State will be exposed from its dissolution."[78] By the start of April 1788, Hamilton, Madison, and Jay had published their first seventy-seven papers. The next eight would be published before the end of that summer, by which point all of the earlier papers were also available in book form. Like their opponents, they wrote under a pseudonym chosen from ancient Rome, Publius, one of the Romans who, according to Livy and Plutarch, joined together in 509 BC to overthrow Rome's monarchy and found the Roman Republic. It was a fitting pseudonym for men hoping to begin, rather than preserve, a republic. These letters—officially titled *The Federalist,* but often referred to as *The Federalist Papers*—provided the definitive response to the Anti-Federalists' criticisms.

The Constitutional Convention had decided that for the Constitution to become law, nine of the thirteen states would have to ratify it. Ratification was not a given.[79] The Federalists, led by Madison and Hamilton, were going to have to convince enough other Americans that the new Constitution would make the United States a better place. Part of that argument concerned Congress's ability to "call forth" the militia, as even that measure had drawn the ire of Anti-Federalists, who saw in any national regulations on state militias the seed of a standing army.[80] Just as the Revolution's causes were broader than just the presence of professional British soldiers in North America, so too, the debate over the Constitution was about more than just the militia. That larger debate went beyond what can be covered in this chapter. But the debates about the militia were central to the concerns that had helped spur the Revolution in the first place and had shaped the initial encounters at Lexington and Concord. Those debates would also help determine the kind of nation the United States wanted to be. The United States had identified itself as a citizenry in arms, fighting against a professional army that went so far as to hire foreign mercenaries. In the aftermath of that war, this American identity remained strong. So when the Anti-Federalists began criticizing the militia clause, they were able to draw on themes and ideals that went to the core of the beliefs that had led the Americans to fight in the first place.

The Constitution's "federalization" of the militia was a fairly moderate proposal from today's perspective, but this federal intrusion on what had been state institutions—and, before that, colonial institutions specific to each colony—was still a shift that the Anti-Federalists took seriously.[81] The Federalists defended the militia cause and often ridiculed their opponents while doing so. But looking only at the disagreements in this debate—and knowing how bitter those debates were at times—risks missing the forest for the trees. There was an enormous amount of agreement between the two sides, about the dangers of a standing army, the need for limits on the executive, and the importance of having a citizenry that contributed to maintaining some notion of public order. The two sides also agreed that the civil authorities needed to have control over military power. The questions revolved around how best to achieve that, and *which* civil authorities—the states or the federal government—should control the militia.

The authors of *The Federalist* positioned the Constitution's approach to the militia as a sort of realistic republicanism, suitable for a realistic republic. The United States would indeed rely on its militia, but *The Federalist* authors made it clear that they were not looking to re-create the societies of the ancient world. "Sparta was little better than a well-regulated camp; and Rome was never sated of carnage and conquest," Hamilton wrote.[82] Such a "nation of soldiers" was incompatible with the "industrious habits of the people of the present day, absorbed in the pursuits of gain, and devoted to the improvements of agriculture and commerce."[83] Beyond that, they were not interested in "the deceitful dream of a gold age." Nor were they interested in the "reveries" of "political doctors,"[84] or "a zeal for liberty more ardent than enlightened,"[85] let alone "the inflammatory ravings of incendiaries or distempered enthusiasts."[86] In other words, their opponents were dreamers with unrealistic goals; the Federalists hoped to set up a more realistic society. And while Fletcher and his friends had argued that soldiers made better citizens due to the discipline they learned while training, Hamilton told his readers that "the scheme of disciplining the whole nation must be abandoned as mischievous or impracticable."[87] The government needed a way to enforce its law and to protect against invasions, but it had to accept that relying on "governing at all times by the simple force of law (which we have been told is the only admissible principle of republican government)" would not work any better in the future, than it had in addressing Shays's Rebellion.

As for that rebellion, Hamilton, Madison, and Jay got all the mileage they could out of the threat Shays's insurrection had posed to the United States. It had taught the nation "how little the rights of a feeble government are likely to be respected, even by its own constituents. And it teaches us, in addition to the rest, how unequal parchment provisions are to a struggle with public necessity."[88] And as badly as things had gone in Massachusetts, Hamilton warned, "Who can determine what might have been the issue of her late convulsions, if the malcontents had been headed by a Caesar or by a Cromwell?"[89]

In other words, the Articles of Confederation had not done a good enough job at providing peace and stability to the United States over the last few years, and matters would only get worse going forward. Hamilton, Madison, and Jay were unwilling to chase after unrealistic dreams of a rejuvenated citizenry, and they were also unwilling to look past the militia's recent shortcomings. Responding to the idea that "the militia of the country is its natural bulwark, and would be at all times equal to the national defense," Hamilton responded that "the facts which, from our own experience, forbid a reliance of this kind, are too recent to permit us to be the dupes of such a suggestion. The steady operations of war against a regular and disciplined army can only be successfully conducted by a force of the same kind." In other words, they rejected the claim that the militia's strongest advocates had made—going back to Machiavelli—that the motivations of part-time soldiers defending their homes and their families would allow them to defeat better-trained professional soldiers fighting only for money. While during the war, militias did show their valor on "numerous occasions," for Hamilton "the bravest of them feel and know that the liberty of their country could not have been established by their efforts alone, however great and valuable they were."[90] The key, for matters both internal and external, was to establish a unified force able to maintain order on the national level—but not so powerful that it would go on to oppress the people. As Jay put it, the nation needed "security for the preservation of peace and tranquility, as well as against dangers from FOREIGN ARMS AND INFLUENCE, as from dangers of the LIKE KIND arising from domestic causes."[91] Hence the Constitution's plan, which *The Federalist* defended, to "place the militia under one plan of discipline, and, by putting their officers in a proper line of subordination to the Chief Magistrate, will, as it were, consolidate them into one corps, and thereby render them more efficient than if divided into thirteen or into three or four distinct independent companies."[92] This was the arrangement that Hamilton, Madison, and Jay defended. Their answer was not the idealistic approach of a Fletcher or a Trenchard or of the more radical of the Anti-Federalists.

And yet the Federalists still shared the concern that military forces that were too strong would "bear a malignant aspect to liberty."[93] The questions at the base of their proposal were still the same: How can a society defend itself without being threatened by its defenders? How can a society maintain its systems of domination without creating a force capable of turning on those who had created it? In arguing against the Anti-Federalists, Hamilton, Madison, and Jay took the side of a stronger government and a more regimented militia. But they accepted the same overall frame of the debate, which saw risks in a military that was too strong. Between the Federalists and the Anti-Federalists, it was a matter of degree: the Federalists were more willing to err on the side of a stronger military, but only in comparison to their political opponents. They agreed with their opponents on the dangers of standing armies, and, therefore, on the need for citizens to participate in the militias. Strengthening the national control over the militia, rather than being the crypto-standing army its critics claimed, was the best way to prevent Americans from needing, or even desiring, a standing army.

The key passage came in *The Federalist* 29, where Hamilton wrote,

> If a well-regulated militia be the most natural defense of a free country, it ought certainly to be under the regulation and at the disposal of that body which is constituted the guardian of the national security. If standing armies are dangerous to liberty, an efficacious power over the militia, in the body to whose care the protection of the State is committed, ought, as far as possible, to take away the inducement and the pretext to such unfriendly institutions. If the federal government can command the aid of the militia in those emergencies which call for the military arm in support of the civil magistrate, it can the better dispense with the employment of a different kind of force. If it cannot avail itself of the former, it will be obliged to recur to the latter. To render an army unnecessary, will be a more certain method of preventing its existence than a thousand prohibitions upon paper.[94]

National authority over the militia, which their opponents criticized as a nascent standing army, instead became the best way to prevent the United States from needing a standing army. It was a choice between an armed citizenry organized into a militia on one hand and a professional standing army on the other. The Federalists chose the militia.

And while Hamilton rejected the idea of "disciplining" the entire citizenry, he did tie in the militia to the role that writers had been giving it—that of the protector of the people's liberties. "Let a regular army, fully equal to the resources of the country, be formed," he wrote, "and let it be entirely at the devotion of the federal government; still it would not be going too far to say, that the State governments, with the people on their side, would be able to repel the danger."[95] Any army that the government formed, meanwhile, would find itself facing

> a militia amounting to near half a million of citizens with arms in their hands, officered by men chosen from among themselves, fighting for their common liberties, and united and conducted by governments possessing their affections and confidence. . . . Besides the advantage of being armed, which the Americans possess over the people of almost every other nation, the existence of subordinate governments, to which the people are attached, and by which the militia officers are appointed, forms a barrier against the enterprises of ambition, more insurmountable than any which a simple government of any form can admit of.[96]

The Federalists did not endorse insurrections, any more than the Constitution they were defending did. The Constitution's militia clause made that clear: the role of the militia was to "suppress Insurrection." Nothing in *The Federalist* changed that. Hamilton did note that "if the representatives of the people betray their constituents, there is then no resource left but in the exertion of that original right of self-defense which is paramount to all positive forms of government." Should such an action become necessary, though, it would be the right of the people "through the medium of their State governments, to take measures for their own defense."[97] Should there ever be a situation where a national government fielded a professional army and set it against the citizens, those citizens would not only have their weapons, training, and hierarchy in place; they would also have state governments to lead them.

This was the vision of the nation, the militia, and the citizenry that the Federalists put forth in 1787–88. Like everything in the United States, this vision was in some senses new, while still building on the traditions of colonial society. The idea of sharing power between national and state governments would take some thinking through. Harrington and Fletcher had had a vision of power in the hands of the nobility, limiting the power of the Crown; in *The Federalist,* things shifted—power would be shared between the states and the national government. State governments, with their militias, would remain in place as the protection against an overly aggressive central government. The situation they did endorse, though, was all but guaranteed to be unstable. The Federalists rejected the possibility of disciplining the entire population, which they considered to be unrealistic. But they also embraced a vision of citizenry "little, if at all, inferior to [an army] in discipline and the use of arms, who stand ready to defend their own rights and those of their fellow-citizens."[98] The result would be that for the most part, US militias would remain what they had been during the colonial era.

In other words, rather than focusing only on the disagreements between the Federalists and their opponents, it is worth highlighting the agreement between the two sides. The terms of the debate no longer concerned the viability of a standing army, as they had in 1783. The moment for the US Constitution to embrace or endorse even a small standing army had come and gone. The success of the Continental army in the war, the shortcomings of the militia in that same war, the personal prestige that Washington had put behind his plan for a "Peace Establishment"—none of those had been enough to make the United States abandon its fear of standing armies. The problems Shays's Rebellion had posed led the authors of the Constitution to find new ways to suppress any sort of repetitions of such an event—but a professional military force would not be one of them.

In July 1788, Alexander Hamilton wrote what would be the penultimate issue of *The Federalist.* There he brought up one of the earliest and strongest criticisms of the Constitution and the first one that Jefferson had pointed to in his letter to Madison: the lack of a Bill of Rights. For Hamilton, the Constitution did not need such a bill. England's 1689 Bill of Rights, Hamilton wrote, had been an agreement between the king and the people, like the Magna Carta had been. There was no need for such an agreement in a Constitution "founded upon the power of the people, and executed by their immediate representatives and servants." Adding one, he added, would be "not only unnecessary . . . but would even be dangerous."[99] In Hamilton's argument, there was no reason to prevent the federal government from doing things it had no power to do in the first place. Read charitably, Hamilton was giving the states more power in the new Constitution than his opponents were, by pointing to the many state bills of rights and the limits of the national government. Read less charitably, it was just sophistry from Hamilton, a way of telling his opponents that what was in fact happening was not what was happening. It was, in any case, a lost battle for Hamilton—but only part of a much larger war that the Federalists won. In December 1787, before Hamilton, Madison, and Jay had written a third of their essays, Delaware became the first state to ratify the Constitution. By June 1788, as Hamilton was writing his argument against a Bill of Rights, nine states had ratified it. The Constitution was now the law of the land. Virginia would soon follow. The new government began meeting in early 1789.

Even then, not everything was settled. Many of the states had suggested additions and alterations to the Constitution, including Virginia. Yes, the Federalists had won, but not all of the Anti-Federalists had lost. Again, among the opponents of the Constitution, some wanted it rejected in its entirety; others only hoped to add a Bill of Rights.[100] Those hoping for rejection had lost. Those hoping for the addition of a Bill of Rights, though, were still very much in the game. They also had a new player on their team. After the Constitution was ratified, James Madison ran for a seat in the new House of Representatives. As part of his platform, he announced that he, too, supported adding a Bill of Rights.[101] This would allow him again to take center stage in the process of writing and shaping the laws of the United States. The road to the Bill of Rights—and, with it, the Second Amendment—was approaching its end.

TEN

Congress Amends the Constitution
1789–1791

THE GEORGE Mason who wrote Virginia's Declaration of Rights was one in a long line of George Masons. In 1827, James Madison received a letter from another of those Georges—a young man trying to learn about his grandfather and seeking out those who, like Madison, had known him. By that point, Madison himself was in his mid-seventies. The eight years he served as president had ended a decade earlier. The George Mason with whom Madison had served in both Virginia and national politics was twenty-five years older than Madison and had died in 1792. Madison offered what information he could to the grandson. He started out by noting that it was a shame that "highly distinguished as he was," Mason seemed to have left fewer traces "than of many of his contemporaries, far inferior to him in intellectual powers, and in public services."[1] Madison's point was a valid one. Both of the men had been prominent Virginia politicians at a time when Virginia had been the most important of the colonies and then the most important state of the new republic. Many of Virginia's leading politicians—including Madison, but also including Washington, Jefferson, and others—had parlayed their prominence in Virginia politics into a leading role in national politics. Mason's focus remained on Virginia. He had even opted against serving in the Continental Congress, despite the urging of his fellow Virginia politicians.[2]

Madison went on to point to two occasions during which he had worked with the elder Mason. The first was the 1776 Virginia Convention in Williamsburg. "Being young & inexperienced, I had of course but little agency in those proceedings," Madison wrote. But he added that "I retain however a perfect impression that [Mason] was a leading champion for the Instruction; that he was the Author of the Declaration as originally drawn, and with very slight variations adopted." The second occasion would come eleven years later at the Constitutional Convention. Of that, Madison wrote,

> The public situation in which I had the best opportunity of being acquainted with the genius, the opinions, and the public labours, of your Grandfather, was that of our co-service in the Convention of 1787, which formed the Constitution of the U. S. The objections which led him to withold his name from it, have been explained by himself. But none who differed from him on some points, will deny that he sustained, throughout the proceedings of the Body, the high character of a powerful Reasoner, a profound Statesman, and a devoted Republican.[3]

These were, perhaps, overly polite words that an older man might use to describe a younger man's grandfather. George Mason had been one of only three men who served as a delegate to the Constitutional Convention and then refused to sign the Constitution. Mason had argued against the Constitution on a number of grounds. Like Jefferson, Mason wanted the Constitution to include a Bill of Rights and like Jefferson, thought it had insufficient protections against a standing army. Unlike Jefferson, Mason had participated in the Convention itself.

Mason also went on to argue against the ratification, putting him head to head against Madison in the heated debates of Virginia's Ratifying Convention. Though Mason lacked the prickly offensiveness of his fellow Anti-Federalist Patrick Henry, also a participant in Virginia's Ratifying Convention, he and Madison had still been leading men on opposite sides of a heated debate. As Mason's biographer writes, the defeat was "bitter" for Mason, who, "always disdainful of ordinary politics . . . had none of the ambitions that might have tempered his resentments."[4] It seems hardly by chance that Madison left out of his letter any discussion of Virginia's ratification debates at which Mason and Madison had squared off.

The younger Mason's query was decades later, of course. Men who had fought against each other in the political sphere during previous decades, provided they had not shot each other, had had plenty of time to move past any lingering grudges from the founding era. John Adams and Thomas Jefferson had been friends, then bitter rivals, then ended their lives as friends again.[5] But Madison's fond recollections—"his conversations were always a feast to me"—also pointed to the significant overlap between the two men, who shared much in their outlook, politics, and philosophy. Both men were republicans who saw the risks of an overly powerful executive, and both agreed that a standing army, in the hands of that executive power or in the hands of its generals, was a threat to civil society.[6]

Both men were also slave owners. And while each claimed to have various misgivings about the institution of slavery, neither man was eager to see enslaved people stockpiling weapons and ammunition or holding musters, let alone rising up against their enslavers.[7] Quite the contrary. Theirs was a vision of a republic that would serve the interests of white citizens and would clamp down on violence from enslaved African Americans, free blacks, and Native Americans. They only disagreed on some of the means to put their republic into place and to safeguard it. It was a debate on how to reconcile liberty—for some—and stability. In the debates of the 1780s, some leading politicians were more willing to err on the side of stability and order; others were more willing to err on the side of liberty, even if that meant that the society would be less stable. These were differences of degree, and once the heat of the debate was over, it was possible to look back on the points on which they had agreed—hence Madison's fond recollections of those debates decades later. The overlap between their positions would help shape history. The Bill of Rights, including the Second Amendment, was built on the work of both men. It started with the work that Mason had done in the 1770s and then moved on to Madison's use of Mason's earlier work to write the first drafts of the Bill of Rights.

Mason's leading role in writing Virginia's Declaration of Rights at the Virginia Convention of 1776 is well established. Fearing that his colleagues would come up with "a Plan form'd of heterogenious, jarring & unintelligible Ingredients," Mason took charge of the writing process and came up with a plan that, according to another of the politicians who was there, "swallowed up all the rest, by fixing the grounds and plan, which after great discussion and correction, were finally ratified."[8] The declaration's sixteen articles were a classic statement of the colonists' beliefs as they started on the road to independence, generally consistent with the ideas in England's 1689 Bill of Rights but also showing the influence of eighteenth-century ideas about inherent rights and religious freedom.[9] Thirteen years later, Madison used Virginia's Declaration of Rights as the framework for the draft of a Bill of Rights that he presented to Congress in June 1789.[10] Madison's draft, in turn, formed the basis for the twelve amendments that Congress sent out for ratification in September 1789.

The ten of those amendments that were ratified over the following two years became the Bill of Rights that is still in place today.

The Virginia Declaration of Rights was a broader document than the Bill of Rights would wind up being. As Rakove writes, "Madison's project of 1789 was to compile a list of restrictions on the powers of the national government. By contrast, Mason's purpose was to define the duties of the republican citizens of Virginia, and in so doing, to describe who they were as a people." As a result, Mason included "deeper purposes that would today seem entirely out of place in a constitutional text,"[11] such as statements about the relationship between the different branches of the government and philosophical statements about the nature of government, including the community's "unalienable right to . . . abolish it" should that become necessary.[12] But even the most superficial reading of the Virginia declaration would show the overlap between Mason's goals in that document and the goals that Madison brought into his first draft of the Bill of Rights and the way that Madison adopted specific articles from Virginia's declaration. Both guaranteed the freedom of the press and some form of freedom of religion; both guaranteed citizens the right to a trial by jury and the protection from arbitrary laws. And, of course, both placed the onus for the society's safety—"defense" in the Virginia declaration, "security" in the Bill of Rights—on the people. Mason's phrasing in the Virginia Declaration of Rights is especially useful for seeing the ideas behind the Second Amendment's later formulation—which was both more concise and, at least in today's world, more enigmatic. Mason's wording also showed more clearly the links between the "well regulated militia" and the tradition of criticisms of the standing army that go back to the writers of seventeenth-century Britain. Again, the full article reads, "That a well regulated militia, composed of the body of the people, trained to arms, is the proper, natural, and safe defense of a free state; that standing armies, in time of peace, should be avoided as dangerous to liberty; and that, in all cases, the military should be under strict subordination to, and be governed by, the civil power."[13] As shown in chapter 8, it was an article that Fletcher or Trenchard themselves might have written. It insisted on the civil authorities' ability to control the military. It accomplished that by insisting that the people themselves be both armed and trained—allowing the colony to avoid having a peacetime army. It did not go as far as some of the British theorists did—there is no statement there that soldiers make better citizens or that citizens make better soldiers—but Mason's formulation still advocated that any military obligations would fall to citizens who served as part-time soldiers rather than to the professional soldiers of a part-time army.

Nothing in the Constitution that Madison and the rest of the Constitutional Convention had just written contradicted any of this. But the Constitution, as it first became the law of the land, did not guarantee any of this either. It established that there would be a militia, and it gave the legislature—not the executive—control over any funding for a national military. But for many leading critics of the Constitution, that was not enough, nor were they comfortable with any level of national control over what had been distinct and separate colonial institutions before 1775 and had remained separate state institutions under the Articles of Confederation.

To understand the Anti-Federalists' criticisms of the Constitution's militia clause, but also to understand what Madison and Mason did and did not agree on, it is worth looking at the event where the two men squared off on that very issue: Virginia's Ratifying Convention, which began in June 1788. By that time, eight states had already ratified. With one more, the Constitution would become law. Virginia, though, was not just any state; its ratification was important for the nation, and for many of its leaders, starting with George Washington himself. But the Virginians leading the arguments against ratification were influential men—starting with Mason and Patrick Henry—and it would not be an easy fight for either side.[14] Much of the debate lay beyond the scope of this book. Still, the arguments about the future of the militia, the fear of a standing army, and, beyond that, the question of a Bill of Rights, led straight to the heart of the disagreements between the supporters and opponents of ratification.

What, then, did the Anti-Federalists find to criticize about the Constitution's militia clause? Henry complained that the militia clause amounted to a "mutual concurrence of powers" between the national government and the state governments that would "carry on into endless absurdity." Henry had twice been governor of Virginia and had been involved in revolutionary politics as long as anyone. And he was an advocate of the militia, which he called "this great bulwark, this noble palladium of safety," and "our ultimate safety. We can have no security without it."[15] Henry worried that the dual command over the militias would lead to confusion and contradictory obligations. It was here that Henry said, "The great object is, that every man be armed." His point in that sentence was to prevent the confusion that would follow from requirements that militiamen would be subject to both state and federal regulations—a situation that, he speculated, would lead to "two sets of arms, double sets of regimentals, &c.; and thus, at a very great cost, we shall be doubly armed,"[16] even though previous efforts at arming all citizens had consistently fallen short. The objection seems strange in retrospect—but the idea of Federalism, and of shared authority between state and national governments, was something the United States was still thinking through. Henry opposed ratification, period. "Who authorized them to speak the language of, *we the people*," he asked, "instead of *we, the states?*"[17] In asking that question, Henry went to the very foundation of the Constitution itself.

Mason's views were less extreme. He was willing to accept some sort of new Constitution, just not the one that the convention had produced.[18] Many of his criticisms revolved around the lack of a Bill of Rights along with his disagreements with the Constitution's militia clause. For Mason, the Constitution's militia clause provided insufficient means to prevent the establishment of a standing army. Mason was not alone in this fear. There were a few scenarios that Mason and other Anti-Federalists proposed that might lead from the new Constitution to a standing army on American soil. In one, the federalized militia became, for all intents and purposes, a standing army. By sending the militia from one state to another, the national government could, according to one Maryland writer, "send the militia of Pennsylvania, Boston, or any other state or place, to cut your throats, ravage and destroy your plantations, drive away your cattle and horses, abuse your wives, kill your infants, and ravish your daughters, and live in free quarters."[19] In the other scenario, the national government would institute polices determined to undermine the militia. Mason also speculated that the national government could "render the service and use of militia odious to the people themselves—subjecting them to unnecessary severity of discipline in time of peace, confining them under martial law, and disgusting them so much as to make them cry out, 'Give us a standing army!' "[20] In another version of that scenario—which Henry alluded to—the national government could maneuver the militia into such a state of neglect that the people would no longer have sufficient arming and training to be able to accomplish the tasks required of a militia, thereby artificially creating a need for a professional army where none had previously existed.[21]

In his responses, Madison disputed Mason's claims that the new Constitution threatened the militia, along with Henry's view that the dual authority would pose a threat to the militia. "I cannot conceive," he told the other deputies, "that this Constitution, by giving the general government the power of arming the militia, takes it away from the state governments. The power is concurrent, and not exclusive." He also stated that

> I most cordially agree . . . that a standing army is one of the greatest mischiefs that can possibly happen. It is a great recommendation for this system, that it provides against this evil more than any other system known to us, and, particularly, more than the old system of confederation. The most effectual way to guard against a standing army, is to render it unnecessary. The most effectual way to render it unnecessary, is to give the general government full power to call forth the militia, and exert the whole natural strength of the Union, when necessary.[22]

In other words, for Madison the way to prevent a standing army was to make sure that the state militias remained strong. That was best done at the national level. Madison justified the "federalization of the militia" in this argument as the best alternative to a standing army. It was one more sign of the enormous unpopularity of standing armies at the time.[23]

Madison's arguments were not enough to satisfy Mason or Henry, but he and his fellow Federalists won the day. In late June Virginia's Ratifying Convention voted to ratify the Constitution. It was the tenth state to do so. New York would soon follow.[24] Virginia would be a full and willing member of the United States—and a leading member at that. It would go on to provide five of the first six presidents. Still, things were not fully settled. As discussed in the last chapter, the ratification of the Constitution did not mean that there would be no additions made to it. While the Constitution that the states ratified in 1788 was far enough from his principles that Mason refused to sign it, he would live to see a Constitution that, once amended with the Bill of Rights, showed his influence.

The idea of a Bill of Rights for the entire United States had come up during the writing of the Constitution itself and then later during the ratification debates. Given the existence of state bills of rights, and the legacy of England's 1689 Bill of Rights, such a complaint had made sense—and was not limited to ardent Anti-Federalists. By the time Congress first met in 1789, there was real momentum for a Bill of Rights. Several states that ratified also proposed amendments or modifications to the Constitution, including Virginia and New York. North Carolina's Ratifying Convention, which met after Virginia's, declined to ratify but instead called on Congress to add a "Declaration of Rights" and

"Amendments to the most ambiguous and exceptional Parts of the said Constitution of Government" before it would ratify.[25] Five of these states included proposals about the issues that the Second Amendment would eventually address. All five included language criticizing or calling for limits on standing armies. Four states declared that the "well regulated militia" was the "proper, natural and safe defence of a free state." Four of these states also recommended that the amendments guarantee the people's right to keep and bear arms.[26]

It was clear, then, that many Americans—including supporters of the Constitution—wanted it to be amended to have a Bill of Rights.[27] It was also clear that one of those amendments would concern the militia. By the time Madison returned from the Constitutional Convention to his home state of Virginia, it was clear to him as well. He had a few motives in this, not least that he felt endorsing the idea of a Bill of Rights would help him get elected to the House of Representatives, where he could play a role in shaping those amendments.[28] On both of these counts, Madison succeeded. He was elected to the House of Representatives, and in March 1789 he headed north to New York City where the US Congress first met.

In June of 1789, Madison addressed Congress and called for amendments to be added to the Constitution, including those that would repeat the rights guaranteed in various—though not all—state constitutions. "Notwithstanding the ratification of this system of government by eleven of the thirteen United States, in some cases unanimously, in others by large majorities," Madison told Congress, "yet still there is a great number of our constituents who are dissatisfied with it; among whom are many respectable for their talents, their patriotism, and respectable for the jealousy they have for their liberty, which, though mistaken in its object, is laudable in its motive."[29] Just as he had done with the Constitution itself, Madison would again take a leading role in the process of formulating the Bill of Rights. Madison had a double goal: he wanted to amend the Constitution with a Bill of Rights, but he also wanted to make sure that the amendments would not undo any of the work of the Constitution itself. "I should be unwilling to see a door opened for a re-consideration of the whole structure of the government, for a re-consideration of the principles and the substance of the powers given," he wrote, and that position guided the amendments themselves. Above all, Madison wanted to avoid having a second Constitutional Convention. "I doubt, if such a door was opened, if we should be very likely to stop at that point which would be safe to the government itself,"[30] he warned.

With those criteria in mind, Madison then listed a number of changes to make in the Constitution, including the rights that would become the basis of the Bill of Rights. Again, Madison's was a collection of rights quite similar to those Mason had proposed, including protections of individuals in legal matters (no excessive bail, no cruel and unusual punishments, and the right to trial by jury); the freedom of the press and of religion; and Madison's version of what would become the Second Amendment: "The right of the people to keep and bear arms shall not be infringed; a well armed, and well regulated militia being the best security of a free country: but no person religiously scrupulous of bearing arms, shall be compelled to render military service in person."[31]

It was June 1789 when Madison made his speech proposing the Bill of Rights. For all of the urgency of the issue during the ratification debates, it was not the only item on the politicians' plates as they gathered in New York City for the first meeting of Congress. It would take more than a month before the House of Representatives began discussing the issue among themselves, then another month after that before the House finalized its list of seventeen and sent them off to the Senate.

The House of Representatives discussed the amendment dealing with the militia and the right to bear arms in August 1789. On 24 August 1789, the House of Representatives approved the following version: "A well regulated militia, composed of the body of the people, being the best security of a free State, the right of the people to keep and bear arms, shall not be infringed, but no one religiously scrupulous of bearing arms, shall be compelled to render military service in person."[32] The Senate began its discussions of the amendment early in September. Quakers were still a significant presence in several states, so delegates would not have been surprised to see Madison's language about a person "religiously scrupulous of bearing arms." Similar language had been present in earlier colonial militia regulations. Still, while that phrase survived the House's discussion, the senators removed the clause exempting pacifists from bearing arms. They also removed the phrase "composed of the body of the people." Several days later they changed "the best" to "necessary for the," and the amendment took on the wording that it has had ever since.[33]

Once Congress decided to put a Bill of Rights into the Constitution, the presence of some sort of amendment dealing with the militia was inevitable. Its exact wording was not. Some Anti-Federalists tried to get more explicit language about the standing army into the amendment. In the House of Representatives, Elbridge Gerry chimed in on this issue, telling his fellow congressmen, "What, sir, is the use of a militia? It is to prevent the establishment of a standing army, the bane of liberty." His problem with the Federalists' wording of the Second Amendment was that "Congress could take such measures with respect to a militia, as to make a standing army necessary."[34] Another representative proposed adding the phrase "a standing army of regular troops in time of peace is dangerous to public liberty, and should not be supported in time of peace, except by the consent of two thirds of each house of legislature." The House did not support those proposed changes.[35] In the Senate there were also efforts to insert language that explicitly mentioned standing armies, including a motion declaring them "dangerous to liberty" and requiring two-thirds of both houses to approve them—along with language prohibiting any soldier from being "enlisted for any longer term than the continuance of the war."[36] The Senate rejected these motions. The senators also shortened the entire Bill of Rights. The House had sent them seventeen amendments, which the senators whittled down to twelve over two weeks, leading to a conference committee to finalize the list and the wording. Before the end of September, Congress sent the final wordings of those twelve amendments out to the states to be ratified.[37] That ratification process would take over two years, but before the end of 1791, it was done. The first two did not survive the process; the other ten all did. From that point on, the US Constitution has declared that a well-regulated militia being necessary for the security of a free state, the right to keep and bear arms shall not be infringed.

In adding that amendment, Congress endorsed a tradition of republican thought that had elevated militias to a place of honor and glory well above what their lackluster military achievements, including those of the Revolution itself, would suggest. Congress also endorsed a tradition of militias that went back to the start of British colonization of North America. With the ratification of the Bill of Rights, citizens also endorsed these decisions and enshrined them into law. The United States, considering itself a free state, was trusting its security not to a professional army but to the citizens' militia. For all of the impact that the Revolution had on American life, the Second Amendment was also an endorsement of a state of affairs that predated the Revolution—one in which citizens had access to weapons and participated in the militia and were expected to look after their own military needs. It was also an endorsement of a society where most of the inhabitants were not citizens and where being a member of the militia entailed the responsibility for policing the behavior of those who were not.

At first, the Second Amendment's importance was largely symbolic.[38] As George Washington had noted, the United States could not afford the cost of a standing army during peacetime. The Constitution's militia clause also made clear that the United States would rely on its militia for both domestic policing and any external threats. Everyone expected the militia to remain a key part of policing the enslaved population as well. But the phrasing itself stood at the end of this long tradition of thought, endorsing one of its central ideas: that only a society with a well-regulated militia could be both secure and free.

Relying on the militia—whether due to the Second Amendment or to the Constitution's militia clause—also meant accepting a state of affairs where those men who were tasked with policing the population could at times cause problems of their own. The aftermath of Shays's Rebellion in Massachusetts showed that while the leaders of the founding generation were worried about uprisings from the men who made up the militia, they were also willing to tolerate that violence more than they had admitted in the lead-up to the Constitutional Convention. Earlier, when Jefferson had written to Madison that "the late rebellion in Massachusetts has given more alarm than I think it should have done," he had also added, "Calculate that one rebellion in 13 states in the course of 11 years, is but one for each state in a century & a half. No country should be so long without one. Nor will any degree of power in the hands of government prevent insurrections."[39]

As discussed in the last chapter, in terms of the words spoken, Jefferson's response was quite a bit different than the Federalists' had been. Washington wrote to a friend that he was "mortified beyond expression," and feared that Shays's Rebellion, and the government's weakness in handling it, would "render ourselves ridiculous and contemptible in the eyes of all Europe."[40] And it was perhaps easy for politicians like Madison and Washington, still in the United States, to dismiss the overconfidence of a man who was only witnessing the events from across the ocean. But sometimes actions do speak louder than words, and the actions that the various authorities took in the aftermath of Shays's Rebellion showed that political leaders in the United States—including Massachusetts—sided with Jefferson in thinking that they had taken things too far in the original crackdown on Shays's Rebellion and on Daniel Shays himself.[41]

In the immediate aftermath of the rebellion, Shays had fled to Vermont. Two other men who had played leading roles in the rebellion were hanged in

December 1787, one day before Delaware became the first state to ratify the Constitution.

Then the tide turned. More and more states ratified the Constitution. Shays's Rebellion looked less like the existential threat to the republic than it had appeared. In February 1788, Massachusetts ratified the Constitution. Massachusetts also began moving away from the hard line it had taken toward Shays and the rest of the protesters. John Hancock, who had resigned from the governorship before the rebellion had begun, returned to public life and was elected, once again, to be governor. Hancock began extending "offers of grace and mercy to the penitent citizen[s]" and releasing them from all "pains, penalties, disqualifications and disabilities of the law in such case," provided they take an oath of allegiance and promise not to again take up arms against the state. Hancock's first proclamation did exclude Shays and some others, "whose crimes are so attrocious, and whose obstinancy so great, as to exclude them" from the offer.[42] But soon enough, Hancock offered a pardon to Shays as well, and the one-time would-be Caesar returned from Vermont to Massachusetts. The press in Boston still held him in little regard, but Shays did get a pension from the government for the time he had spent fighting in the Continental army.[43]

Shays's Rebellion had shown the weakness of relying on a militia: the men Massachusetts needed to put the insurrection down were the ones fomenting it in the first place. Moreover, neighboring militias were not eager to help—their allegiance was as much with the insurgents as it was with the government. In all this, the events of Shays's Rebellion had loosely followed the script of Bacon's Rebellion. What would turn out to be the one distinctive aspect of the earlier rebellion, though, was Governor Berkeley's punitive response. Berkeley had had many of Bacon's followers and allies executed.[44] (Judging by the large number of Virginians who had been unwilling to join Berkeley in suppressing the rebellion, it seems likely that those men also disagreed with the executions.) No other uprising of white colonists would see such harsh punishments. The British colonies in North America would show that they were willing to tolerate an enormous amount of violence from white citizens. This was especially true if the victims of that violence were enslaved peoples, in which case the violence of the enslavers toward the enslaved was explicitly written into the laws. It was also true when victims were Native Americans, in which case there might be a certain amount of hand-wringing should an allied tribe suffer, as had been the case in the aftermath of the Paxton Boys or the massacre of the Lenape in 1782, but neither of those cases led to the perpetrators being punished.[45] Hancock's leniency toward Shays and his followers showed that this indulgence of white Americans' violence would be treated with leniency, even when the victims of that violence were other white citizens.

By trusting the enforcement of the laws to a portion of the citizens, the United States committed itself to a certain amount of unpredictability from those citizens. Many of the people living in the United States, though—or along its western borders—were not citizens and were not part of the militia. As shown in chapter 7, colonial militia codes required white men to participate in the militia; the colonies expected these men to have access to firearms and other weapons, to have some level of training, and to participate in periodic musters—along with serving in actual conflicts when needed. Those same militia codes either kept African Americans and Native Americans out of the militias completely or restricted them to specific roles such as drummers or scouts. In the slave societies of the South, those same militia codes also required the men in the militia to inspect the living quarters of the enslaved population and confiscate weapons that they found there. As the thirteen former colonies, now states, issued new and updated militia codes, those codes wound up looking a lot like the colonial codes that preceded them. South Carolina's 1794 Act to Organize the Militia Throughout the State of South Carolina, in Conformity with the Act of Congress required every male citizen eighteen years or older to participate in the militia, including "any white apprentice or man servant" and to fight against "invasions" or "insurrections" should they occur, with the traditional list of men exempt, including legislators and clerics. Any "free negroes, Indians . . . , Moors, mulattoes, and mestizos" would be required to participate as well, but only as "fatigue men and pioneers."[46] In Virginia, militias would continue to "patrol and visit all negro quarters" and break up any illegal gatherings.[47] The militia was still a white man's activity, and explicitly so. This was true at the national level as well. The 1792 Militia Act declared that "each and every free able-bodied white male citizen of the respective states, resident therein, who is or shall be of the age of eighteen years, and under the age of forty-five years (except as is herein after excepted) shall severally and respectively be enrolled in the militia."[48] The militia's role in patrolling the slave population in the new republic would continue to be what it had been during the colonial era.[49] The citizens of the United States would be armed. An armed citizenry, however, is not the same as an armed population, and it remained one of the main requirements of the armed citizens that they police the actions of those parts of the population that were, by law, unarmed. As Hadden has shown, in Virginia and the Carolinas, militias had always been intertwined with slave patrols and had always policed the enslaved populations; they had also always included, as part of their purview, the need to search the quarters of enslaved peoples for weapons and confiscate any that were found. In that history, the American Revolution represented a moment of crisis, which stressed the states' resources; it did not, however, represent a break with past practices. Once the fighting was over, the militias returned to their previous tasks.[50]

One of the main debates in Second Amendment scholarship concerns the relationship between the amendment and southern slavery. Some scholars have pointed to the role that militias played in policing the enslaved populations and have argued that this "hidden" reason was the basis for the Second Amendment, which was meant "to assure the Southern states that Congress would not undermine the slave system by using its newly acquired constitutional authority over the militia to disarm the state militia and thereby destroy the South's principal instrument of slave control."[51] The argument is a complicated one worth paying attention to. At its base are two key interlocking points: first, the key role the militia played in policing the enslaved population; second, the "curious silence" that surrounded the question of slavery during the Constitutional Convention. There is little to argue with on the first point; in slave states, the militia did play that role, before, during, and after the Revolution. One might even add that while slavery had become a southern phenomenon by the 1780s, few in the North were abolitionists, and even fewer would have supported the prospect of an uprising by enslaved people. The question then becomes, if the role of the Second Amendment was to protect slavery, why does the historical record not make that clearer? The answer to that relies on the ability of the men who wrote the Constitution to discuss slavery without mentioning it, all while putting in place laws meant to bolster slavery.[52] When Mason raised the threat that Virginia's militia would be marched to New Hampshire, for instance, the implied message was that white Virginians would then be unable to defend themselves against an uprising by the enslaved people. Moreover, this message would be "obvious to everyone in the audience."[53] The main advantage of this interpretation is the emphasis it gives to the racial politics of early America. It helps highlight that during the eighteenth century, the militias were a domestic police force far more often than they were a citizens' army.

There are limits to this interpretation, though. First, the militia was a popular cause in the North as well as the South. Its popularity in the North went well beyond northerners' lack of sympathy for the people living in slavery in the southern states. Unlike the three-fifths compromise, neither the Second Amendment nor the militia clause were the result of a compromise between northerners and southerners. Yes, the militia was important to slave owners like Mason and Henry, but it was also important to northerners like Elbridge Gerry or Samuel Adams. Beyond that, while one of the advantages of this interpretation is the way that it highlights the racial politics of the early republic, and their importance for the formulation of the Second Amendment, there was more to those racial politics of the early republic than slave patrols. Highlighting the role of racial politics in the formulation of the Second Amendment, along with the importance of the militia in maintaining white Americans' dominant status, also involved more than slave patrols.

Violence between white Americans and Native Americans was happening along the frontier in the North and the South. Even people like Washington or Hamilton who, during the 1780s, had championed the cause of a small permanent army, did not anticipate a force large enough to protect the settler communities that kept encroaching onto Native American territory. Those Americans who wished to settle along the frontier would have to look after their own military affairs. As American settlement pushed further west, the conflicts between the settlers and the Native American communities continued, and the militias continued to be at the center of those conflicts, with the leaders of the United States uneager to provide the sort of permanent force that would make those militias unnecessary, nor to rein in those militias when they committed crimes against the Native American populations.[54]

Militia membership was at once a symbol of white domination in American society and the institution that enforced that domination when need be. Relying on the militia to enforce social domination meant relying on an institution that was at times unpredictable and even dangerous. Shays had proved that. And as the United States started out, its leaders were willing to tolerate that unpredictability and be lenient toward violent white Americans. Shays's pardon had proved that. So, too, did the Constitution and the Bill of Rights, by relying on militias to execute the laws of the union and suppress insurrections and repel invasions and by declaring those militias necessary for the security of a free state.

Once Congress decided to add a Bill of Rights, it was inevitable that the Bill of Rights would have some version of the Second Amendment. Its exact wording was not inevitable. As shown above, before the Second Amendment became final, it went through a number of different versions, and historians, lawyers, and concerned citizens alike have pored over the relations between all of these phrasings. The differences in the wording are important: the final version is part of the Constitution; the earlier versions are not. There is less material than one might wish about the debates over the wording, especially in the Senate.[55] But there is a continuity that should not be overlooked, and the earlier wordings show the intellectual pathways that led to the final wording. Earlier versions show how fears of a standing army led Virginia—and then the United States—to present the militia as an alternative to a standing army. Similarly, though Mason did not include the term "right to bear arms" in the Virginia declaration, the idea of a "body of the people, trained in arms" would be difficult to accomplish without those people having access to weapons of war. All of the wordings were based in the same general view of society. All of them stress the need for a citizens' militia and, beyond that, a citizenry familiar with and trained in the use of arms.

If measured against the standards that a Fletcher or a Trenchard would have held it to, the Second Amendment fell somewhat short of Mason's 1776 formulation. Neither the Second Amendment nor the Constitution itself explicitly mentioned standing armies. The Federalists did not fear a small standing army the way that Mason had; Washington's and Hamilton's attempts in the 1780s to institute some sort of professional, full-time force showed their desire for a professional force, as long as it was small. But they saw the same need for citizens to be armed and trained and to be members of the militia. Federalists and Anti-Federalists alike saw the same dangers of a large standing army that could be turned against the people and the need for the people to be able to defend themselves. And though they did not speak of it often, they saw the same risks of an uprising by enslaved people that the Anti-Federalists did, and they saw the same need to expropriate American Indian lands. And they both showed a willingness to tolerate the excesses of the men who made up those militias. Machiavelli had written that "if you want to make a populace numerous and well-armed, so that they can conquer a vast empire, then you must accept that you will not be able to get them to do everything you want."[56]

At a certain level, Madison and Mason, Washington and Jefferson, all agreed on this principle.

The Second Amendment began—and begins—by declaring that a well-regulated militia is necessary for the security of a free state. The meaning of that phrase stood at the end of a long line of writers and politicians who had called for an armed and organized citizenry and who had criticized the habit of paying professional soldiers, be they local-born men seeking a career at arms or foreign mercenaries. To rely on such soldiers meant that a society was no longer truly free; not only could that professional force turn on the citizens themselves, but such a development was an inevitability. In that situation, the civil authorities would be unable to control the military. To ignore the need for any sort of military troops, though, meant that the society could not be secure. The only way for a society to be both free and secure was to rely on citizens trained in "discipline and the use of arms, who stand ready to defend their own rights and those of their fellow-citizens."[57] For a century, men of the British Empire had been asking, How can a society defend itself from its enemies, without being threatened by its defenders? The best answer they had come up with was the citizens' militia. Part of the appeal of that answer lay in the justification it provided for an institution that maintained its members' superiority in the social order. But it was a justification with a long intellectual pedigree, along with a long institutional history. The road to the Second Amendment, which went back to the origins of colonial America and the intellectual traditions of seventeenth-century England, and which claimed for itself the lessons of the ancient world, ended with a twenty-seven-word statement declaring that if people wanted to be free, they had to spend some of their time as soldiers.

EPILOGUE

The Long Road from the Second Amendment

In September 1791, a tax collector named Robert Johnson was making his rounds in western Pennsylvania's Washington County. It was a time when it was difficult to be a tax collector anywhere west of the Appalachian Mountains, but western Pennsylvania was especially hostile to men like Johnson. As Alexander Hamilton would later describe it, "A party of men armed and disguised way-laid him . . . seized, tarred and feathered him, cut off his hair, and deprived him of his horse, obliging him to travel on foot a considerable distance in that mortifying and painfull situation." Johnson could not have been completely surprised. At the time, "the people in general in the Western part of the state" were "in such a ferment on Account of the Act of Congress for laying a duty on distilled Spirits & so much opposed to the execution of the said Act."[1]

Hamilton had initiated that whiskey tax as a way to raise revenue during Washington's presidency. Like many economic policies formulated during the colonial era had done, it hit Americans closer to the frontier harder than it did those living closer to the Atlantic, and it hit rural folks harder than those in the cities. In those western communities many people were angry about the tax. That anger had spread to enough of the community that even after Johnson identified his attackers, local government officials had a difficult time punishing them. One man who attempted to serve the papers fared no better than Johnson had and was himself "seized whipped tarred and feathered and after having his Money and horse taken from him was blindfolded and tied in the Woods, in which condition he remained for five hours."[2]

These attacks on tax collectors were part of the events that, together, would become known as the Whiskey Rebellion—the latest uprising of white citizens from frontier counties against their own governments. The parallels to Shays's Rebellion were many: both were in the western part of the state, both concerned economic policy, and both were insurrections that the community itself could not—or would not—suppress. Officially, the task of suppressing such rebellions still fell to the local militia, but that militia was made up of men who were taking part in the insurrection. Or, as one of western Pennsylvania's leading men at the time wrote, the fear was that "government would call out the militia, and we were the militia ourselves, and have to be at war with one another."[3] It was the same dilemma that the Massachusetts governor had faced in Shays's Rebellion, and it was the same dilemma Berkeley had faced in Bacon's Rebellion. Robert Johnson had tried to collect taxes from men who were poor, indebted, discontented, and armed, and it had not gone well. As Saul Cornell notes, the rebels even went to great pains to present themselves as a militia, using militia rituals and rhetoric. Though people outside the region looked at the rebels as a "mob," the rebels themselves tried to "convince the government that we are no mob, but a regular army, and can preserve discipline, and pass thro' a town, like the French and American armies, in the course of the last war, without doing the least injury to persons or property."[4]

It took the national government several years to resolve the problems in the region. Eventually, George Washington would come to the same conclusion that Hamilton had come to years earlier: the national government had to call out troops to put down the rebellion once and for all. In September 1794, Washington issued a proclamation in which he stated that "the moment is now come when . . . every form of conciliation not inconsistent with the being of Government has been adopted without effect." The "serious consequences of a treasonable opposition" had led him to use the powers he had and to summon into service the militia from not only Pennsylvania but New Jersey, Maryland, and Virginia as well.[5]

The subsequent crackdown on the rebels in western Pennsylvania was what the authors of the Constitution hoped for when they'd written the militia clause and then, later, the Second Amendment. Washington gathered an army of over ten thousand militiamen from those states and rode out with them to western Pennsylvania. Most leaders of the rebellion fled further west. Those who remained faced arrest by the men Washington had assembled. There would be no full-scale armed confrontation, though: the scale of Washington's forces convinced the rebels in Pennsylvania that such a confrontation would not go well for them. Militarily speaking, that was the end of the Whiskey Rebellion. The government would still have trouble collecting the taxes on whiskey, and it would be some time before the reach of its enforcement would extend into Kentucky. But the period of open rebellion was over.[6]

One goal of the US Constitution had been to put the government in a better position to crack down on events like Shays's Rebellion, and the Whiskey Rebellion had presented an opportunity to test its new powers. As noted in earlier chapters, the Constitution gave Congress the power "to provide for calling forth the Militia to execute the Laws of the Union, suppress Insurrections and repel Invasions." That federalization of the militia, against which Henry and Mason had fought, had been the law of the land since 1789.[7] The Second Amendment, which declared those militias necessary to the security of a free state, had been law since 1791. And the following year, Congress added a Militia Act that gave the president a power that previously only Congress had enjoyed—that of calling forth the militia. The president could invoke that power in case of "imminent danger of invasion from any foreign nation or Indian tribe." He could also invoke it "whenever the laws of the United States shall be opposed or the execution thereof obstructed, in any state, by combinations too powerful to be suppressed by the ordinary course of judicial proceedings." In those cases, the act continued, "it shall be lawful for the President of the United States . . . to call forth and employ such numbers of the militia of any other state or states most convenient thereto, as may be necessary."[8] President Washington had done just that.

In the immediate aftermath of the Whiskey Rebellion, some of the insurrection's leaders were arrested. There was no serious attempt to track down those who had fled further west. And as had been the case—eventually, at least—after Shays's Rebellion, there were few punishments of the men who had taken part in the rebellion. Though some men were arrested, they were subsequently either acquitted or pardoned.[9]

In describing the militia's arrival in western Pennsylvania to Congress, Washington was able to take pride in the accomplishment of the men who had heeded his call: "It has been a spectacle, displaying to the highest advantage, the value of Republican Government to behold the most and the least wealthy of our citizens standing in the same ranks, as private Soldiers; preeminently distinguished by being the army of the Constitution. . . . Nor ought I to omit to acknowledge the efficacious and patriotic cooperation, which I have experienced from the chief magistrates of the States, to which my requisitions have been addressed."[10] From there, he took a moment to call for Congress to do something he had been hoping for since his 1783 *Sentiments on a Peace Establishment:* enact the kind of reforms that would put each state's militia on a better footing: "The devising and establishing of a well regulated militia, would be a genuine source of legislative honor, and a perfect title to public gratitude. I therefore, entertain a hope, that the present Session will not pass, without carrying to its full energy the power of organizing, arming, and disciplining the militia; and thus providing, in the language of the Constitution, for calling them forth to execute the laws of the Union, suppress insurrections, and repel invasions."[11] Washington's plea would go unheeded, though—as would a similar plea from Jefferson some years later. The Constitution's militia clause and the 1792 Militia Act had added a new element to American life—the national government's ability to call forth the militia and to rely on different states to pitch in. Otherwise, the state militias would continue to be what the colonial militias had been: a domestic police force that could at times cause more problems than it solved.

The Whiskey Rebellion had shown that the new system could better handle such unrest than the old system had; it also showed that the new system would not prevent such unrest from happening. Even the success of Washington's actions against the Whiskey Rebellion raised the question of how much of that success lay in Washington himself, in his charisma and the respect he had enjoyed ever since the war ended. Washington had thought himself retired following the Revolution itself, until the Constitutional Convention brought him back in. He would go on to serve two terms as president before retiring once again and returning, once again, to his estate. Many of the most ardent rebels were citizens of Pennsylvania's Washington County. Washington knew his history, and he thought about his legacy. He was the American politician who most easily could have turned Caesar. Instead, he chose—quite consciously—the path of Cincinnatus.[12]

There would be other rebellions during the early years of the republic, both while Washington was in office and after he left. But not all insurrections were created equal. In 1800, as John Adams's term as president was winding down, word that there was another rebellion on the way reached the authorities in Virginia, including the governor, James Monroe. This time, though, the echoes were not of Shays's Rebellion or of Bacon's, but of Stono. The white population did not sympathize with the rebels, and the government was not lenient in its punishments.

For several years already, the fear of a revolt by enslaved people hitting the United States had been higher than usual. The French Revolution had spread to its Caribbean colony of San Domingue, leading eventually to an uprising there that would end French rule, free all enslaved people, and end with black rule of the independent nation of Haiti. White Americans feared that this spirit of rebellion would reach their shores. Already in 1793, a New York newspaper wrote of South Carolina "that the NEGROES have become very insolent, in so much that the citizens are alarmed, and the militia keep a constant guard. It is said that the St. Domingo negroes have sown those seeds of revolt, and that a magazine has been attempted to be broken open."[13] That was the context for the conspiracy led by an enslaved African American named Gabriel living near Richmond, Virginia.

Gabriel had planned an insurrection, but his plans were thwarted, in part by storms on the day he had chosen for the revolt, in part because several enslaved people informed their enslavers, who in turn informed the authorities. Gabriel fled but was captured. As historian Michael Nicholls notes, "Neither the geographical extent of the plot nor the number of insurgents in the conspiracy was revealed. In fact, the initial task for Republican governor James Monroe, beyond sending out some patrols, was to determine if the conspiracy even existed." Monroe told Virginia's General Assembly that he had "endeavored to give the affair as little importance as the measures necessary for defence would permit," in the hopes that "it would even pass unnoticed by the community."[14] But word soon spread. With fears high, the militia responded to the potential, yet thwarted, rebellion by doing everything a militia was supposed to do: springing into action, engaging the rebels, defeating them, punishing them, and restoring order to the colony. Militia leaders in the region "demanded to be called into service," according to Douglas Egerton, and "for the better part of the month, several hundred men . . . crashed about the county harassing blacks but finding virtually no conspirators. Finally growing tired of this sport, the Twenty-third agreed to be mustered out," though not before presenting the governor with a bill for their time and services.[15]

As for the leniency that the men of the other rebellions enjoyed, there would be no such treatment for Gabriel's men. The local courts tried, convicted, and hanged at least twenty-five men for having participated in the plot. As had been the case since the colonial era, American citizens' tolerance for violence could extend along the social ladder of white society; it did not extend to Native Americans or to African Americans. The state militias would continue to be what they had been: unpredictable armed military organizations aimed at establishing and maintaining racial domination.

As the republic began, then, there was every sign that its militias were going to continue to be more or less what they had been during the colonial era. The limited ability of the national government to call on the militias of several states when needed had proved useful. But in the aftermath of the Revolution, the armed citizens of the new republic were acting a lot like the armed citizens of the colonies had. Nor was there any sign that the United States would begin to embrace the idea of a standing army any more than it had in the past. When Thomas Jefferson became president in 1801, he brought into the office a genuine sympathy for the citizens' militia. Jefferson had declared in 1799 that "I am for relying, for internal defense, on our militia solely, till actual invasion . . . and not for a standing army, in time of peace."[16] Like Washington, he had hoped to get Congress to pass a significant restructuring of the militia. He was less concerned than his predecessors had been about the occasional insurrection or "trifling mutiny."[17] In his 1808 State of the Union address, he told Congress that "for a people who are free, and who mean to remain so, a well organized and armed militia is their best security. It is therefore incumbent on us at every meeting to revise the condition of the militia." Some states, Jefferson noted, "have paid a laudable attention to this object, but every degree of neglect is to be found among others." But while he urged Congress to "present this as among the most important objects of their deliberation," Jefferson, too, got nowhere on this. Like Washington, he was unable to get Congress to reform the militia.[18] He did succeed, however, in establishing the United States' first military academy at West Point, as his way of helping ensure that the nation's military growth took place in as republican a way as possible.[19]

The United States began the nineteenth century with its vision of a nation of citizen-soldiers still largely intact, even if the militia was not the institution that its advocates dreamed it might become. The permanent army was still small. The militia musters continued to be occasions for men to show their patriotism and demonstrate their citizenship, especially a muster on the Fourth of July.[20] Being a citizen-soldier remained at once an idealized status for those who wrote about it and an unwanted burden for many of the men who participated. And in the South, the militias continued to serve as slave patrols, searching the quarters of enslaved people for weapons and policing their movements between plantations.[21] This would not be the society of which Fletcher and Trenchard had dreamed. The Federalists had rejected the idea of disciplining the nation, and the nation had shown no signs that it wanted to be disciplined. But it remained a nation that relied on its citizens to serve as its police force and, on occasion, as its army as well. And it remained a nation where most of the political elite still believed that for a nation to be both free and secure, its citizens would have to spend part of their time as soldiers.

The United States of today is a far cry from the nation that emerged out of the eighteenth century. It would be hard to imagine otherwise; human society as a whole has changed more during those two-plus centuries than it had during any previous time. Most of those transformations lie well beyond the scope of this book. Several, however, are worth pointing out because of the direct influence they had on the themes of this book, starting with the abolition of slavery. During the first half of the nineteenth century, slave state militias retained their roles as slave patrols. The Civil War put an end to that. The militia in the southern states would not survive this change, especially since the Militia Act of 1862 not only included "all able-bodied male citizens between the ages of eighteen and forty-five" but specified that this would include "persons of African descent." In the aftermath of the war, southern whites balked at serving in the militia. Some were barred from serving for having served in the Confederate Army. Others had no interest in serving alongside African Americans. The southern militias, as official state institutions, would never again be what they had been. Instead, white southerners began organizing voluntary, unofficial militias—groups of men who took it upon themselves to continue to "police" the free black population much as their predecessors had policed the enslaved black population before the war.[22]

The end of slavery and the inclusion of African Americans in the militia were part of a broader movement that changed the nature of American citizenship. At the start of the republic, citizenship was a privileged status to which only whites and males were eligible; most inhabitants of the United States were not full citizens. That is no longer the case. Starting with the Fourteenth Amendment and through the Nineteenth Amendment and the Civil Rights Act, the laws of the United States now guarantee that that anyone born in the United States is a citizen and that all citizens are equal in rights. The reality of both race and gender relations in the United States, however, has fallen short of equality. And while much of the racial and gender politics of the United States lies outside the scope of this book, guns and gun ownership always played a major role in America's divisions and continue to do so today. The history of gun rights and gun control has gone hand in hand with racial politics. As long as the laws could, they made this link explicit: the militia codes of the antebellum South, for instance, encouraged white men to have weapons and participate in the militia but forbade most African Americans from both.[23] The passage of the Fourteenth Amendment ended such explicit racial laws.[24] Those old patterns have not disappeared, though. Gun ownership remains higher among whites than among people of color. It also remains higher among men than among women.[25] Nonwhites are expected to justify their possession of firearms in ways that white gun owners are not.[26] The American public also continues to react differently to gun violence depending on the race of the victims and to tolerate higher levels of violence when the victims are people of color or when the perpetrators are white.[27] Yet even mass shootings that claim white victims, as at Sandy Hook in 2012 or Las Vegas in 2017, have led only to minimal changes in the laws regulating gun ownership. Just as Shays's Rebellion and the Whiskey Rebellion did not lead the early republic to abandon the militia system, so too the toll of American gun violence—both the mass shootings that make the headlines and the daily toll of violence that make up the overwhelming majority of casualties—has not led the United States to change its approach to arming civilians. The United States remains an armed society, and citizen gun ownership remains high, as it was during the colonial era, even as that ownership has since become untethered from any membership in the state militia.[28]

The United States remains an armed society, but it is no longer an organized society. Its citizens are no longer organized into militia units, as they had been during the colonial era and the first decades of the republic. Instead, the United States became the kind of society that the Second Amendment was meant to prevent: a society with a large standing army under the authority of the executive branch, an army that is often segregated from civilian life and an untrained citizenry. Meanwhile, the time when Americans feared a standing army is long gone. The United States' permanent standing army has become the most powerful fighting force the world has ever seen. The appropriate size of the military budget, military commitments across the world, and engagement in specific wars remain key elements of political debates, but the existence of a permanent army does not. Any politician who proposed eliminating the permanent army would be laughed off of the podium. So, too, would any officer who proposed reinstating mandatory militia duty. Jefferson's attempt to reorganize the militia might have been its last chance to look anything like the battle-ready unit that he, and other militia advocates, would have liked.

The militia remained an important institution over the course of the nineteenth century, but it became clear that it would never be a full substitute for an external army. Nor would it be a full substitute for an internal police force. Here, too, the nineteenth century saw the growth of professional police forces, first in cities and then across the nation.[29] As skepticism toward professional soldiers and policemen declined, so too did acceptance of the idea that most citizens should spend a part of their time in militia training.

The Militia Act of 1903 put the new reality into law by reforming the militia into two categories, only one of which entailed any sort of duty at all. Just as Washington, Jefferson, and others had called for, there would now be a two-tiered militia, where one portion of the citizenry would be trained to a higher standard. The second tier would exist in name only. According to that act, the militia would consist of "every able-bodied male citizen . . . who is more than eighteen and less than forty-five years of age." But most of those able-bodied men were militiamen in name only; there would be no musters and no registers, and millions of men have lived and died without realizing that they were a part of the militia at all; the 1903 Militia Act simply said of them, "the remainder to be known as the Reserve Militia." As for the "organized militia," those citizens would still be part-time soldiers, but their training would be similar to the training that permanent soldiers received. Since 1903, the organized militia of the United States has been called the National Guard.[30]

In today's United States, the Second Amendment has come to take on meanings well beyond those intended by the men of the eighteenth century. There has been an enormous shift over these centuries from viewing the amendment as a way to ensure that the state militias remained strong to an amendment that guarantees individual gun ownership. The modern gun rights movement places far more emphasis on the second half of the Second Amendment and its declaration that "the right of the people to keep and bear arms shall not be infringed." That shift in emphasis reflects the decline of the militia in American life since 1791. In the 2008 *DC v. Heller* case, the US Supreme Court made this shift from the amendment's first clause to its second official by ruling that the Second Amendment protected an individual's right to bear arms. Viewed from this book's perspective, the Supreme Court's 2008 ruling was not a return to the amendment's "original understanding," as the court claimed.[31] Rather, that ruling endorsed the transformations of

American society that have occurred since. A Second Amendment limited to its second clause is an amendment tailored for a society where most citizens are not citizen-soldiers and where participation in the militia is the exception.

There is perhaps no better measure of how the meaning of the Second Amendment has changed since 1791 than the way in which organizations who view themselves as protectors of the Second Amendment go out of their way to praise both the armed forces and the police. Professional soldiers have become paragons of patriotism, and politicians of any stripe criticize the army at their own risk. In the aftermath of the Revolutionary War, Alexander Hamilton complained about "Republican . . . hostility to an army whatever be their merits." As a result of that hostility, American society only acknowledged soldiers' contributions "with unwillingness and . . . reluctance."[32] The men of the eighteenth century who clamored for a Bill of Rights believed in the importance of a citizens' militia; today, however, people associate the amendment with private gun ownership. The United States has become a society where few people know what the militias of the founding era were, nor does the average American understand why the founders considered those militias to be necessary to the security of a free state. In other words, the United States has become a society where the Second Amendment no longer makes sense.

NOTES

Introduction

1. These men usually served as part of a provincial troop rather than in their existing militia units. See, for example, Richard Hall, *Atlantic Politics, Military Strategy, and the French and Indian War* (Palgrave Macmillan, 2016), 69, 167.

2. The relevant portions can be found in Article I, Section 8, which gave Congress the following powers: "To raise and support Armies, but no Appropriation of Money to that Use shall be for a longer Term than two Years; To provide and maintain a Navy; To make Rules for the Government and Regulation of the land and naval Forces; To provide for calling forth the Militia to execute the Laws of the Union, suppress Insurrections and repel Invasions; To provide for organizing, arming, and disciplining, the Militia, and for governing such Part of them as may be employed in the Service of the United States, reserving to the States respectively, the Appointment of the Officers, and the Authority of training the Militia according to the discipline prescribed by Congress." Though comparative word count is no definitive measure of importance, the priority of militia over army is clear: Congress's role with the militia was to establish a minimum level of preparedness; its goal with the army was to prevent its growth by controlling its purse strings.

3. John Fitzpatrick, ed., *The Writings of George Washington,* 39 vols. (Washington, DC, 1931–44), 26:375.

4. Fitzpatrick, *The Writings of George Washington,* 6:110–12.

5. Fitzpatrick, *The Writings of George Washington,* 26:387.

6. Fitzpatrick, *The Writings of George Washington,* 26:392, 387.

7. Fitzpatrick, *The Writings of George Washington,* 26:388.

8. John Robertson, ed., *Andrew Fletcher: Political Works* (Cambridge, 1997), 13.

9. Fitzpatrick, *The Writings of George Washington,* 26:375.

10. Mark Smith, *Stono: Documenting and Interpreting a Slave Revolt* (Columbia: University of South Carolina Press, 2005), 15.

11. Micah Alpaugh, "A Self-Defining 'Bourgeoisie' in the Early French Revolution: The *Milice Bourgeoise,* the Bastille Days of 1789, and Their Aftermath," *Journal of Social History* 47:3 (2014): 696–720.

1. Julius Caesar Crosses the Rubicon

1. Jefferson told this story in an 1811 letter to Dr. Benjamin Rush, available in *The Writings of Thomas Jefferson,* ed. Paul Leicester Ford, 12 vols. (New York and London,

1904–5), 9:296. See also the discussion in Thomas P. Govan, "Alexander Hamilton and Julius Caesar: A Note on the Use of Historical Evidence," *William and Mary Quarterly*, 3rd ser., 32:3 (July 1975): 475–80.

2. Barry Strauss, *The Death of Caesar: The Story of History's Most Famous Assassination* (New York, 2015), 33.

3. For ancient sources on Julius Caesar, the best starting places remain Plutarch's "Life of Caesar," included in his *Parallel Lives*, and Suetonius's chapter on Julius Caesar in in his *Twelve Caesars*, along with Julius Caesar's own writings, *The Gallic Wars* and *The Civil War*. For secondary works, see Strauss, *The Death of Caesar*; Jeremy Patterson, "Caesar the Man," in *A Companion to Julius Caesar*, ed. Miriam Griffin (Oxford, 2009), 126–40. For eighteenth-century views of Julius Caesar, addressed in more depth later in this book, there is a useful summary in Margaret Malamud, "Manifest Destiny and the Eclipse of Julius Caesar," in *Julius Caesar in Western Culture*, ed. Maria Wyke (Oxford, 2006), 148–53; and Nicholas Cole, "Republicanism, Caesarism, and Political Change," in Griffin, *A Companion to Julius Caesar*, 418–30.

4. See Gordon Wood, "The Legacy of Rome in the American Revolution," in *The Idea of America: Reflections on the Birth of the United States* (New York, 2011); Eran Shalev, *Rome Reborn on Western Shores: Historical Imagination and the Creation of the American Republic* (Charlottesville, VA, 2009); and Bernard Bailyn, *The Ideological Origins of the American Revolution* (Cambridge, MA, 1992), 23–26.

5. Charles Louis de Secondat, Baron de Montesquieu, *Considerations on the Causes of the Greatness of the Romans and Their Decline*, trans. David Lowenthal (Ithaca, NY, 1965), 92.

6. Alexander Hamilton, James Madison, and John Jay, *The Federalist Papers* (Oxford, 2008), hereafter *FP*. Page numbers refer to this edition.

7. For Cincinnatus, see Livy [Titus Livius], *Ad Urbe Condita Libri*, book 3, chapters 26–29; quoted here from Livy, *History of Rome*, trans. B. O. Foster, 14 vols. (Cambridge, MA, 1919–59), 2:89–95.

8. Shalev, *Rome Reborn*, 221; Julia Osman, "Cincinnatus Reborn: The George Washington Myth and French Renewal during the Old Regime," *French Historical Studies* 38:3 (August 2015): 421–46; Laura Auricchio, "Two Versions of 'General Washington's Resignation': Politics, Commerce, and Visual Culture in 1790s Philadelphia," *Eighteenth-Century Studies* 44:3 (Spring 2011): 388.

9. Livy is again the best source for information on the Punic Wars. Ten of the thirty-five extant books from his *Ad Urbe Condita Libri* cover the Second Punic War (books 21 through 30). They have been published as one volume, Livy, *The War with Hannibal*, trans. Aubrey de Selincourt, ed. Betty Radice (Middlesex, 1965). Quotations here are from Livy, *History of Rome*, vol. 5. Secondary works on the wars include Adrian Goldsworthy, *The Punic Wars* (London, 2000), 143–328; and Lawrence Keppie, *The Making of the Roman Army: From Republic to Empire* (Norman, OK, 1984), 25–32.

10. As the peoples of pre-Roman northern Europe did not write, there are fewer records of them than there are of the peoples of the Mediterranean. The most valuable primary sources are Julius Caesar's *The Gallic Wars* and Tacitus's *Germania*, which

Tacitus wrote more than a century after Caesar's death—and therefore well after the Punic Wars were over. Investigations beyond those are generally the purview of archeologists rather than historians, though Norman Davies's *Europe: A History* (Oxford, 1996), 215–20, provides a useful introduction.

11. For a history of Carthage and its use of mercenaries, see Serge Yalichev, *Mercenaries of the Ancient World* (London, 1997), 204–30; and Paul Erdkamp, "Manpower and Food Supply in the First and Second Punic Wars," in *A Companion to the Punic Wars,* ed. Dexter Hoyos (Chichester, 2011), 58–76.

12. Livy, *History of Rome,* 5:355–57. For accounts of Cannae, along with Livy's description, see Goldsworthy, *Punic Wars,* 197–221. Goldsworthy estimates the combined forces at over 125,000 men and 16,000 horses in a five-to-six-square-mile area. For the background to the Punic Wars, see Cyril Robinson, *A History of Rome: From 753 B.C. to A.D. 410* (London, 1935), 56–62.

13. Polybius, *The Rise of the Roman Empire,* trans. Ian-Scott Kilvert (London, 1979), 272.

14. The figure of eight thousand Roman prisoners of war comes from Goldsworthy, *Punic Wars,* 216.

15. Livy, *History of Rome,* 5:375.

16. Livy, *History of Rome,* 5:369. Though Livy felt otherwise, subsequent writers have questioned the feasibility of Hannibal marching on Rome right after Cannae, though Rome was certainly quite weak. Others have questioned whether or not marching on Rome was ever part of Hannibal's plans. See John Briscoe, "The Second Punic War," in *The Cambridge Ancient History*, ed. A. E. Astin, F. W. Walbank, M. W. Frederiksen, and R. M. Ogilvie, 14 vols. (Cambridge, 1970–2005), 8:53.

17. Livy, *History of Rome,* 5:405.

18. See Edward Lengel, *General George Washington. A Military Life* (New York, 2005), 149–50.

19. *The Histories of Polybius,* trans. Evelyn Shuckburgh, 2 vols. (London and New York, 1889), 1:502. See also Briscoe, "The Second Punic War," 75.

20. Horace, *Satires, Epistles, Ars Poetica,* trans. H. Rushton Fairclough (London, 1929), 409 (*Epistulae* II:1:156)

21. For the cultural ties between Greece and Rome (from a more dialogical perspective than the one Horace suggested), see Andrew Wallace-Hadrill, *Rome's Cultural Revolution* (Cambridge, 2008), 23.

22. Erich Gruen is particularly critical of the "golden haze of idealization" surrounding Rome's citizens' army. See his *The Last Generation of the Roman Republic* (Berkeley, 1995), 366–74.

23. Mary Beard and Michael Crawford, *Rome in the Late Republic,* 2nd ed. (London, 1999), 5–6.

24. For the Marian reforms, see Beard and Crawford, *Rome in the Late Republic,*7–8; Keppie, *The Making,* 57–58, 61–63; Robinson, *A History,* 134; and Andrew Lintott, "Political History, 146–95 B.C.," in *The Cambridge Ancient History*, 9:92, ed. J. A. Crook, Andrew Lintott, and Elizabeth Rawson.

25. Montesquieu, *Considerations on the Causes,* 91.

26. Suetonius, *The Lives of the Twelve Caesars; An English Translation, Augmented with the Biographies of Contemporary Statesmen, Orators, Poets, and Other Associates,* ed. J. Eugene Reed and Alexander Thomson (Philadelphia, 1889), 93.

27. For the relationships between Caesar, Brutus, and Cato, see their respective chapters in *Plutarch's Lives,* trans. John Dryden, 2 vols. (New York, 2006), especially 2:259, 340–43, 627; for a more recent view, see Strauss, *The Death of Caesar,* 15–23.

28. Suetonius, *The Lives,* 63. See also Jeremy Patterson, "Caesar the Man," 127–30, which includes a broader discussion of his habits, character, and appearance.

29. Suetonius, *The Lives,* 11.

30. For Caesar's battles in Gaul and his travel to Britain, the best place to start remains Caesar's own account: Caesar, *The Conquest of Gaul,* trans. S. A. Handford (London, 1951). See also see Keppie, *The Making,* 80–95, 101–2. For an assessment of Caesar as a "both conventional and unique" general and military leader, see Nathan Rosenstein, "General and Imperialist," in Griffin, *A Companion to Julius Caesar,* 85–99.

31. *Plutarch's Lives,* 2:240.

32. Appian, *Roman History,* vol. 3, *The Civil Wars,* trans. Horace White (Cambridge, MA, 1913), 293.

33. Suetonius, *The Lives,* 45.

34. For the civil war, see Keppie, *The Making,* 103–12.

35. *Plutarch's Lives,* 2:258–59.

36. See Strauss, *The Death of Caesar,* 215–36.

37. For Rome in the early Empire, see Robinson, *A History,* 243–65.

38. Jean-Jacques Rousseau, *The Government of Poland,* trans. Willmoore Kendall (Indianapolis, 1985), 80.

2. Niccolò Machiavelli Retires to His Estate

1. Niccolo Machiavelli, *The Prince,* trans. Harvey Mansfield (Chicago, 1985), 29, 30. For an account of d'Orco's execution, including Machiavelli's proximity to the events as a Venetian diplomat at the time, see Paul Strathern, *The Artist, the Philosopher, and the Warrior: The Intersecting Lives of Da Vinci, Machiavelli, and Borgia and the World They Shaped* (New York, 2009), 187–88. D'Orco's last name is often written as de Lorqua or de Lorca.

2. Machiavelli, *The Prince,* 27.

3. Machiavelli, *The Prince,* 38.

4. Machiavelli, *The Prince,* 10–11.

5. The best peek at Machiavelli's life comes from the impressive collection of correspondence translated and published as Niccolò Machiavelli, *Machiavelli and His Friends: Their Personal Correspondence,* trans. and ed. James B Atkinson and David Sices (Dekalb, IL, 1996). For secondary works on Machiavelli's life, see Strathern, *The Artist*; Charles D. Tarlton, *Fortune's Circle: A Biographical Interpretation of Niccolò*

Machiavelli (Chicago, 1970), esp. 25–35; and Corrado Vivanti, *Niccolò Machiavelli: An Intellectual Biography*, trans. Simon MacMichael (Princeton, NJ, 2013).

6. This topic will be discussed in more depth later in this chapter. Good introductions to the topic include R. Claire Snyder, *Citizen Soldiers and Manly Warriors: Military Service and Gender in the Civic Republican Tradition* (Lanham, MD, 1999), and, more critically, Mark Jurdjevic, "Machiavelli's Hybrid Republicanism," *English Historical Review* 122:499 (December 2007): 1228–57.

7. John Robertson, ed., *Andrew Fletcher: Political Works* (Cambridge, 1997), 20. For more on Fletcher, see chapter 7.

8. John Fitzpatrick, ed., *The Writings of George Washington*, 39 vols. (Washington, DC, 1931–44), 26:394.

9. Quoted from the University of Chicago's very useful page on the Virginia Ratifying Convention debates, at http://press-pubs.uchicago.edu/founders/documents/a1_8_12s27.html.

10. Quotation from Vivanti, *Niccolò Machiavelli*, 3. For Machiavelli as a civil servant, see Vivanti, *Niccolò Machiavelli*, 41–54. For the Florentine militia, see Mikael Hörnqvist, "*Perché non si usa allegare i Romani:* Machiavelli and the Florentine Militia of 1506," *Renaissance Quarterly* 55:1 (2002): 148–91.

Niccolò Machiavelli, *Tercets on Ambition*, from *Machiavelli: The Chief Works and Others*, trans. Allan Gilbert, 3 vols. (Durham, NC, 1989), 2:737.

11. For the history of militias in Italy at the time, see Michael Mallett, "Mercenaries," in *Medieval Warfare: A History*, ed. Maurice Keen (Oxford, 1999), 223–29. As Mallett points out, Florence was somewhat behind its neighbors, and Machiavelli did have some difficulty justifying his respect for the Swiss with their status as the leading mercenaries of their day. See also Tarlton, *Fortune's Circle*, 23; and Adorno et al., *The World of Renaissance Florence*, trans. Walter Darwell (Florence, 1999), 202–5.

12. Machiavelli, *Tercets on Ambition*, 2:737.

13. As Strathern points out, Machiavelli was able to rise quickly as a civil servant and diplomat in the small world of Florentine politics, but his experience as a diplomat would show him how little weight Florence pulled in larger European struggles. When he was sent on a diplomatic mission to the French court, his eight-day journey over the Alps was followed by a thirteen-day wait to meet with King Louis XII, who was much more concerned with Spain. Strathern, *The Artist*, 53.

14. Again, the best source is Machiavelli's own letters, collected in *Machiavelli and His Friends*. Quotations here are from letters 204 (13 March 1513) and 206 (18 March 1513), both to Francesco Vettor from Niccolò Machiavelli, *Machiavelli and His Friends*, 221, 222. See also Tarlton, *Fortune's Circle*, 32, 34. Tarlton describes Machiavelli's crisis of 1512–13 as "of unrelenting significance to an understanding of Machiavelli's life, and especially to an understanding of the relationship between his life and his writings," adding that Machiavelli retained "a sense of bitterness, a resentment against Fortune, which had toyed so maliciously with his life and the happiness of his city, and against the Medici who had been such a willing instrument of Fortune."

15. Machiavelli, *Machiavelli and His Friends,* letter 224, 262–65. This letter is also widely available online.

16. Machiavelli, *Machiavelli and His Friends,* letter 224, 265.

17. Niccolò Machiavelli, *Discourses on Livy,* trans. Harvey C. Mansfield and Nathan Tarcov (Chicago, 1996).

18. For more discussion of Livy, see chapter 1. See also J. Patrick Coby, *Machiavelli's Romans: Liberty and Greatness in the "Discourses on Livy"* (Lanham, MD, 1999).

19. Machiavelli, *The Prince,* 10.

20. Machiavelli, *Discourses on Livy,* 5.

21. Machiavelli, *Discourses on Livy,* 6.

22. Machiavelli, *Discourses on Livy,* 33.

23. Many scholars have pointed out Machiavelli's frequent use of gendered language in his writings and his concern with citizens' being sufficiently masculine. The starting point in this debate remains Hannah Fenichel Pitkin, *Fortune Is a Woman: Gender and Politics in the Thought of Niccolò Machiavelli* (Berkeley, 1984). Pitkin notes that for Machiavelli "republican activism seems to be linked to 'manly' heroism and military glory, and to disdain for the household, the private, the personal, and the sensual," and "political, military and sexual achievement are somehow merged. Political power and military conquest are eroticized, and Eros is treated as a matter of conquest and domination." Pitkin, *Fortune Is a Woman,* 5, 25. But see also the essays in Maria J. Falco, ed., *Feminist Interpretations of Niccolo Machiavelli* (University Park, PA, 2004).

24. Machiavelli, *Discourses on Livy,* 271.

25. Machiavelli, *Discourses on Livy,* 272.

26. Machiavelli, *Discourses on Livy,* 9.

27. Machiavelli, *Discourses on Livy,* 91.

28. Machiavelli, *Discourses on Livy,* 91.

29. Machiavelli, *Discourses on Livy,* 91.

30. As Coby points out, "Perhaps nothing so attracts Machiavelli to ancient Rome as that city's reliance upon citizen-soldiers." Machiavelli was "a stickler for military training," including peacetime training, which allowed for "stoic-like equanimity in the face of good and bad fortune." Coby, *Machiavelli's Romans,* 130–31.

31. Niccolò Machiavelli, *The Art of War,* in *Machiavelli: The Chief Works and Others,* trans. Allan Gilbert, 3 vols. (Durham, NC, 1989), vol. 2.

32. Machiavelli, *The Art of War,* 570.

33. Machiavelli, *The Art of War,* 567.

34. Machiavelli, *The Art of War,* 572.

35. Machiavelli, *The Art of War,* 578.

36. Machiavelli, *The Art of War,* 570.

37. Machiavelli, *The Art of War,* 576.

38. Machiavelli, *The Art of War,* 576.

39. Machiavelli, *The Art of War,* 566.

40. Machiavelli, *Discourses on Livy,* 21–22.

41. Machiavelli, *The Art of War,* 585.

42. Machiavelli, *The Art of War,* 578.

43. J. G. A. Pocock, *The Machiavellian Moment: Florentine Political Thought and the Atlantic Republican Tradition* (Princeton, 1975); Bernard Bailyn, *The Ideological Origins of the American Revolution* (Cambridge, MA, 1992 [first published 1967]); Gordon Wood, *The Creation of the American Republic, 1776–1787* (Chapel Hill, NC, 1969). See also Asher Horowitz and R. K. Matthews, "A Narcissism of the Minor Differences: What Is at Issue and What Is at Stake in the Civic Humanism Question," in *The World Turned Upside Down: The State of Eighteenth-Century American Studies at the Beginning of the Twenty-First Century,* ed. Michael Kennedy and William Shade (Bethlehem, PA, 2001), 224–53. Some important criticisms include Ryan Balot and Stephen Trochimchuk, "The Many and the Few: On Machiavelli's 'Democratic Moment,'" *Review of Politics* 74:4 (October 2012): 559–88; Mark Jurdjevic, "Machiavelli's Hybrid Republicanism," *English Historical Review* 122:499 (December 2007): 1228–57; and John P. McCormick, "Machiavelli against Republicanism: On the Cambridge School's 'Guiccardinian Moments,'" *Political Theory* 31:5 (October 2003): 615–43.

44. Machiavelli, *The Prince,* 83.

45. Machiavelli, *The Prince,* 49.

46. Machiavelli, *The Prince,* 48.

47. Machiavelli, *The Prince,* 48–49.

48. Machiavelli, *The Prince,* 83.

49. Machiavelli, *Discourses on Livy,* 33.

50. Machiavelli, *The Art of War,* 587.

51. In chapter three, for example, Machiavelli blames France's King Louis XII for allowing Spain to become powerful at its own expense. Machiavelli, *The Prince,* 16.

3. The Fall of La Rochelle

1. David Parker, *La Rochelle and the French Monarchy: Conflict and Order in Seventeenth-Century France* (London, 1980), 6–8.

2. David Parrott, *Richelieu's Army: Government and Society in France, 1624–1642* (Cambridge, 2001), 9–15.

3. The starting point for the historiography of French absolutism remains William Beik, *Absolutism and Society in Seventeenth-Century France: State Power and Provincial Aristocracy in Languedoc* (Cambridge, 1985). See also David Parker, "Sovereignty, Absolutism and the Function of the Law in Seventeenth-Century," *Past and Present* 122 (1989): 36–74; and Mark Greengrass, *Conquest and Coalescence: The Shaping of the State in Early Modern Europe* (London, 1991).

4. Quoted in Richard Bonney, *Society and Government in France under Richelieu and Mazarin, 1642–61* (London, 1988), 7–8. Mack Holt also attributes the letter to Richelieu. Mack Holt, *The French Wars of Religion, 1562–1629* (Cambridge, 2005), 184.

5. Parrott, *Richelieu's Army,* 164–65; Beik, *Absolutism*, 280–85; William Church, *Richelieu and Reason of State* (Princeton, NJ, 1972), 175.

6. Parker, *La Rochelle,* 171.

7. Richard Bonney, *The European Dynastic States, 1494–1660* (Oxford, 1992); Geoffrey Parker, ed., *The Thirty Years' War* (London, 1987).

8. Thomas Cogswell, "Prelude to Ré: The Anglo-French Struggle over La Rochelle, 1624–1627," *History* 71:231 (1986): 6.

9. See, for instance, Georges Duby, *Le Dimanche de Bouvines* (Paris, 1973); Duby, *France in the Middle Ages, 987–1460,* trans. Juliet Vale (Oxford, 1991); and Maurice Keen, "The End of the Hundred Years War: Lancastrian France and Lancastrian England," in *England and Her Neighbors, 1066–1453,* ed. Michael Jones and Malcolm Vale (London, 1989).

10. The transformations of the seventeenth century have been the subject of a number of overarching interpretations. See, for instance, Geoffrey Parker and Lesley Smith, eds., *The General Crisis of the Seventeenth Century* (London, 1978); Peter Burke, *Popular Culture in Early Modern Europe* (London, 1978); Geoffrey Parker, *Global Crisis: War, Climate Change and Catastrophe in the Seventeenth Century* (New Haven, CT, 2013); J. Michael Hayden and Malcolm R. Greenshields, "Les Réformations catholiques en France: le témoignage des statuts synodaux," *Revue d'histoire moderne et contemporaine* 48:1 (2001): 5–29, esp. 25. All point, one way or another to the transformations that occurred in Europe during the middle of the seventeenth century.

11. For an overview, see Clifford Rogers, "The Practice of War," in *A Companion to the Medieval World,* ed. Carol Lansing and Edward English (Malden, MA, 2009), 435–54.

12. See John Elliott, *Richelieu and Olivares* (Cambridge, 1984), 60; Perry Anderson, *Lineages of the Absolutist State* (London, 2013), 48; and Victor Tapie, *France in the Age of Louis XIII and Richelieu*, trans. D. Lockie (New York, 1975), 190.

13. Parker, *La Rochelle,* 115; James Collins, *The State in Early Modern France*, 2nd ed. (Cambridge 2009), 20, 115–16.

14. On this topic, see the discussions in chapters 4 and 6.

15. Lois Schwoerer, *"No Standing Armies!": The Antiarmy Ideology in Seventeenth-Century England* (Baltimore, 1974).

16. Linda Colley, *Britons: Forging the Nation, 1707–1837* (New Haven, CT, 1992), 17, 368. See also Gerald Newman, *The Rise of English Nationalism: A Cultural History, 1740–1830* (New York, 1987).

17. See the discussions of John Trenchard and Andrew Fletcher of Saltoun in chapter 6.

18. See the discussions in Parker, *Global Crisis,* chapters 10–12.

19. Jean-Vincent Blanchard, *Éminence: Cardinal Richelieu and the Rise of France* (New York, 2011), 96.

20. James Wood, *The King's Army: Warfare, Soldiers and Society during the Wars of Religion in France, 1562–1576* (Cambridge, 1996), esp. 4–5.

21. Holt, *The French Wars of Religion,* 179–83.

22. Parker, *La Rochelle,* 99.

23. Quoted in Bonney, *Society and Government,* 95.

24. Blanchard, *Éminence,* 99–104.

25. Blanchard, *Éminence,* 100–102.

26. Blanchard, *Éminence,* 92, 95, 100; Cogswell, "Prelude to Ré," 15–17.

27. Greg Koabel, "Youth, Manhood, Political Authority, and the Impeachment of the Duke of Buckingham," *Historical Journal* 57:3 (2014): 597–98, 602. For a more sympathetic view of Buckingham, see Mark Kishlansky, *A Monarchy Transformed: Britain, 1603–1714* (London, 1997), 96–98, 110.

28. Kishlansky, *Monarchy Transformed,* 96–98, 107–8.

29. Roger Manning, *An Apprenticeship in Arms: The Origins of the British Army, 1585–1702* (Oxford, 2006), 117–18.

30. Quoted in Mark Fissel, *English Warfare, 1511–1642* (London, 2001), 267.

31. Laurence Spring, *The First British Army, 1624–1628: The Army of the Duke of Buckingham* (Devon, 2016), 198; Blanchard, *Éminence,* 91.

32. Blanchard, *Éminence,* 104.

33. Blanchard, *Éminence,* 102, 107.

34. For the best overview of Roberts's theories and their reception, see Geoffrey Parker, "The 'Military Revolution,' 1560–1660—a Myth?" *Journal of Modern History* 48:2 (June 1976), 195–214. See also David Parrott, "Cultures of Combat in the Ancien Régime: Linear Warfare, Noble Values, and Entrepreneurship," *International History Review,* 27:3 (September 2005): 518–33.

35. Parker, "The Military Revolution."

36. Parker, "The Military Revolution," 206.

37. Steve Pincus, *1688: The First Modern Revolution* (New Haven, CT, 2009), 314.

38. For overviews of the Protestant Reformation, see Ulinka Rublack, *Reformation Europe* (Cambridge, 2017); and Thomas Brady, *The Politics of the Reformation in Germany: Jacob Sturm (1489–1553) of Germany* (Atlantic Highlands, NJ, 1997).

39. For overviews of the French Reformation and Wars of Religion, see Barbara Diefendorf, *Beneath the Cross: Catholics and Huguenots in Sixteenth-Century Paris* (Oxford, 1991); and Robert Kingdon, *Myths about the Saint Bartholomew's Day Massacres, 1572–1576* (Cambridge, MA, 1988).

40. I borrow the term "culture of revolt" from Brian Sandberg, *Warrior Pursuits: Noble Culture and Civil Conflict in Early Modern France* (Baltimore, 2010), 189–93.

41. Sandberg, *Warrior Pursuits,* 223.

42. Quentin Skinner, *The Foundations of Modern Political Thought,* 2 vols. (Cambridge, 1978), 2:302–38.

43. Parker, *La Rochelle,* 99.

44. Wood, *The King's Army,* 4–5. See also the classic essay by Natalie Zemon Davis, "The Rites of Violence," in *Society and Culture in Early Modern France* (Palo Alto, CA, 1975), 152–88.

45. Good overviews of the period include Holt, *The French Wars of Religion;* and Diefendorf, *Beneath the Cross.*

46. Elliott, *Richelieu and Olivares,* 35–38.

47. Parker, *La Rochelle,* 31.

48. Anthony Levi, *Cardinal Richelieu and the Making of France* (NY, 2000).

49. Elliott, *Richelieu and Olivares,* 18.

50. Elliott, *Richelieu and Olivares,* 36.

51. As Elliot has noted, the *Political Testament* "can safely be taken as an expression of his own ideas and of the self-image which he wished to transmit to posterity," even if it was "in large part the work of others." Elliott, *Richelieu and Olivares,* 4.

52. Armand Jean du Plessis, duc de Richelieu, *The compleat statesman, or, The political will and testament of that great minister of state, Cardinal Duke de Richelieu from whence Lewis the XIV . . . has taken his measures and maxims of government: in two parts* (London, 1695), 1–2.

53. Richelieu, *The compleat statesman,* 12.

54. Wood, *The King's Army,* 44.

55. Richelieu, *The compleat statesman,* 52.

56. Richelieu, *The compleat statesman,* 51.

57. Richelieu, *The compleat statesman,* 51–52.

58. Richelieu, *The compleat statesman,* 64.

59. Richelieu, *The compleat statesman,* 55.

60. Richelieu, *The compleat statesman,* 57.

61. Richelieu, *The compleat statesman,* 110.

62. Richelieu, *The compleat statesman,* 111.

63. Richelieu, *The compleat statesman,* 109.

64. Bonney, *Society and Government,* 163.

65. Parker, *La Rochelle,* 115.

66. Parrott, *Richelieu's Army,* 182, 220. As Parrot notes, these estimates are considerably lower than the previously accepted totals of 100,000–120,000 soldiers.

67. Parrott, *Richelieu's Army,* 222.

68. Perry Anderson, *Lineages of the Absolutist State* (London, 2013), 48.

69. François-André Isambert et al., *Recueil générale des anciennes lois françaises depuis l'an 420 jusqu'à la Révolution de 1789,* 29 vols. (Paris, 1821–33), 1:246.

70. John Trenchard, "A Letter from the Author of the Argument against a Standing Army, to the author of the Ballancing Letter," in *A Collection of State Tracts Published during the Reign of King William III* (London, 1706), 2:591.

71. See, for instance, Saul Cornell, "The Right to Keep and Carry Arms in Anglo-American Law: Preserving Liberty and Keeping the Peace," *Law and Contemporary Problems* 80 (2017): 11–54; and Joyce Malcolm, *To Keep and Bear Arms: The Origins of an Anglo-American Right* (Cambridge, MA, 1996).

72. Helen Nicholson, *Medieval Warfare: Theory and Practice of War in Europe, 300–1500* (London 2004), 46–48.

73. See Thomas Macaulay's classic history of England, where he attributed England's freedom to its lack of a standing army, made possible by its physical separation from the continent. Lord Macaulay, *The History of England from the Accession*

of James the Second, ed. C. Firth, 6 vols. (New York 1968), 1:38, discussed further in chapter 4.

74. Discussed in chapter 6.

4. England's Parliament Debates the Militia Act

1. Mark Kishlansky, *A Monarchy Transformed: Britain, 1603–1714* (London, 1997), 113–212.

2. K. J. Kesselring, ed., *The Trial of Charles I: A History in Documents* (Peterborough, ON, 2016), 64.

3. The period of Charles I's trial was actually a setback in that process; during the late 1640s and into the 1650s, France saw a major uprising by the nobility, after the death of Louis XIII but before Louis XIV began his personal reign. That revolt would be short lived; Cardinal Mazarin, Richelieu's successor, was able to regain control. Orest Ranum, *The Fronde: A French Revolution, 1648–1652* (New York, 1993).

4. See, for instance, J. G. A. Pocock, *The Ancient Constitution and the Feudal Law* (Cambridge, 1957).

5. Kishlansky, *Monarchy Transformed,* 115–23.

6. Kesselring, *The Trial of Charles I,* 34.

7. Henry Reece, *The Army in Cromwellian England, 1649–1660* (Oxford, 2013), 6. This total includes deaths in battle as well as from accident or disease.

8. Kesselring, *The Trial of Charles I,* 34.

9. Kesselring, *The Trial of Charles I,* 36.

10. Kesselring, *The Trial of Charles I,* 66.

11. *A Complete History of England, with the Lives of all the Kings and Queens Thereof* (London, 1706), 2:172.

12. Geoffrey Parker, *Global Crisis: War, Climate Change and Catastrophe in the Seventeenth Century* (New Haven, CT, 2013), 328–32.

13. Quoted in David Sharp, *Oliver Cromwell* (Oxford, 2003).

14. Quoted in J. P. Kenyon, *The Stuart Constitution: Documents and Commentary* (Cambridge, 1966), 340.

15. Jack Rakove, *Declaring Rights: A Brief History with Documents* (Boston, 1998), 6–12.

16. Steve Pincus, *1688: The First Modern Revolution* (New Haven, CT, 2009), 4–5; Charles-Édouard Levillain, "Thomas Macaulay ou comment s'en débarrasser. Autour d'un ouvrage de Steven Pincus : nouvelles perspectives historiographiques sur la Glorieuse Révolution (1688)," *Histoire, économie & société,* 30:1 (March 2011): 3–22.

17. See, for example, the Declaration and Resolves of the First Continental Congress, October 14, 1774, available at Yale Law School, Lillian Goldman Law Library, https://avalon.law.yale.edu/18th_century/resolves.asp. See also Rakove, *Declaring Rights,* 12–13.

18. Lord Macaulay, *The History of England from the Accession of James the Second,* ed C. Firth, 6 vols. (New York, 1968), 36.

19. This line of argument is covered in depth in chapter 6.

20. Helen Nicholson, *Medieval Warfare: Theory and Practice of War in Europe, 300–1500* (London, 2004), 2–6.

21. Nicholson, *Medieval Warfare,* 47.

22. Nicholson, *Medieval Warfare,* 47–8.

23. Nicholson, *Medieval Warfare,* 48.

24. R. H. Hilton, *Class Conflict and the Crisis of Feudalism: Essays in Medieval Social History* (London, 1985), 155–59.

25. See, for instance, Desmond Seward, *A Brief History of the Wars of the Roses* (London, 1995).

26. See the discussion of Andrew Fletcher of Saltoun in chapter 6, as well as the discussion of Harrington later in this chapter.

27. Michael Braddick, *State Formation in Early Modern England, c. 1550–1700* (Cambridge, 2000), 182.

28. Victor Stater, *Noble Government: The Stuart Lord Lieutenancy and the Transformation of English Politics* (Athens, GA, 1994), 12–13.

29. Braddick, *State Formation,* 190.

30. Stater, *Noble Government,* 15.

31. Braddick, *State Formation,* 185, 187, 192.

32. Neil Younger, "If the Armada Had Landed: A Reappraisal of England's Defences in 1588," *History* 93:3 (July 2008): 329–30.

33. Stater, *Noble Government,* 25.

34. Charles-Édouard Levillain, *Un glaive pour un royaume. La querelle de la milice dans l'Angleterre du XVIIe siècle* (Paris, 2014), 52–56; Lois Schwoerer, "'The Fittest Subject for a King's Quarrel': An Essay on the Militia Controversy 1641–1642," *Journal of British Studies* 11:1 (November 1971), 58.

35. William Cobbett, *The Parliamentary History of England,* 36 vols. (London, 1806–20), 2:1083.

36. Schwoerer, "'The Fittest Subject,'" 45.

37. Quoted in Cobbett, *The Parliamentary History of England,*2:1129.

38. Schwoerer, "'The Fittest Subject,'" 75.

39. Cobbett, *The Parliamentary History of England,* 2:1355.

40. Kishlansky, *Monarchy Transformed,* 151; Joyce Malcolm, "A King in Search of Soldiers: Charles I in 1642," *Historical Journal* 21:2 (1978): 265: "A more politically inept motto than this, with its rigid insistence upon absolute obedience even to a tyrant, could scarcely have been chosen, but in the four days it was displayed at Nottingham, few were to see it."

41. Braddick, *State Formation,* 214.

42. Levillain, *Glaive,* 117–18.

43. It was, as historian Charles-Édouard Levillain puts it, "a militarization of the state apparatus." Levillain, *Glaive,* 118.

44. Braddick, *State Formation,* 195.

45. Kishlansky, *Monarchy Transformed,* 160.

46. Kishlansky, *Monarchy Transformed,* 152; Malcolm, "A King in Search of Soldiers," 254–57.

47. David Armitage, "The Cromwellian Protectorate and the Languages of Empire," *Historical Journal* 35:3 (1992): 532–33.

48. Martyn Bennett, *Cromwell at War: The Lord General and His Military Revolution* (London, 2017); Peter Gaunt, *Oliver Cromwell* (New York, 2004); Malcolm Wanklyn and Frank Jones, *A Military History of the English Civil War, 1642–1646* (Great Britain, 2005); John Milton, *The Annotated Milton: Complete English Poems,* ed. Burton Raffel (New York, 1999), 40.

49. Levillain, *Glaive,* 117.

50. Levillain, *Glaive,* 121.

51. Levillain, *Glaive,* 131–32.

52. Caroline Robbins, *The Eighteenth-Century Commonwealthman: Studies in the Transmission, Development and Circumstance of English Liberal Thought from the Restoration of Charles II until the War with the Thirteen Colonies* (Cambridge, MA, 1959), 3.

53. Pocock had a different vision of Harrington's importance and described *Oceana* as "one of those works that transcend their immediate context," and "paradigmatic breakthrough." After that, scholarly interest in Harrington followed a familiar path for things intellectual: a flurry of enthusiasm, followed by a wave of skepticism. *Oceana* has since found its place in the canon of English intellectual history, with interest in Harrington higher than it was before Pocock wrote, but a far cry from what it was in the 1980s—which is probably the appropriate place. Pocock, *Machiavellian Moment,* 384.

54. James Harrington, *"The Commonwealth of Oceana" and "A System of Politics,"* ed. J. G. A. Pocock (Cambridge, 1992), 8–9.

55. Harrington, *"The Commonwealth of Oceana,"* 60.

56. Harrington, *"The Commonwealth of Oceana,"* 207.

57. Robbins, *The Eighteenth-Century Commonwealthman,* 22, 34.

5. Bacon's Rebels Burn Jamestown to the Ground

1. The classic account and interpretation of Bacon's Rebellion is Edmund Morgan, *American Slavery, American Freedom: The Ordeal of Colonial Virginia* (New York, 1975), chapter 13. Morgan's influence will be discussed later in the chapter. Other accounts of the rebellion include Daniel Richter, *Before the Revolution: America's Ancient Pasts* (Cambridge, MA, 2011), 265–77; Wilcomb Washburn, *The Governor and the Rebel: A History of Bacon's Rebellion in Virginia* (Chapel Hill, NC, 1957); James Rice, "Bacon's Rebellion in Indian Country," *Journal of American History* 101:3 (2014): 726–50; Kathleen Brown, *Good Wives, Nasty Wenches, and Anxious Patriarchs: Gender, Race, and Power in Colonial Virginia* (Chapel Hill, NC, 1996), chapter 5; Ethan Schmidt, *The Divided Dominion: Social Conflict and Indian Hatred in Early Virginia*

(Boulder, CO, 2015), chapter 6; and Thomas Jefferson Wertenbaker, *Torchbearer of the Revolution: The Story of Bacon's Rebellion and Its Leader* (Princeton, NJ, 1940).

2. Quoted in *The Beginning, Progress, and Conclusion of Bacon's Rebellion in Virginia, In the Years 1675 and 1676, by T.M., a planter from Northumberland and an Assembly member,* in *Tracts and Other Papers Relating Principally to the Origin, Settlement, and Progress of the Colonies in North America, from the Discovery of the Country to the Year 1776,* ed. Peter Force, 3 vols. (Washington, DC, 1836–46), 1:17. (Note that each item in Force's useful collection is separately paginated.)

3. Quoted in *The Beginning, Progress, and Conclusion,* 1:17.

4. Quoted in Warren Billings, ed., *The Old Dominion in the Seventeenth Century: A Documentary History of Virginia, 1606–1700* (Chapel Hill, NC, 2007), 345.

5. Historians often cite this quotation from Berkeley. It is quoted here from Washburn, *The Governor and the Rebel,* 39. Washburn cites a letter Berkeley wrote to "Mr. Secretary" [Thomas Ludwell], 1 July 1676. See also Stephen Webb, *1676: The End of American Independence* (New York, 1984), 16.

6. For the relationship between Berkeley and Bacon, see the useful if dated account in Wertenbaker, *Torchbearer of the Revolution,* 39–60. See also Washburn, *The Governor and the Rebel*, 17–18; and Richter, *Before the Revolution*, 270–71.

7. Billings, *The Old Dominion,* 344.

8. Quoted in Schmidt, *The Divided Dominion,* 161. For more on Bacon as a "Cambridge-educated thirty-something ne'er-do-well" see Richter, *Before the Revolution*, 268.

9. For background on Berkeley and his vision for Virginia, see Richter, *Before the Revolution,* 270–73; for his military background, and his pre-1676 approach to relations with the indigenous population, see Schmidt, *The Divided Dominion*, 153.

10. For the history of "gentility" in colonial Virginia and its ties to different codes of masculinity, see Brown, *Good Wives, Nasty Wenches,* 247–82. As Brown points out, there would eventually be a "genteel" Virginia elite, but not until the eighteenth century. During the seventeenth century, "elite codes for gentlemanly conduct were irrelevant to the concept of honor driving" Bacon and his supporters. Brown, *Good Wives, Nasty Wenches*, 172.

11. For the history of Virginia before Bacon, aside from the works by Morgan and Brown already cited, see Alan Taylor, *American Colonies: The Settling of North America* (New York, 2001), 118–48.

12. Morgan, *American Slavery,* chapters 6–7; Taylor, *American Colonies*, 136–37.

13. For the population numbers, see Morgan, *American Slavery,* 159.

14. Taylor, *American Colonies,* 136, 153–57.

15. Brown, *Good Wives, Nasty Wenches*, 80–82; Taylor, *American Colonies*,141, 148.

16. Morgan, *American Slavery,* 216.

17. Walter Hening, ed., *The Statues at Large: Being a Collection of All the Laws of Virginia, from the First Session of the Legislature, in the Year 1619,* 13 vols. (New York, 1809–1823), 2:126.

18. Brown, *Good Wives, Nasty Wenches.* As Brown points out, long guns had long been pervasive in Virginia culture, and denying a man the right or ability to arm himself amounted to an "exclusion from the community of male householders" (177).

19. See Philip Bruce, *Institutional History of Virginia in the Seventeenth Century,* 2 vols. (Gloucester, MA, 1964), 2:2–5, 61–64.

20. Quoted in Hening, *Statutes,* 1:94.

21. "Instructions to Sir William Berkeley, August 1641," in *The Old Dominion in the Seventeenth Century,* 63.

22. The classic starting point for histories of the colonial militia remains John Shy, *A People Numerous and Armed: Reflections on the Military Struggle for American Independence* (Ann Arbor, MI, 1990), 29–43. See also Lawrence Cress, *Citizens in Arms: The Army and the Militia in American Society to the War of 1812* (Chapel Hill, NC, 1982); William Shea, *The Virginia Militia in the Seventeenth Century* (Baton Rouge, 1983); and Sally Hadden, *Slave Patrols: Law and Violence in Virginia and the Carolinas* (Cambridge, MA, 2001).

23. Quoted in *The Beginning, Progress, and Conclusion,* 8. As Richter points out, Bacon's Rebellion was "exceedingly confusing, for those who lived through it no less than for those who have since tried to make sense of it." Richter, *Before the Revolution*, 265. The following narrative draws on Richter's own, along with the other works cited in note 1 above. Citations in the following narrative are limited to direct quotations.

24. Quoted in *The Beginning, Progress, and Conclusion,* 9.

25. Rice, "Bacon's Rebellion," 736.

26. Quoted in *The Beginning, Progress, and Conclusion,* 10.

27. *An Account of our Late Troubles in Virginia, Written by Mrs. An. Cotton, of Q. Creeke,* in Force, *Tracts and Other Papers*, 4.

28. Quoted in Rice, "Bacon's Rebellion," 739.

29. Quoted in *The Beginning, Progress, and Conclusion,* 12.

30. *A Narrative of the Indian and Civil Wars in Virginia in the Years 1675 and 1676* (Boston, 1814), in Force, *Tracts and Other Papers*, 10.

31. William Berkeley, "Declaration against the Proceedings of Nathaniel Bacon, 1676," in Ronald Bayor, ed., *The Columbia Documentary History of Race and Ethnicity in America* (New York, 2004), 61, 62.

32. *A Narrative of the Indian and Civil Wars,* 15.

33. Hening, *Statutes,* 2:543.

34. Saul Cornell discusses this tension with regard to Shay's Rebellion. "Was the militia an agent of government authority, or was it a popular institution that might serve as a check on government?" Saul Cornell, *A Well-Regulated Militia: The Founding Fathers and the Origins of Gun Control in America* (New York, 2006), 33.

35. Quoted in *The Beginning, Progress, and Conclusion,* 20. See also Webb, *1676*, 45.

36. *A Narrative of the Indian and Civil Wars,* 24–26.

37. Webb, *1676,* 12.

38. See, however, Webb, *1676*, xvi, 4. Webb argues that the events of 1676, including Bacon's Rebellion, transformed the nature of British colonialism in the New World.

39. These themes run through the entire book, but Morgan addresses them most centrally in chapter 18.

40. Morgan, *American Slavery*, 269.

41. Brown, *Good Wives, Nasty Wenches*, 178.

42. Every book and journal article on the topic published since 1975 has situated itself in some way vis-à-vis Morgan's book, but one of the most interesting conversations can be found in an episode of the Junto podcast discussing the book's legacy. As of this writing, that podcast is available at https://thejuntocast.com/archives/ep-17-morgans-american-slavery-american-freedom/.

43. Rice, "Bacon's Rebellion," 737.

44. Morgan, *American Slavery*, 327.

45. On this topic, see especially Brown, *Good Wives, Nasty Wenches*, 180–88, 211.

46. Brown, *Good Wives, Nasty Wenches*, 178–79; Taylor, *American Colonies*, 156–57.

6. Andrew Fletcher of Saltoun Publishes *A Discourse of Government with Relation to Militias*

1. For narratives of the Monmouth Rebellion, see Steve Pincus, *1688: The First Modern Revolution* (New Haven, CT, 2009), 104–5; and Christopher Scott, *The Maligned Militia: The West County Militia of the Monmouth Rebellion, 1685* (Burlington, VT, 2015). For more on Fletcher's role in the rebellion, and for Fletcher's life in general, see G. W. T. Omond, *Fletcher of Saltoun* (New York, 1897).

2. Mark Kishlansky, *A Monarchy Transformed, Britain 1630–1714* (London, 1997), 270–71.

3. Quoted in Scott, *The Maligned Militia*, 22. Scott takes issue with James's (and historians') assessment of the militia's unfairly "maligned" response to the Monmouth Rebellion. See also John Miller, "The Militia and the Army in the Reign of James II," *Historical Journal* 16:4 (1973): 661–62.

4. John Tincey, *Sedgemoor, 1685: Marlborough's First Victory* (Barnsley, South Yorkshire, 2005), 41.

5. John Robertson, ed., *Andrew Fletcher: Political Works* (Cambridge, 1997), introduction; T. C. Smout, "A New Look at the Scottish Improvers," *Scottish Historical Review* 91:231 (2012): 125–49 (discussion of his library on 127).

6. Kishlansky, *Monarchy Transformed*, 277.

7. William Beik, *Absolutism and Society in Seventeenth-Century France: State Power and Provincial Aristocracy in Languedoc* (Cambridge, 1985); David Parker, "Sovereignty, Absolutism and the Function of the Law in Seventeenth-Century," *Past & Present* 122 (1989): 36–74.

8. See the discussion in David Parker, "Absolutism, Feudalism and Property Rights in the France of Louis XIV," *Past & Present* 179 (2003): 62–63.

9. Along with the discussion in chapter 3, see John Lynn, "Recalculating French Army Growth during the Grand Siecle," *French Historical Studies* 18:4 (1994): 881–906.

10. David Bell, *The First Total War: Napoleon's Europe and the Birth of Warfare as We Know It* (Boston, 2007), 32.

11. John Miller, *James II* (New Haven, CT, 2000), chapter 2.

12. Steve Pincus, *1688: The First Modern Revolution* (New Haven, CT, 2009), 125.

13. Pincus, *1688,* 178; Michael Printy, *Enlightenment and the Creation of German Catholicism* (Cambridge, 2009), 36–42.

14. Pincus, *1688,* 6.

15. Miller, "The Militia," 659, 663.

16. Pincus, *1688,* 144.

17. Quoted in Tincey, *Sedgemoor,* 78.

18. Miller, "The Militia," 663–64.

19. Neal Garnham, *The Militia in Eighteenth-Century Ireland: In Defence of the Protestant Interest* (Rochester, NY, 2012), 7–10.

20. Quoted in John Miller, "The Earl of Tyrconnel and James II's Irish Policy, 1685–1688," *Historical Journal* 20:4 (1977): 806, 815–18. Tyrconnell probably went even further in reversing Ireland's traditional policies than his king would have wished.

21. In E. Neville Williams, ed., *The Eighteenth-Century Constitution, 1688–1815: Documents and Commentary* (Cambridge, 1970), 8.

22. Charles-Edouard Levillain, "William III's Military and Political Career in Neo-Roman Context, 1672–1702," *Historical Journal,* 48:2 (2005): 336. Kishlansky also notes that since the age of twenty-two, William of Orange "had spent every waking moment combating the menace of Catholic France." Kishlansky, *Monarchy Transformed*, p. 277.

23. For the events of the Glorious Revolution, see, for example, Kishlansky, *Monarchy Transformed,* 277–90.

24. Levillain, "William III's," 328–29.

25. Quoted in Jack Rakove, *Declaring Rights: A Brief History with Documents* (Boston, 1998), 45.

26. Joyce Lee Malcolm wrote that "the right of ordinary citizens to possess weapons . . . was born in 1689 with its inclusion in that document and perpetuated, with modifications, in the American Bill of Rights a century later." Joyce Lee Malcolm, *To Keep and Bear Arms: The Origins of an Anglo-American Right* (Cambridge, MA, 1994), ix. Lois Schwoerer called 1689 the climax of English gun culture, and also wrote that "at no time prior to 1689 did anyone in print claim the right of English subjects to arms. The idea lacks historical, political, and legal precedent." Lois Schwoerer, *Gun Culture in Early Modern England* (Charlottesville, VA, 2016), 157. See also Adam Winkler, *Gunfight: The Battle over the Right to Bear Arms in America* (New York, 2011), 100–103.

27. The text is widely available, including as an appendix to Lois Schwoerer, *The Declaration of Rights, 1689* (Baltimore, 1981), 295–98.

28. See, for example, Schwoerer, *Gun Culture,* 156–70; David Thomas Konig, "The Second Amendment: A Missing Transatlantic Context for the Historical Meaning of 'The Right of the People to Keep and Bear Arms,'" *Law and History Review* 22:1 (Spring 2004): 119–59; and Lawrence Delbert Cress, *Citizens in Arms: The Army and the Militia in American Society to the War of 1812* (Chapel Hill, NC, 1982), chapter 2.

29. Schwoerer, *Gun Culture,* 159.

30. Schwoerer, *Gun Culture,* 156–70.

31. There were occasional attempts in colonial North America to prevent Catholics from owning weapons or participating in the militia, especially around the time of the French and Indian War. See, for example, Virginia's 1756 An Act for disarming Papists, and reputed Papists, refusing to take the oaths to the government, in Walter Hening, ed., *The Statues at Large: Being a Collection of All the Laws of Virginia, from the First Session of the Legislature, in the Year 1619,* 13 vols. (New York, 1809–23), 7:35. The infinitely more common restrictions, however, were along racial lines between European settlers, the indigenous population, and especially the enslaved African population, as shown in the next chapter.

32. In Rakove, *Declaring Rights,* 41–45.

33. This tradition, and its relevance for American law, is the subject of a huge literature from both historical and legal scholars. Jack Rakove provides a good introduction to the topic in his introduction to *Declaring Rights,* 5–40.

34. Saul Cornell, *A Well-Regulated Militia: The Founding Fathers and the Origins of Gun Control in America* (New York, 2006), 12.

35. Kishlansky, *Monarchy Transformed,* 306–10.

36. John Brewer, *The Sinews of Power: War, Money and the English State, 1688–1783* (London, 1989), 30.

37. John Trenchard and Walter Moyle, *An argument, shewing that a standing army is inconsistent with a free government and absolutely destructive to the constitution of the English monarchy* (London, 1697), 1, 3.

38. Robertson, *Andrew Fletcher,* xvi.

39. As Sullivan points out, Walter Moyle's history of Rome was "a vessel for the transmission of a stern, aggressive republicanism very much indebted to Machiavelli. . . . [Moyle] tends to couple Machiavelli's name with other, more reputable thinkers, when, in fact, Machiavelli alone deserves the credit for these distinctive teachings." Vickie Sullivan, "Walter Moyle's Machiavellianism, Declared and Otherwise, in *An Essay upon the Constitution of the Roman Government,*" *History of European Ideas* 37:2 (2012): 121. Petrina adds that in England, the problem of how to reconcile "good" and "bad" versions of Machiavelli "does not seem to have troubled either the Florentine's defenders or his attackers." Alessandra Petrina, *Machiavelli in the British Isles: Two Early Modern Translations of "The Prince"* (Burlington, VT, 2009), 4.

40. Machiavelli, *The Prince,* 48–49.

41. Robertson, *Andrew Fletcher,* 13.

42. Robertson, *Andrew Fletcher,* 3.

43. Robertson, *Andrew Fletcher,* 3–4.

44. Robertson, *Andrew Fletcher,* 6.
45. See the discussion in chapter 3.
46. Robertson, *Andrew Fletcher,* 5.
47. Robertson, *Andrew Fletcher,* 7.
48. Robertson, *Andrew Fletcher,* 6.
49. Robertson, *Andrew Fletcher,* 6.
50. Robertson, *Andrew Fletcher,* 7.
51. Robertson, *Andrew Fletcher,* 9.
52. Robertson, *Andrew Fletcher,* 9.
53. Robertson, *Andrew Fletcher,* 13.
54. Robertson, *Andrew Fletcher,* 10.
55. Robertson, *Andrew Fletcher,* 19.
56. Robertson, *Andrew Fletcher,* 23.
57. Robertson, *Andrew Fletcher,* 20.
58. Robertson, *Andrew Fletcher,* 13.
59. Robertson, *Andrew Fletcher,* 23.
60. Robertson, *Andrew Fletcher,* 24–25.
61. Cornell, *A Well-Regulated Militia,* 66. See also the discussion in Mark Pitcavage, "An Equitable Burden: The Decline of the State Militias, 1783–1858," PhD diss., Ohio State University, 1995, 36–44. For France see Albert Depréaux, "Les régiments provinciaux et l'ordonnance du 19 Octobre 1773," *Revue d'histoire moderne* 13:4 (July–September 1938): 267–86. See also the plans of Rousseau and of Servan, discussed in Julia Osman, *Citizen Soldiers and the Key to the Bastille* (New York, 2015), 62–63.
62. Robertson, *Andrew Fletcher,* 18.
63. Robertson, *Andrew Fletcher,* 61.
64. Robertson, *Andrew Fletcher,* 31.
65. Robertson, *Andrew Fletcher,* 26.
66. Schwoerer, *Gun Culture,* 201–3.
67. Robertson, *Andrew Fletcher,* 22.
68. Robertson, *Andrew Fletcher,* 14.
69. Robertson, *Andrew Fletcher,* 22.
70. Trenchard and Moyle, *An argument,* 8–10.
71. Walter Moyle, *Democracy Vindicated. An Essay on The Constitution & Government of The Roman State* (Norwich, 1796), not paginated.
72. Levillain, "William III's," 346.
73. John Fitzpatrick, ed., *The Writings of George Washington,* 39 vols. (Washington, DC, 1931–44), 26:388.
74. John Toland, *The militia reform'd, or, An easy scheme of furnishing England with a constant land-force capable to prevent or to subdue any forein power, and to maintain perpetual quiet at home without endangering the public liberty* (London, 1699), 18.
75. Toland, *The militia reform'd,* 19.
76. Toland, *The militia reform'd,* 21.

77. Andrew Fletcher, "Two Discourses Concerning the Affairs of Scotland," in Robertson, *Andrew Fletcher,* 58–66.

78. Machiavelli, *The Prince,* 83.

79. Omond, *Fletcher of Saltoun,* 121–22.

80. Robertson, *Andrew Fletcher,* xvii–xviii.

81. Jean-Jacques Rousseau, *Collected Writings of Rousseau,* vol. 11, *Plan for Perpetual Peace, On the Government of Poland, and Other Writings on History and Politics,* ed. Christopher Kelly (Hanover, NH, 2005), 217–21.

82. Jean-Jacques Rousseau, *The Social Contract,* trans. Christopher Betts (Oxford, 1994), 58.

83. Lois G. Schwoerer, "The Role of King William III of England in the Standing Army Controversy—1697–1699," *Journal of British Studies,* 5:2 (May, 1966): 93–94.

84. William Fields and David Hardy, "The Third Amendment and the Issue of the Maintenance of Standing Armies: A Legal History," *American Journal of Legal History* 35:4 (1991): 409. See also Blackstone's *Commentaries on the Laws of England,* which notes that "it has also for many years past been annually judged necessary by our legislature, for the safety of the kingdom, the defence of the possessions of the crown of Great Britain, and the preservation of the balance of power in Europe, to maintain even in time of peace a standing body of troops, under the command of the crown; who are, however, ipso facto disbanded at the expiration of every year, unless continued by parliament." Blackstone, *Commentaries on the Laws of England,* book 1, chapter 13, quoted in Yale Law School, Lillian Goldman Law Library, https://avalon.law.yale.edu/18th_century/blackstone_bk1ch13.asp.

85. Brewer, *Sinews of Power,* remains the classic study of the growth of England's army during the eighteenth century.

86. Lois Schwoerer, "The Literature of the Standing Army Controversy, 1697–1699," *Huntington Library Quarterly* 28:3 (1965): 197.

87. Hannah Smith, "Politics, Patriotism, and Gender: The Standing Army Debate on the English Stage, circa 1689–1720," *Journal of British Studies* 50:1 (2011): 48–75, quote on 54.

88. Caroline Robbins, *The Eighteenth-Century Commonwealthman: Studies in the Transmission, Development and Circumstance of English Liberal Thought from the Restoration of Charles II until the War with the Thirteen Colonies* (Cambridge, MA, 1959), 3.

89. For England's militia during the eighteenth century, see Matthew McCormack, *Embodying the Militia in Georgian England* (Oxford, 2015). For Scotland's, see Konig, "The Second Amendment," 127–30.

7. The Stono Rebels Head for Florida

1. Thomas Cooper and David McCord, eds., *The Statutes at Large of South Carolina,* 22 vols. (Columbia, SC, 1836–41), 9:640. An identical act was passed again in 1734, mentioned on 9:641.

2. Winthrop Jordan, *White over Black: American Attitudes toward the Negro, 1550–1812* (New York, 1977), 110. See also Robert Parkinson, *The Common Cause: Creating Race and Nation in the American Revolution* (Chapel Hill, NC, 2016), 79–82.

3. Jordan, *White over Black,* 114.

4. "Lieutenant Governor Bull's Eyewitness Account." This text, along with the other primary texts that form the documentary basis of this chapter, is available in the invaluable work of Mark Smith, *Stono: Documenting and Interpreting a Slave Revolt* (Columbia, SC, 2005).

5. Quoted in Smith, *Stono,* 15, 17.

6. Quoted in Smith, *Stono,* 17.

7. Julie Anne Sweet, "The British Sailors' Advocate: James Oglethorpe's First Philanthropic Venture," *Georgia Historical Quarterly* 91:1 (Spring 2007): 10–11, 21.

8. Quoted in Smith, *Stono,* 14–15.

9. Quoted in Smith, *Stono,* 17.

10. Quoted in Smith, *Stono,* 15.

11. Smith, *Stono,* xiii.

12. Quoted in Smith, *Stono,* 8.

13. Quoted in Smith, *Stono,* 14, 16.

14. John Thornton, "African Dimensions of the Stono Rebellion," *American Historical Review* 96:4 (1991): 1101–13.

15. Quoted in Smith, *Stono,* 55–56.

16. Smith, *Stono,* xiv.

17. William Styron, *The Confessions of Nat Turner* (London, 2004). See also Patrick Breen, *The Land Shall Be Deluged in Blood: A New History of the Nat Turner Revolt* (Oxford, 2015).

18. As Edward Pearson notes, Stono "did not prompt Anglo-Carolinians to pick up their pens and record their thoughts on paper." Edward A. Pearson, "'A Countryside Full of Flames': A Reconsideration of the Stono Rebellion and Slave Rebelliousness in the Early Eighteenth-Century South Carolina Lowcountry," *Slavery and Abolition* 17:2 (1996): 23.

19. Michael Mullin's *Africa in America: Slave Acculturation and Resistance in the American South and the British Caribbean, 1736–1831* (Urbana, IL, 1995), pays relatively little attention to Stono, as does Eugene Sirman's *Colonial South Carolina: A Political History, 1663–1763* (Williamsburg, VA, 1966), long considered the standard history of colonial South Carolina. Peter Wood, though, describes Stono as a "turning point in the history of South Carolina's black population." Peter H. Wood, *Black Majority: Negroes in Colonial South Carolina from 1670 through the Stono Rebellion* (New York, 1974), 309.

20. Berkeley himself was not indulgent toward Bacon and his followers. In the aftermath of the rebellion, Berkeley had many of those men hanged. This sort of reprisal would disappear over the course of the eighteenth century.

21. See the discussion of Shay's Rebellion and the Whisky Rebellion in chapter 9 and the epilogue.

22. See Sally Hadden, *Slave Patrols: Law and Violence in Virginia and the Carolinas* (Cambridge, MA, 2001); and Daragh Grant, "'Civilizing' the Colonial Subject: The Co-Evolution of State and Slavery in South Carolina, 1670–1739," *Comparative Studies in Society and History* 57:3 (2015): 606–36.

23. For histories of colonial Virginia, see Edmund Morgan, *American Slavery, American Freedom: The Ordeal of Colonial Virginia* (New York, 1975); Kathleen Brown, *Good Wives, Nasty Wenches, and Anxious Patriarchs: Gender, Race, and Power in Colonial Virginia* (Chapel Hill, NC, 1996); Alan Taylor, *American Colonies: The Settling of North America* (New York, 2001), chapters 6, 12–15.

24. Population numbers from https://web.viu.ca/davies/h320/population.colonies.htm. For further estimates of colonial populations, see J. Worth Estes, "Population Growth Tables for the United States since Colonial Times," *Journal of American Studies* 21:2 (1987): 255–63.

25. Quoted in Wilcomb Washburn, *The Governor and the Rebel: A History of Bacon's Rebellion in Virginia* (Chapel Hill, NC, 1957), 39.

26. This was not true of the other British colonies, however. North Carolina, for instance, would see the Regulators movement bring the colony to the brink during the 1760s. See Carole Troxler, *Farming Dissenters: The Regulator Movement in Piedmont North Carolina* (Raleigh, NC, 2011).

27. For the distinction between slave societies and societies with slavery, see Ira Berlin, *Many Thousands Gone: The First Two Centuries of Slavery in North America* (Cambridge, MA, 1998), 8.

28. Brown, *Good Wives, Nasty Wenches,* 132–35.

29. Simon P. Newman, *A New World of Labor: The Development of Plantation Slavery in the British Atlantic* (Philadelphia, 2013), 66.

30. Taylor, *American Colonies,* 237.

31. Taylor, *American Colonies,* 237.

32. Pearson, "'A Countryside Full of Flames,'" 37.

33. Patrick Riordan, "Finding Freedom in Florida: Native Peoples, African Americans, and Colonists, 1670–1816," *Florida Historical Quarterly* 75:1 (Summer 1996): 24–43.

34. Joel S. Berson, "How the Stono Rebels Learned of Britain's War with Spain," *South Carolina Historical Magazine* 110:1/2 (2009): 53–68.

35. See Benjamin Martyn, *An impartial enquiry into the state and utility of the province of Georgia* (London, 1741), 27. See also the discussion in Alan Taylor, *The Internal Enemy: Slavery and War in Virginia, 1772–1832* (New York, 2013), 23: James Madison had warned that the British would try to foment a slave revolt, as "that is the only part in which this Colony is vulnerable."

36. Wood, *Black Majority,* 128. See also An Act for Raising and Enlisting such Slaves as shall be thought serviceable to this Province in Time of Alarms, in *The Earliest Printed Laws of South Carolina, 1692–1734,* ed. John Cushing (Wilmington, DE, 1978), 116.

37. John Shy, "A New Look at Colonial Militia," *William and Mary Quarterly,* 3rd ser., 20:2, (1963): 131.

38. Hadden, *Slave Patrols,* 11.

39. Stanley Engerman, Seymour Drescher, and Robert Paquette, eds., *Slavery* (Oxford, 2001), 105.

40. See the discussion in chapter 6.

41. As militia codes were issued colony by colony, and often reissued with little or no change after several years, there are many such codes available, including in collections of laws and statues compiled later. For South Carolina, these are gathered in Cooper and McCord, *Statutes,* vol. 9, though these are best read in conjunction with the slave codes, which are collected in vol. 7. See also Cushing, *The Earliest Printed Laws of South Carolina,* 470. For Virginia, the militia codes are included in Walter Hening, *The Statutes at Large: Being a Collection of All the Laws of Virginia, from the First Session of the Legislature, in the Year 1619,* 13 vols. (New York, 1809–23). The Virginia laws are in chronological order; some of the militia codes can be found at 3:335, 4:118, 5:16, 6:421. Some other colonial collections include *The Colonial Laws of New York from the Year 1664 to the Revolution* (Albany, 1896), 220, 500; John Cushing, ed., *The Earliest Printed Laws of North Carolina,* 2 vols. (Wilmington, DE, 1977), 1:161; and Cushing, ed., *The Earliest Laws of the New Haven and Connecticut Colonies, 1639–1673* (Wilmington, DE, 1977), 44, 123.

42. Cooper and McCord, *Statutes,* 9: 634.

43. Bernard Bush, ed., *Laws of the Royal Colony of New Jersey,* 5 vols. (Trenton, NJ, 1977), 2:289.

44. Hening, *Statutes,* 4:119.

45. Nathaniel Shurtleff, ed., *Records of the Governor and Company of the Massachusetts Bay in New England,* 5 vols. (New York, 1853–54), 4:257.

46. Hening, *Statutes,* 5:17.

47. *The Colonial Laws of New York from the Year 1664,* 506.

48. John Cushing, ed., *The Laws of the Province of Maryland* (Wilmington, DE, 1978), 116.

49. Cushing, *The Laws of the Province of Maryland,* 125.

50. Cooper and McCord, *Statutes,* 7:386.

51. Shurtleff, *Records,* 4:257; Hening, *Statutes,* 4:119. For laws limiting Indians' and blacks' access to weapons, see Shy, "A New Look" 175–85; Hadden, *Slave Patrols,* 2–4; Philip Morgan and Andrew O'Shaughnessy, "Arming Slaves in the American Revolution," in *The Arming of Slaves: Classical Times to the Modern Age,* ed. Christopher Brown and Philip Morgan (New Haven, CT, 2007), 183; and Bernard Nalty and Morris MacGregor, eds., *Blacks in the Military: Essential Documents* (Wilmington, DE, 1981), 3–15. The many militia regulations available for the American colonies repeatedly show the restrictions on nonwhites. In Maryland, for instance, the laws stated that "all Negroes and Slaves whatsoever shall be exempted the duty of training or other military service" and that "no Negro or other slave within this Province, shall

be permitted to carry any Gun, or any other offensive Weapon from of their Masters Land, without License from their said Master." Cushing, *The Laws of the Province of Maryland*, 116, 125. In New Jersey, the 1704 militia act specified "that this act, nor any article or clause herein contained, shall be construed or taken to allow or give liberty to any Negro, Indian or Malatto Slave or Servant to be listed, or to do any Duty in the Militia of this Province." Bush, *Laws of the Royal Colony of New Jersey*, , 2:19, 4:238. And in Virginia, the colonial government also wrote in 1748 that "no negroe, mulattoe, or Indian whatsoever shall keep, or carry any gun, powder, shot, club, or other weapon, whatsoever." Hening, *Statutes*, 1:441, 525, 6:109.

52. Cooper and McCord, *Statutes,* 9:617.

53. Hening, *Statutes,* 5:16.

54. Hening, *Statures,* 6:530.

55. *Acts and laws, of His Majesties province of the Massachusetts-Bay, in New-England* (Boston, 1699), 47.

56. Hening, *Statutes,* 6:112.

57. Hadden, *Slave Patrols,* 18; Engerman, Drescher, and Paquette, *Slavery,* 106.

58. Cooper and McCord, *Statutes,* 7:343, 345.

59. Cooper and McCord, *Statutes,* 7: 352.

60. Hadden, *Slave Patrols,* 20–21.

61. Smith, *Stono,* 15, 17.

62. See, for instance, Bartlett James and Franklin Jameson, eds., *Journal of Jasper Danckaerts* (New York, 1913), 239: "They were excercised in military tactics, but I have never seen anything worse of the kind"; Alexander Salley, ed., *Narratives of Early Carolina, 1650–1708* (New York, 1911), 295–96; and Timothy Pickering, *An Easy Plan of Discipline for a Militia* (Salem, MA, 1775), 6, 10. Jefferson noted that Virginia's militia laws were "indifferently complied with." Thomas Jefferson, *Notes on the State of Virginia* (Philadelphia, 1788), 98.

63. Hening, *Statutes,* 5:16. See also Shy, "A New Look," 179.

64. Quoted in Smith, *Stono,* 17.

65. Quoted in Smith, *Stono,* 15.

66. Wood, *Black Majority,* 323.

67. Smith, *Stono,* 20–27.

68. Quoted in Smith, *Stono,* 27.

69. Riordan, "Finding Freedom," 24–43.

70. Wood, *Black Majority,* 325.

71. Cooper and McCord, *Statutes,* 7:397. See also Brown, *Good Wives, Nasty Wenches*, 132–35.

72. Grant, "'Civilizing' the Colonial Subject," 615.

73. Wood, *Black Majority,* 127.

74. William Berkeley, "Declaration against the Proceedings of Nathaniel Bacon, 1676," in *The Columbia Documentary History of Race and Ethnicity in America,* ed. Ronald Bayor (New York, 2004), 61, 62.

75. Taylor, *American Colonies,* 226.

76. Taylor, *American Colonies,* 241–43.

77. Riordan, "Finding Freedom," 31–36.

78. Riordan, "Finding Freedom," 34–41. For a broader study of maroon colonies, see Ruma Chopra, *Almost Home: Maroons between Slavery and Freedom in Jamaica, Nova Scotia, and Sierra Leone* (New Haven, CT, 2018).

79. Wood, *Black Majority,* 309.

80. For the English militia in the eighteenth century, see Matthew McCormack, *Embodying the Militia in Georgian England* (Oxford, 2015), esp. 5–8, 116–20.

8. The Minutemen Turn Back the Redcoats at Concord Bridge

1. David Hackett Fischer, *Paul Revere's Ride* (New York, 1995); Robert Gross, *The Minutement and Their World* (New York, 1976), 116; Manuscript of the Letter From Col. Paul Revere to the Corresponding Secretary (Jeremy Belknap), 1798, Paul Revere Heritage Project, http://www.paul-revere-heritage.com/ride-letter-to-Belknap.html. See also Michael Greenburg, *The Court-Martial of Paul Revere: A Son of Liberty and America's Forgotten Military Disaster* (Lebanon, NH, 2014), 46–55.

2. Fischer, *Paul Revere's Ride,* 84–85.

3. Gross, *Minutemen,* 69–73; Mary Fuhrer, "The Revolutionary Worlds of Lexington and Concord Compared," *New England Quarterly* 85:1 (March 2012): 109, 114.

4. For England and the Seven Years' War, see John Brewer, *The Sinews of Power: War, Money and the English State, 1688–1783* (London, 1989), 175.

5. Manuscript of the Letter from Col. Paul Revere to the Corresponding Secretary (Jeremy Belknap), 1798.

6. Gross, *Minutemen,* 6.

7. Andrew O'Shaughnessy, *The Men Who Lost America: British Leadership, the American Revolution, and the Fate of the Empire* (New Haven, CT, 2013), 84.

8. Quoted in Fischer, *Paul Revere's Ride,* 85.

9. O'Shaughnessy, *The Men Who Lost America,* 23, 84.

10. Both quotes from Fischer, *Paul Revere's Ride,* 37.

11. Quoted in Ray Raphael, *The First American Revolution: Before Lexington and Concord* (New York, 2002), 167.

12. Gross, *Minutemen,* 114. Another recent account stresses that Gage's options were limited and his goal was less to succeed in the expedition than to prove to his superiors in London that he had done enough to retain his position. George Daughan, *Lexington and Concord: The Battle Heard Round the World* (NY, 2018), 184–5.

13. Quoted in O'Shaughnessy, *The Men Who Lost America,* 84.

14. Testimony of John Robins, *Journals of the American Congress: From 1774 to 1788,* 4 vols. (Washington, 1823), 1:59–60.

15. "A British Officer at Lexington and Concord, April 19, 1775," Library of Congress, http://www.loc.gov/teachers/classroommaterials/presentationsandactivities/presentations/timeline/amrev/shots/concord.html.

16. Gross, *Minutemen,* 117–18.

17. Gross, *Minutemen,* 118.

18. From the memoir of Joseph Hosmer, quoted in Gross, *Minutemen,* 125.

19. Quoted in Gross, *Minutemen,* 119.

20. Gross, *Minutemen,* 125.

21. See the discussion in chapter 6.

22. Brewer, *Sinews of Power,* 137.

23. England and France were at war from 1689 to 97, from 1702 to 13, from 1739 to 63, and from 1775 to 83. They would also be at war for most of the period from 1793 to 1815. See Brewer, *Sinews of Power,* 27.

24. See, for instance, Matthew McCormack, *Embodying the Militia in Georgian England* (Oxford, 2015); and Linda Colley, *Britons: Forging the Nation, 1707–1837* (New Haven, CT 1992), 287. As Colley notes, this reform was "only patchily effective and was profoundly unpopular. As in France, the burden of militia service fell overwhelmingly on the illiterate poor."

25. Brewer, *Sinews of Power,* 30. As Brewer points out, those numbers "have to be treated with some caution" but the overall trajectory is unmistakable. The war that began in 1702 was known in Europe as the War of Spanish Succession and in North America as Queen Anne's War.

26. Aaron Graham and Patrick Walsh, introduction to *The British Fiscal-Military States, 1660–c. 1783* (London, 2016), 14–20; Brewer, *Sinews of Power,* 137.

27. Brewer, *Sinews of Power,* 45. "In Britain . . . military power had little or no autonomous existence; it was subordinate to those civilians who wielded political authority."

28. Brewer, *Sinews of Power,* 55.

29. Brewer, *Sinews of Power,* 53.

30. See, for example, Stephen Conway, "The Eighteenth-Century British Army as a European Institution," in *Britain's Soldiers: Rethinking War and Society, 1715–1815,* ed. Kevin Linch and Matthew McCormack (Liverpool, 2014), 32–38.

31. Bernard Bailyn, *The Ideological Origins of the American Revolution* (Cambridge, MA, 1992), 62–63; Lawrence Cress, "Radical Whiggery on the Role of the Military: Ideological Roots of the American Revolutionary Militia," *Journal of the History of Ideas* 40:1 (1979): 49–50, 54.

32. *Plutarch's Lives,* trans. John Dryden, 2 vols. (New York, 2006), 2:309.

33. Quoted from *Cato's Letters* (London, 1723), 2:147; Bailyn, *Ideological Origins,* 62; Cress, "Radical Whiggery," 54.

34. Alan Taylor, *American Revolutions: A Continental History, 1750–1804* (New York, 2016), 92–93; Lawrence Delbert Cress, *Citizens in Arms: The Army and the Militia in American Society to the War of 1812* (Chapel Hill, NC, 1982), 35; Ronald Hamowy, "Cato's Letters, John Locke, and the Republican Paradigm," *History of Political Thought* 11:2 (1990): 273–94.

35. Gary L. McDowell, "The Language of Law and the Foundations of American Constitutionalism," *William and Mary Quarterly,* 3rd ser., 55:3 (1998): 378.

36. John Grenier, *The First Way of War: American War Making on the Frontier, 1607–1814* (Cambridge, 2005), 33–35, 55–63.

37. Wayne E. Lee, *Crowds and Soldiers in Revolutionary North Carolina* (Gainesville, FL, 2001), chapter 2.

38. James Green, "Ethan Allen and Daniel Shays: Contrasting Models of Political Representation in the Early Republic," *Early American Literature* 48:1 (2013): 125–51.

39. See, for instance, Wendy Warren, *New England Bound: Slavery in Early New England* (New York, 2016), 6–13.

40. Ann Little, *Abraham in Arms: War and Gender in Colonial New England* (Philadelphia, 2007), 166, 172, 178.

41. John D. Cushing, ed., *Massachusetts Province Laws, 1692–1699* (Wilmington, DE, 1978), 13.

42. *Acts and laws, of His Majesties province of the Massachusetts-Bay, in New-England* (Boston, 1699), 47.

43. Nathaniel Shurtleff, ed., *Records of the Governor and Company of the Massachusetts Bay in New England,* 5 vols. (New York, 1853–4), 5:47.

44. *The acts and resolves, public and private, of the province of the Massachusetts Bay: to which are prefixed the charters of the province: with historical and explanatory notes, and an appendix,* 21 vols. (Boston, 1869–85), 1:684.

45. *The acts and resolves,* 1:130. See also *The Militia Act; together with the rules and regulations for the Militia* (Boston, 1776), 2.

46. Cushing, *Massachusetts Province Laws,* 65.

47. Shurtleff, *Records,* 4:86.

48. Shurtleff, *Records,* 4:257.

49. *The acts and resolves,* 1:606.

50. Shurtleff, *Records,* 4:295.

51. Shurtleff, *Records,* 5:211.

52. Kyle Zelner, *A Rabble in Arms: Massachusetts Towns and Militiamen during King Philip's War* (New York, 2009), chapter 2.

53. Alan Taylor, *American Colonies: The Settling of North America* (New York, 2001), xiii.

54. Quoted in Edmund Morgan, *American Slavery, American Freedom: The Ordeal of Colonial Virginia* (New York, 1975), 379.

55. William Lincoln, ed., *Journals of Each Provincial Congress of Massachusetts in 1774 and 1775* (Boston, 1838), 71.

56. Lincoln, *Journals,* 71.

57. *The Militia Act,* 2.

58. Quoted in Josiah Adams, *An Address Delivered at Acton, July 21, 1835: Being the First Centennial . . .* (Boston, 1835) 45. Adams notes that from November 1774, "a Company of Minute Men was raised by voluntary enlistment" and "by agreement, met for discipline, twice in each week." Adams, *An Address,* 16.

59. Don Higginbotham, "The Early American Way of War: Reconnaissance and Appraisal," *William and Mary Quarterly,* 3rd ser., 44:2 (April 1987): 235.

60. Fred Anderson, *Crucible of War: The Seven Years' War and the Fate of British North America, 1754–1766* (New York, 2007), 168, 288.

61. George Washington to John Augustine Washington, 31 May 1754, available at National Archives, Founders Online, https://founders.archives.gov/documents/Washington/02-01-02-0058.

62. Philip Morgan and Andrew O'Shaughnessy, "Arming Slaves in the American Revolution," in *The Arming of Slaves: Classical Times to the Modern Age,* ed. Christopher Brown and Philip Morgan (New Haven, CT, 2007), 186.

63. Quoted in R. S. Stephenson, "Pennsylvania Provincial Soldiers in the Seven Years' War," *Pennsylvania History: A Journal of Mid-Atlantic Studies* 62: 2 (Spring 1995): 200.

64. Higginbotham, "Early American," 243–44.

65. Jared Sparks, ed., *The Writings of George Washington,* 12 vols. (Boston, 1833–39), 2:1–2.

66. Zelner, *A Rabble in Arms,* chapter 2.

67. Higginbotham, "Early American," 247.

68. Higginbotham, "Early American," 236. See also Justin du Rivage, *Revolution against Empire: Taxes, Politics, and the Origins of American Independence* (New Haven, CT, 2017), 86.

69. David Preston, *Braddock's Defeat: The Battle of the Monongahela and the Road to Revolution* (Oxford, 2015), 256–57.

70. Taylor, *American Revolutions,* 94.

71. The classic account remains Edmund S. Morgan and Helen M. Morgan, *The Stamp Act Crisis: Prologue to Revolution* (Chapel Hill, 1995). Peter D. G. Thomas, "The Stamp Act Crisis and Its Repercussions, Including the Quartering Act Controversy," in *A Companion to the American Revolution,* ed. Jack P. Greene and J. R. Pole (New York, 2008), provides a good recent overview. See also Andrew David Edwards, "Grenville's Silver Hammer: The Problem of Money in the Stamp Act Crisis," *Journal of American History* 104:2 (1 September 2017): 337–62.

72. Many histories of the buildup to the American Revolution cover this material; see, for instance, Gordon Wood, *The American Revolution: A History* (New York, 2003), 27–38.

73. See "Great Britain : Parliament—The Declaratory Act; March 18, 1766," Yale Law School, Lillian Goldman Library, http://avalon.law.yale.edu/18th_century/declaratory_act_1766.asp.

74. Wood, *American Revolution,* 39.

75. Higginbotham, "Early American," 248–49.

76. Benjamin Carp, *Defiance of the Patriots: The Boston Tea Party and the Making of America* (New Haven, CT, 2010), chapter 1.

77. These quotes, along with those from Preston and Bliss in the following paragraph, come from Captain Thomas Preston's Account of the Boston Massacre (13 March 1770), from British Public Records Office, C.O. 5/759, Reprinted in *English Historical Documents,* 12 vols., ed. Merrill Jensen (London, 1955–77), 9:750–53, accessed at AMDOCS: Documents for the Study of American History, http://www.vlib.us/amdocs/texts/preston.html; and Deposition of Theodore

Bliss, accessed at Boston Massacre Historical Society, http://www.bostonmassacre.net/trial/d-bliss.htm.

78. See the recent discussion in Eric Hinderaker, *Boston's Massacre* (Cambridge, MA, 2019).

79. Benjamin Carp, *Defiance of the Patriots: The Boston Tea Party and the Making of America* (New Haven, CT, 2010), 196–98.

80. Alan Taylor, *The Internal Enemy: Slavery and War in Virginia, 1772–1832* (New York, 2013), 23–26.

81. Adams, *An Address,* 30.

82. For the fighting, see Gross, *The Minutemen,* 118–30; and Arthur Tourtellot, *Lexington and Concord: The Beginning of the War of the American Revolution* (New York, 1959), 149–67.

83. Adams, *An Address,* 45.

84. Smith in Adams, *An Address,* 45. In Gross, *Minutemen*, the quote is "Fire, fellow soldiers, for God's sake fire" (125).

85. Adams, *An Address,* 44.

86. Gross, *The Minutemen,* 127.

87. Smith in Adams, *An Address,* 17.

88. "A British Officer at Lexington and Concord, April 19, 1775."

89. Thomas Paine, *Common Sense and Plain Truth,* 4th ed. (Philadelphia, 1776), 23.

90. "A British Officer at Lexington and Concord, April 19, 1775."

91. John Robertson, ed., *Andrew Fletcher: Political Works* (Cambridge, 1997), 10.

92. Lincoln, *Journals,* 71.

93. "Continental Congress: Declarations and Resolves, October 14, 1774," in *Declaring Rights: A Brief History with Documents,* ed. Jack Rakove (Boston, 1998), 66.

94. *Massachusetts Spy,* 3 May 1775, accessed at http://www.teachushistory.org/node/333.

95. Rakove, *Declaring Rights,* 84.

96. Pamela Copeland and Richard McMaster, *The Five George Masons: Patriots and Planters of Virginia and Maryland* (Fairfax, VA, 2016), 216.

97. Rakove, *Declaring Rights,* 87.

98. For the different state declarations of rights, see the collection of texts at Yale Law School, Lillian Goldman Law Library, https://avalon.law.yale.edu/subject_menus/18th.asp. For context on the Vermont constitution, see Willard Randall, *Ethan Allen: His Life and Times* (New York, 2011), 442–45.

99. James Kirby Martin and Mark Edward Lender, *A Respectable Army: The Military Origins of the Republic, 1763–1789,* 2nd ed. (Wheeling, IL, 2006), 4–5.

100. Martin and Lender, *Respectable Army,* 45–46.

101. Gross, *Minutemen,* 151. See also Henry Baird, ed., *General Washington and General Jackson on Negro Soldiers* (Philadelphia, 1863), 1–5.

102. O'Shaughnessy, *The Men Who Lost America,* 86.

103. Greenburg, *The Court-Martial,* 188–209; William Seymour, *The Price of Folly: British Blunders in the War of American Independence* (London, 1995), 55–56;

Donald Proctor, "John Hancock: New Soundings on an Old Barrel," *Journal of American History* 64:3 (1 December 1977): 669.

9. Hamilton, Madison, and Jay Publish *The Federalist*

1. Quoted in Richard H. Kohn, "The Inside History of the Newburgh Conspiracy: America and the Coup d'Etat," *William and Mary Quarterly*, 3rd ser., 27:2 (Apr. 1970): 187–220, quote on 189. See also Michael Meyerson, *Liberty's Blueprint: How Madison and Hamilton Wrote the Federalist Papers, Defined the Constitution, and Made Democracy* (New York, 2009); and James Kirby Martin and Mark Edward Lender, *A Respectable Army: The Military Origins of the Republic, 1763–1789*, 2nd ed. (Wheeling, IL, 2006), 109–11, 187–94.

2. Kohn, "Inside Story," 198; Alan Taylor, *American Revolutions: A Continental History, 1750–1804* (New York, 2016), 317–18.

3. George Washington to Alexander Hamilton, 4 March 1783, National Archives, Founders Online, https://founders.archives.gov/?q=newburgh%20hamilton&s=1111311111&sa=&r=30&sr=.

4. George Washington to Alexander Hamilton, 12 March 1783, National Archives, Founders Online, https://founders.archives.gov/?q=newburgh%20hamilton&s=1111311111&sa=&r=31&sr=.

5. George Washington to Officers of the Army, 15 March 1783, National Archives, Founders Online, https://founders.archives.gov/documents/Washington/99-01-02-10840.

6. Samuel Shaw, *The Journals of Major Samuel Shaw: The First American Consul at Canton* (Boston, 1847), available at https://babel.hathitrust.org/cgi/pt?id=nyp.33433082389820;view=1up;seq=129.

7. Kohn, "Inside History," 220.

8. George Washington to Officers of the Army, 15 March 1783.

9. Alexander Hamilton to George Washington, 25 March 1783, National Archives, Founders Online, https://founders.archives.gov/documents/Hamilton/01-03-02-0194.

10. Ron Chernow, *Alexander Hamilton* (New York, 2004), 72–74, 85, 160–66; Peter Henriques, "The Great Collaboration: The Increasingly Close Relationship between George Washington and Alexander Hamilton," in *Sons of the Father : George Washington and His Protégés*, edited by Robert M. S. McDonald (Charlottesville, VA, 2013), 192–96; Jack Rakove, *Revolutionaries: Inventing an American Nation* (London, 2010), 403–10.

11. Chernow, *Alexander Hamilton*, 108–9.

12. Gordon Wood, *The Radicalism of the American Revolution* (New York, 1991), 261–62; Taylor, *American Revolutions*, 410–11.

13. Rakove, *Revolutionaries*, 416.

14. Quoted in Michael Klarman, *The Framers' Coup: The Making of the United States Constitution* (Oxford, 2016), 24.

15. Thomas Jefferson to Chastellux, 16 January 1784, National Archives, Founders Online, https://founders.archives.gov/documents/Jefferson/01-06-02-0359; Mary

Gallagher, "Reinterpreting the 'Very Trifling Mutiny' at Philadelphia in June 1783," *Pennsylvania Magazine of History and Biography* 119:1/2 (1995): 3–35.

16. Martin and Lender, *Respectable Army*, 43.

17. Samuel Adams to James Warren, 1776, available at Samuel Adams Heritage Society, http://www.samuel-adams-heritage.com/documents/samuel-adams-to-james-warren-1776.html.

18. Martin and Lender, *Respectable Army*, 74.

19. Philip Foner, ed., *The Complete Writings of Thomas Paine*, 2 vols. (New York, 1945), 1:49.

20. Martin and Lender, *Respectable Army*, 91–92. See also Hamilton's proposal that South Carolina arm enslaved African Americans, "to give them freedom with their muskets." Joanne Freeman, ed., *The Essential Hamilton: Letters & Other Writings* (New York, 2017), 43.

21. Martin and Lender, *Respectable Army*, 117; Orville T. Murphy, "The French Professional Soldier's Opinion of the American Militia in the War of the Revolution," *Military Affairs* 32:4 (February 1969): 191–98. See also Laura Auricchio, *The Marquis: Lafayette Reconsidered* (New York, 2014), 55–76; and Taylor, *American Revolutions*, 283–84, 293–96.

22. James Trecothick Austin, *The Life of Elbridge Gerry: With Contemporary Letters*, 2 vols. (Boston, 1828), 1:276.

23. Martin and Lender, *Respectable Army*, 93, 128.

24. By contemporary definitions, as well as those Machiavelli used, the Hessians would have been "auxiliary forces" rather than mercenaries; they were soldiers of their nation, mostly Germany's Hessen-Kassel, whom the British government hired as an army from the Hessen-Kassel government. As Friederike Baer notes, their use in the American Revolution was both consistent with eighteenth century British military practices and controversial in England itself. Friederike Baer, "The Decision to Hire German Troops in the War of American Independence: Reactions in Britain and North America, 1774–1776," *Early American Studies* 13:1 (2015):115–16; Andrew O'Shaughnessy, *The Men Who Lost America: British Leadership, the American Revolution, and the Fate of the Empire* (New Haven, CT, 2013), 11, 92–93, 187–92.

25. For an overview, see Mark V. Kwasny, "Militia, Guerrilla Warfare, Tactics, and Weaponry," in *A Companion to the American Revolution*, ed. Jack Greene and J. R. Pole (Oxford, 2000), 314–19.

26. George Washington to John Hancock, 2 September 1776, National Archives, Founders Online, https://founders.archives.gov/documents/Washington/03-06-02-0162.

27. Martin and Lender, *Respectable Army*, 43.

28. Martin and Lender, *Respectable Army*, 93.

29. John Shy, "A New Look at Colonial Militia," *William and Mary Quarterly*, 3rd ser., 20:2, (1963): 176–85; John Shy, *A People Numerous and Armed: Reflections on the Military Struggle for American Independence*, rev. ed. (Ann Arbor, MI, 1990), esp. 174–77, 236–43.

30. Philip Morgan and Andrew O'Shaughnessy, "Arming Slaves in the American Revolution," in *The Arming of Slaves: Classical Times to the Modern Age*, ed. Christopher Brown and Philip Morgan (New Haven, CT, 2007).

31. Shy, *A People Numerous and Armed*, 174–77.

32. See, for instance, Charles Lee's 1778 proposal, "A Plan for the Formation of the American Army in the least Expensive Manner possible, and at the same Time for rendering their Manoeuvers so little complex that all the Essentials may be learnt, and practiced in a few Weeks," which advocated replacing the Continental army with a large militia force intended to wear down the British army through relentless, but defensive, efforts. In Mark Lender and Garry Stone, *Fatal Sunday: George Washington, the Monmouth Campaign, and the Politics of Battle* (Norman, OK, 2016), 118–21.

33. John Fitzpatrick, ed., *The Writings of George Washington*, 39 vols. (Washington, DC, 1931–44), 26:375, 397. See also Don Higginbotham, "The Federalized Militia Debate: A Neglected Aspect of Second Amendment Scholarship," *William and Mary Quarterly*, 3rd ser., 55:1 (January 1998): 42–43.

34. Fitzpatrick, *The Writings of George Washington*, 26:389.

35. Fitzpatrick, *The Writings of George Washington*, 26:389.

36. Paul David Nelson, "Washington's *Sentiments on a Peace Establishment*," in *The Encyclopedia of the Wars of the Early American Republic, 1783–1812 ed. Spencer Tucker*, 3 vols. (Santa Barbara, CA, 2014) 1:731.

37. See Mark Pitcavage, "An Equitable Burden: The Decline of the State Militias, 1783–1858," PhD diss., Ohio State University, 1995, 35–45.

38. *Journals of the Continental Congress, 1774–1789*, 34 vols. (Washington, DC, 1904–37), 25:722–44.

39. Martin and Lender, *Respectable Army*, 130–31.

40. *Journals of the American Congress: From 1774 to 1778*, 4 vols. (Washington, DC, 1823), 4:438.

41. Klarman, *The Framers' Coup*, 11–24, 70–72.

42. Austin, *The Life of Elbridge Gerry*, 1:462.

43. For the history of the United States under the Articles of Confederation see, for instance, George Van Cleve, *We Have Not a Government: The Articles of Confederation and the Road to the Constitution* (Chicago, 2017), esp. chapter 9; and Klarman, *The Framers' Coup*, chapter 1.

44. Klarman, *The Framers' Coup*, 30; Taylor, *American Revolutions*, 316–17; Van Cleve, *We Have Not a Government*, 99–101.

45. Articles of Confederation available at Yale Law School, Lillian Goldman Law Library, https://avalon.law.yale.edu/18th_century/artconf.asp.

46. Klarman, *The Framers' Coup*, 43–46.

47. Governor James Bowdoin's Proclamation, September 2 1786, quoted in David Brion Davis and Steven Mintz, *The Boisterous Sea of Liberty: A Documentary History of America from Discovery through the Civil War* (New York, 1998), 227.

48. Robert Gross, "The Uninvited Guest: Daniel Shays and the Constitution," in *In Debt to Shays: The Bicentennial of an Agrarian Revolution*, ed. Robert A. Gross (Charlottesville, VA, 1993), 1.

49. James Greene, "Ethan Allen and Daniel Shays: Contrasting Models of Political Representation in the Early Republic," *Early American Literature,* 48:1 (2013): 131.

50. Greene, "Ethan Allen and Daniel Shays," 141.

51. Compare, however, the events described in Krista Camenzind, "Violence, Race and the Paxton Boys," in *Friends and Enemies in Penn's Woods: Indians, Colonists, and the Racial Construction of Pennsylvania,* ed. William Pencat and Daniel Richter (University Park, PA, 2004), 201–20; and Wayne E. Lee, *Crowds and Soldiers in Revolutionary North Carolina* (Gainesville, FL, 2001), chapter 2.

52. James Bowdoin, "AN ADDRESS, To the good People of the Commonwealth," 12 January 1787, Library of Congress, https://www.loc.gov/resource/rbpe.04300600/?st=text.

53. Greene, "Ethan Allen and Daniel Shays," 145–46; Pauline Maier, *Ratification: The People Debate the Constitution, 1787–1788* (New York, 2010), 15–16.

54. Saul Cornell, *A Well-Regulated Militia: The Founding Fathers and the Origins of Gun Control in America* (New York, 2006), 32–34.

55. Klarman, *The Framers' Coup,* 90–93.

56. George Washington to Henry Knox, 3 February 1787, National Archives, Founders Online, https://founders.archives.gov/documents/Washington/04-05-02-0006.

57. Edward Carrington to the governor of Virginia, 8 December 1786, in Edmund Burnett, ed., *Letters of Members of the Continental Congress,* 8 vols. (Washington, DC, 1921), 8:517.

58. Klarman, *The Framers' Coup,* 93.

59. Cornell, *A Well-Regulated Militia,* 30–37.

60. Rob Harper, "Looking the Other Way: The Gnadenhutten Massacre and the Contextual Interpretation of Violence," *William and Mary Quarterly,* 3rd ser., 64:3 (2007): 621–44. As Harper shows, though the Pennsylvania government called for an investigation, the men leading that investigation did all they could to sweep the matter under the rug.

61. Robert Parkinson, *The Common Cause: Creating Race and Nation in the American Revolution* (Chapel Hill, NC, 2016), 534–38.

62. Camenzind, "Violence, Race and the Paxton Boys," 202.

63. There are many histories of the Constitutional Convention available. See, for instance, Klarman *The Framers' Coup,* chapter 3; Jack Rakove, *Original Meanings: Politics and Ideas in the Making of the Constitution* (New York, 1997), 58–93.

64. Jack Rakove, *Revolutionaries: Inventing an American Nation* (London, 2010), 342–43.

65. Jeff Broadwater, *James Madison: A Son of Virginia and a Founder of the Nation* (Chapel Hill, NC, 2012), xi.

66. Rakove, *Original Meanings,* 36–7.

67. Article II, Section 2.1. Emphasis added.

68. Article I, Section 8.15, 16.

69. For the fear that the battles in Lexington and Concord would lead to slave uprisings, for instance, see Parkinson, *The Common Cause,* 78–84.

70. Alan Taylor, *The Internal Enemy: Slavery and War in Virginia, 1772–1832* (New York, 2013), 23–26.

71. Thomas Jefferson to James Madison, 30 January 1787, in*The Republic of Letters: The Correspondence between Jefferson and Madison, 1776–1826,* ed. James Morton Smith, 3 vols. (New York, 1995), 1:461.

72. Thomas Jefferson to James Madison, 20 December 1787, in Smith, *The Republic of Letters,* 1:514.

73. David Waldstreicher, *Slavery's Constitution: From Revolution to Ratification* (New York 2009), 6, 120. See also George Van Cleve, "Founding a Slaveholders' Union, 1770–1797," in *Contesting Slavery: The Politics of Bondage and Freedom in the New American Nation* ed. John Hammond and Matthew Mason (Charlottesville, VA, 2012), 118, 126–28.

74. Thomas Jefferson to James Madison, 20 December 1787, in Smith, *The Republic of Letters,* 1:512.

75. As Cornell notes, "No group in American political history was more heterogeneous than the Anti-Federalists." Saul Cornell, *The Other Founders: Anti-Federalism and the Dissenting Tradition in American, 1788–1828* (Chapel Hill, NC, 1999), 22. See also 26–34.

76. Chernow, *Alexander Hamilton,* 174.

77. Chernow, *Alexander Hamilton,* 305–6.

78. *FP.*

79. Pauline Maier's book remains the most influential account of the ratification process; as she points out, the debates were much broader than just what the leading spokesmen wrote and took place in "taverns, coffeehouses, and over dinner tables" as well. Maier, *Ratification,* ix.

80. Maier, *Ratification,* 282; Higginbotham, "The Federalized Militia Debate," 47–48. See also the discussion of the Virginia Ratifying Convention in chapter 10 of this book.

81. Higginbotham, "The Federalized Militia Debate," 40.

82. *FP* 6, 32.

83. *FP* 8, 41.

84. *FP* 28, 135.

85. *FP* 26, 126.

86. *FP* 29, 142.

87. *FP* 29, 141.

88. *FP* 25, 125.

89. *FP* 21, 102.

90. *FP* 25, 124–125.

91. *FP* 3, 19.

92. *FP* 4, 24.

93. *FP* 8, 39.

94. *FP* 29, 139.

95. *FP* 46, 238.

96. *FP* 46, 238.

97. *FP* 28, 136.

98. *FP* 29, 141.

99. *FP* 84, 420.

100. Cornell, *The Other Founders*, 22.

101. Jack Rakove, *Declaring Rights: A Brief History with Documents* (Boston, 1998), 168–69; Feldman, *Three Lives of James Madison: Genius, Partisan, President* (New York, 2017), 252–54.

10. Congress Amends the Constitution

1. James Madison to George Mason, 29 December 1827, Founders Early Access, https://rotunda.upress.virginia.edu/founders/default.xqy?keys=FOEA-print-02-02-02-1245.

2. Jeff Broadwater, *George Mason, Forgotten Founder* (Chapel Hill, NC, 2006), 74; Noah Feldman, *The Three Lives of James Madison: Genius, Partisan, President* (New York, 2017), 54.

3. James Madison to George Mason, 29 December 1827. For Jeff Broadwater's view of Mason as the chief architect of the declaration, see Broadwater, *George Mason*, 81–85.

4. Broadwater, *George Mason*, 237, 240.

5. See Gordon Wood, *Friends Divided: John Adams and Thomas Jefferson* (New York, 2017), 365.

6. Feldman, *The Three Lives of James Madison*, 25–27, 54.

7. Feldman, *The Three Lives of James Madison*, 235–36.

8. Quoted in Pamela Copeland and Richard McMaster, *The Five George Masons: Patriots and Planters of Virginia and Maryland* (Fairfax, VA, 2016), 216.

9. As Rakove points out, the declaration was "in part" a statement of Virginians' rights as "freeborn heirs of traditions of English liberty," though more than that as well. Jack Rakove, *Revolutionaries: Inventing an American Nation* (London, 2010), 174.

10. Rakove, *Revolutionaries*, 174.

11. Rakove, *Revolutionaries*, 173–74.

12. See Rakove, *Revolutionaries*, 173–81.

13. Jack Rakove, *Declaring Rights: A Brief History with Documents* (Boston, 1998), 84.

14. Pauline Maier, *Ratification: The People Debate the Constitution, 1787–1788* (New York, 2010), 251.

15. Quoted in Neil Cogan, ed., *The Complete Bill of Rights: The Drafts, Debates, Sources, and Origins* (New York and Oxford, 1997), 197.

16. Quoted in Cogan, *The Complete Bill of Rights*, 198.

17. Patrick Henry, Virginia Ratifying Convention, 4 June 1788, http://press-pubs.uchicago.edu/founders/documents/preambles14.html.

18. Maier, *Ratification*, 262.

19. Quoted in Don Higginbotham, "The Federalized Militia Debate: A Neglected Aspect of Second Amendment Scholarship," *William and Mary Quarterly*, 3rd ser., 55:1 (January 1998): 47.

20. Quoted in Cogan, *The Complete Bill of Rights,* 192–96.

21. Cogan, *The Complete Bill of Rights,* 287.

22. Quoted in Cogan, *The Complete Bill of Rights,* 194.

23. Higginbotham, "The Federalized Militia Debate," 50.

24. For the lead-up to Virginia's ratifying convention, see Maier, *Ratification,* 252–57.

25. From "Ratification of the Constitution by the State of North Carolina; November 21, 1789," Yale Law School, Lillian Goldman Law Library, https://avalon.law.yale.edu/18th_century/ratnc.asp. The ratification statements from all thirteen colonies can be found at Yale Law School, Lillian Goldman Law Library, https://avalon.law.yale.edu/subject_menus/18th.asp.

26. These are collected in Cogan, *The Complete Bill of Rights,* 181–83.

27. Jack Rakove, *Original Meanings: Politics and Ideas in the Making of the Constitution* (New York, 1997), 318.

28. Rakove, *Declaring Rights,* 168–69; Feldman, *The Three Lives of James Madison,* 252–54.

29. Madison speech proposing the Bill of Rights, 8 June 1789, American History: From Revolution to Reconstruction and Beyond, http://www.let.rug.nl/usa/documents/1786–1800/madison-speech-proposing-the-bill-of-rights-june-8-1789.php.

30. Amendments to the Constitution, [8 June] 1789, National Archives, Founders Online, https://founders.archives.gov/documents/Madison/01-12-02-0126.

31. Cogan, *The Complete Bill of Rights,* 169, 170.

32. Cogan, *The Complete Bill of Rights,* 173. This discussion of wording and debates draws heavily on the collection of materials in this book, 169–90. See also Helen Veit, Kenneth Bowling, and Charlene Bickford, eds., *Creating the Bill of Rights: The Documentary Record from the First Federal Congress* (Baltimore, 1991), 38.

33. Veit, Bowling, and Bickford, *Creating the Bill of Rights,* 38–39n13.

34. Veit, Bowling, and Bickford, *Creating the Bill of Rights,* 182.

35. Cogan, *The Complete Bill of Rights,* 172.

36. Cogan, *The Complete Bill of Rights,* 174.

37. Robert Rutland, *The Birth of the Bill of Rights, 1776–1791* (New York, 1962), 218–20.

38. For the unimportance of the Second Amendment (but the importance of the militias themselves) in the 1790s, see Saul Cornell, *A Well-Regulated Militia: The Founding Fathers and the Origins of Gun Control in America* (New York, 2006), 84. For the importance of the Fourteenth Amendment to subsequent interpretations of the Bill of Rights, see Adam Winkler, *Gunfight: The Battle over the Right to Bear Arms in America* (New York, 2011), 140–45; and Akhil Amar, "The Bill of Rights and the Fourteenth Amendment," *Yale Law Journal* 101:6 (1992): 1218.

39. James Morton Smith, ed., *The Republic of Letters: The Correspondence between Jefferson and Madison, 1776–1826,* 3 vols. (New York, 1995), 1:514.

40. George Washington to David Humphreys, 22 October 1786, National Archives, Founders Online, https://founders.archives.gov/documents/Washington/04-04-02-0272.

41. Leonard Richards, *Shays's Rebellion: The American Revolution's Final Battle* (Philadelphia, 2003), 43.

42. Quoted from Shay's Rebellion and the Making of a Nation, http://shaysrebellion.stcc.edu/shaysapp/artifact_trans.do?shortName=proclamation_clemency&page=.

43. Robert Gross, "The Uninvited Guest: Daniel Shays and the Constitution," in *In Debt to Shays: the Bicentennial of an Agrarian Rebellion,* ed. Robert Gross (Charlottesville, VA, 1993), 2.

44. Edmund Morgan, *American Slavery, American Freedom: The Ordeal of Colonial Virginia* (New York, 1975), 273–74.

45. Rob Harper, "Looking the Other Way: The Gnadenhutten Massacre and the Contextual Interpretation of Violence," *William and Mary Quarterly,* 3rd ser., 64:3 (2007): 621–44; Krista Camenzind, "Violence, Race and the Paxton Boys," in *Indians, Colonists, and the Racial Construction of Pennsylvania,* ed. William Pencat and Daniel Richter (University Park, PA, 2004), 201–20.

46. Thomas Cooper and David McCord, eds., *The Statutes at Large of South Carolina*, 22 vols. (Columbia, SC, 1836–41), 8:487–89, 496.

47. Hening, *The Statutes at Large: Being a Collection of All the Laws of Virginia, from the First Session of the Legislature, in the Year 1619,* 13 vols. (New York, 1809–23), 13: 351. The law was from 1792. See similar laws from the postrevolutionary period at 11: 489 and 12: 21.

48. Quoted in Peter Force, *Register of the Army and Navy of the United States* (Washington, DC, 1830), 125.

49. See Alan Taylor, *The Internal Enemy: Slavery and War in Virginia, 1772–1832* (New York, 2013), which argues that in Virginia at least, the presence of African Americans in Dunmore's forces led white Virginians to see the enslaved population after the war as "alien enemies rather than potential citizens" and that "white men disdained slaves as degraded and dishonored by their own failure to win freedom" (30).

50. Hadden, *Slave Patrols: Law and Violence in Virginia and the Carolinas* (Cambridge, MA, 2001), 78, 154–66.

51. Carl Bogus, "The Hidden History of the Second Amendment," *UC Davis Law Review* 31:2 (Winter 1998): 309–408, quote on 321.

52. This is the central argument of David Waldstreicher, *Slavery's Constitution: From Revolution to Ratification* (New York 2009). See also Van Cleve, "Founding a Slaveholders' Union, 1770–1797."

53. Bogus, "Hidden History."

54. Robert Parkinson, *The Common Cause: Creating Race and Nation in the American Revolution* (Chapel Hill, NC, 2016), 534–38.

55. Rakove, *Declaring Rights*, 186. See, however, the discussions included in Cogan, *The Complete Bill of Rights*, 169–204.

56. Quoted from *Machiavelli: Political Writings,* trans. and ed. David Wooton (Indianapolis, 2004), 99. The Mansfield and Tarcov translation, which is the one used in chapter 2 of this book, translates this as "If you wish to make a people numerous and armed so as to be able to make a great empire, you make it of such a quality that you can not then manage it in your mode." Niccolò Machiavelli, *Discourses on Livy*, trans. Harvey C. Mansfield and Nathan Tarcov (Chicago, 1996), 21–22.

57. *FP* 29, 141.

Epilogue

1. Alexander Hamilton to George Washington, [5 August] 1794, National Archives, Founders Online, https://founders.archives.gov/documents/Hamilton/01-17-02-0017.

2. Alexander Hamilton to George Washington, 5 August 1794, National Archives, Founders Online, https://founders.archives.gov/documents/Washington/05-16-02-0357. For overviews of the Whiskey Rebellion, see Thomas Slaughter, *The Whiskey Rebellion: Frontier Epilogue to the American Revolution* (Oxford, 1986); William Hogeland, *The Whiskey Rebellion: George Washington, Alexander Hamilton, and the Frontier Rebels Who Challenged America's Newfound Sovereignty* (New York, 2006); and the discussion in Cornell, *Well-Regulated Militia: The Founding Fathers and the Origins of Gun Control in America* (New York, 2006), 78–85.

3. Hugh Brackenridge, *Incidents of the Insurrection in the Western Parts of Pennsylvania, in the Year 1794* (Philadelphia, 1795), 79.

4. Brackenridge, *Incidents,* 58.

5. George Washington, Proclamation of 25 September 1794, Yale Law School, Lillian Goldman Law Library, http://avalon.law.yale.edu/18th_century/gwproc10.asp.

6. Hogeland, *The Whiskey Rebellion,* 235–38.

7. Don Higginbotham, "The Federalized Militia Debate: A Neglected Aspect of Second Amendment Scholarship," *William and Mary Quarterly,* 3rd ser., 55:1 (Jan. 1998): 40–43.

8. US Congress, *The Public Statutes at Large of the United States of America* (Boston, 1845), 1:264.

9. Hogeland, *The Whiskey Rebellion,* 235–38.

10. George Washington to the US Senate and House of Representatives, 19 November 1794, National Archives, Founders Online, https://founders.archives.gov/documents/Washington/05-17-02-0125.

11. George Washington to the US Senate and House of Representatives, 19 November 1794, National Archives, Founders Online, https://founders.archives.gov/documents/Washington/05-17-02-0125.

12. The legacy of Cincinnatus was not without its hazards. In the immediate aftermath of the Revolution, some of the officers created the Society of the Cincinnati as a way of maintaining ties between officers from the French and American armies and chose George Washington as its first president. When the society decided that membership was hereditary, critics quickly accused it of reintroducing nobility into

American society. Washington agreed to remain president only on condition that the society eliminate its rules about hereditary status.

As a side note, not only was hereditary status later reintroduced but the society continues to exist—and its headquarters in Washington, DC, maintains an excellent library for anyone researching militias and citizen-soldiers. See Gary Wills, *Cincinnatus: George Washington and the Enlightenment* (New York, 1984); Gordon Wood, "The Legacy of Rome in the American Revolution," in his *The Idea of America: Reflections on the Birth of the United States* (New York, 2011), 73; and Gerald E. Kahler, *The Long Farewell: Americans Mourn the Death of George Washington* (Charlottesville, VA, 2008), 106–9.

13. Quoted in Jordan, *White over Black: American Attitudes toward the Negro, 1550–1812* (New York, 1977), 381.

14. Quoted in Herbert Aptheker, *American Negro Slave Revolts,* 50th Anniversary ed. (New York, 1993), 157. See also Jordan, *White over Black*, 393.

15. Douglas Egerton, *Gabriel's Rebellion: The Virginia Slave Conspiracies of 1800 and 1802* (Chapel Hill, NC, 1993), 77–78.

16. Quoted in Mark Pitcavage, "An Equitable Burden: The Decline of State Militias, 1783–1858," PhD diss., Ohio State University, 1995, 92.

17. Thomas Jefferson to Chastellux, 16 January 1784, National Archives, Founders Online, https://founders.archives.gov/documents/Jefferson/01-06-02-0359; Mary Gallagher, "Reinterpreting the 'Very Trifling Mutiny' at Philadelphia in June 1783," *Pennsylvania Magazine of History and Biography* 119:1/2 (1995), 3–35; Jefferson to Madison, 30 January 1787, in *The Republic of Letters: The Correspondence between Jefferson and Madison, 1776–1826*, ed. James Morton Smith, 3 vols. (New York, 1995), 1:461.

18. *Journal of the House of Representatives of the United States,* 343; Jeremey Bailey, *Thomas Jefferson and Executive Power*, 272; Pitcavage, "An Equitable Burden," 96–98.

19. Christine McDonald and Robert McDonald, "West from West Point: Thomas Jefferson's Military Academy and the 'Empire of Liberty,'" in *Light and Liberty: Thomas Jefferson and the Power of Knowledge,* ed. Robert McDonald (Charlottesville, VA, 2012), 117–22.

20. David Waldstreicher, *In the Midst of Perpetual Fetes: The Making of American Nationalism, 1776–1820* (Chapel Hill, NC, 1997), 38.

21. Hadden, *Slave Patrols: Law and Violence in Virginia and the Carolinas* (Cambridge, MA, 2001), 78.

22. Hadden, *Slave Patrols,* 205–7.

23. See, for example, Thomas Cooper and David McCord, eds., *The Statutes at Large of South Carolina,* 22 vols. (Columbia, SC, 1836–41), 8:539.

24. See Adam Winkler, *Gun Fight: The Battle over the Right to Bear Arms in America* (New York, 2011), chapter 8.

25. According to the Pew Research Center, "About four in ten men (39%) say they personally own a gun, compared with 22% of women. And while 36% of whites report that they are gun owners, about a quarter of blacks (24%) and 15% of Hispanics

say they own a gun." Kim Parker, Juliana Menasce Horowitz, Ruth Igielnik, J. Baxter Oliphant, and Anna Brown "America's Complex Relationship with Guns: An In-Depth Look at the Attitudes and Experiences of U.S. Adults," Pew Research Center, June 22, 2017, https://www.pewsocialtrends.org/2017/06/22/americas-complex-relationship-with-guns/, 18.

26. Jennifer Carlson, "Legally Armed but Presumed Dangerous: An Intersectional Analysis of Gun Carry Licensing as a Racial/Gender Degradation Ceremony," *Gender & Society,* 32:2 (2018): 204–27.

27. See Jennifer Carlson, "Police Warriors and Police Guardians: Race, Masculinity, and the Construction of Gun Violence," *Social Problems,* 8 August 2019.

28. Robert Churchill, "Gun Ownership in Early America: A Survey of Manuscript Militia Returns," *William and Mary Quarterly,* 3rd ser., 60:3 (July 2003), 615–42; Parker et al., "America's Complex Relationship with Guns."

29. Eric Monkkonen, "History of Urban Police," *Crime and Justice* 15 (1992): 547–80.

30. For an overall history of the National Guard, see John Mahon, *History of the Militia and the National Guard* (New York, 1983).

31. This phrase comes from Justice Antonin Scalia's ruling in the case, available at https://casetext.com/case/dist-of-columbia-v-heller-3.

32. Alexander Hamilton to George Washington, 25 March 1783, National Archives, Founders Online, https://founders.archives.gov/documents/Hamilton/01-03-02-0194.

INDEX